Journal of a Starseed

Charis Brown Malloy

ISBN-13:978-0615500584

ISBN-10: 0615500587

Cover Design: Charis Brown Malloy

Starseed Press 2011

Dedication

This is to Terry, my real-life prince, Mark, my real-life wizard, and all of the other people who make my life magical.

Thank you.

CONTENTS

ACKNOWLEDGMENTS

I'd like to thank everyone who has assisted me on my own path of discovery along the way as I had the experiences that I'll discuss in these pages. Susannah, of course, for teaching me so many things that would prove invaluable over the years and for unlocking the world for me. Rae, for playing tug of war with me over so many things, and helping me along when I needed it (even though I definitely didn't always like it.) To all of my friends and loved ones who I've mentioned in these pages, thanks for letting me write about you. Amanda, Noah (you know who you are, I know you may think I'm crazy nowadays, so thanks for putting up with my ravings from time to time,) Krishanti, AS, Giorgio, Joe and all of the not-quite-named people here who have helped make me who I am, and who showed me that I could be unafraid and open.

My parents. You guys probably think I'm a little nuts too. Thanks for loving me anyway.

Mark, of course, who pushes me so that I often never realized I was being pushed until I looked back and see that I'm in a completely different place as a result of gentle nudges that set me straight and reminded me that the most painful experiences are really just "grist for the mill."

Michal, for all you do and for how well you do it. A true Jane of all trades – where would I be without you?

Ward. I'm grateful for you every day.

Finally, to Terry, my love, who fights with me and loves me and walks with me through all of my days and down all of my twisting and turning paths. I love you.

Introduction: Disclaimers

Before I really get into anything, I'd like to offer forth an explanation that yes, I'm fully aware that the things I'm about to say will sound completely bat guano bonkers crazy. This knowledge, in fact, is what has kept me quiet during this decade-long journey that I'm about to relate to you. Actually, to be more specific, the *fear* of what would happen to me if I "came out of the closet" and actually publicly told the truth of my experience is what has kept me quiet all these years. As my friend and mentor Mark said to me this morning, they used to burn folks like me at the stake. As I replied to him, they probably burned *me* at the stake a good time or two. That, or drowned me. Or maybe I was just hanged. There may have been an Iron Maiden involved. Ugh. Let's not think about it.

These things considered, I feel it necessary to acknowledge that I know how this will sound, or look, as the case may be. Although my subsequent research and digging over the years has uncovered evidence and information that *actually* reveals my experiences as making more sense than the status quo of our culture's knowledge of the things I'll discuss here does, that status quo is quite powerful – and it doesn't like to be nudged. So I'm aware of what can happen to me and my reputation after I publish this book.

However, I'll add that I've also sent out a few feelers here and there, gently (and progressively more directly) mentioning iffy information on social media sites and such, and I've been met with a definitely anticlimactic silence – no one, in actuality, seems to be nearly as freaked out as I'd feared. Combine that with this feeling I've had in recent months that I MUST write my experiences down and make them available for others to read, and you have me sitting here, typing away on this keyboard, not afraid any more. I've happily discovered, over and over again as of late, that I am **not** as unique as I thought. Others **do** experience what I experience, and, like I was, are often afraid to say anything or ask questions about them because they are similarly aware that even mentioning such things is likely to make them sound bat guano bonkers crazy. And that isn't a good look on most people, or so we think.

However, you've gotta do what you've gotta do, and right now, I've gotta write. So let's get started.

1: The Reason

When my awakening crashed upon me like rumbling mental thunder, when I knew things that I couldn't possibly logically know and felt things that I couldn't possibly logically feel, when I finally admitted to myself that yes, I *was* different in a way I'd only seen in movies and when I was seized with voracious cravings for knowledge such that I appeared, even to myself, to match the image of any insane person you may see rifling through papers, wide eyed, focused, me being the same in every detail except for the differences that my manicured fingernails and made-up face created between the street person chic look usually sported by such characters (no offense to street people, many of whom are quite interesting, by the way,) all that searching and rifling and admitting did not earn me any knowledge that actually helped *all that* much. The people I loved the most shook their heads, at a loss for anything to say in reply at best, and at worst, giving me those sidelong glances and the familiar "I believe that *you* believe it" comments that definitely make a person feel like they're going mad and there's nothing to be done about it.

Eventually I did find resources that provided some type of structure and container that my fundamentalist Jehovah's Witness upbringing until adolescence had lacked in the form of nonfiction books by Lynn V. Andrews and Mary Summer Rain, as well as fiction books by Marion Zimmer Bradley and other similar authors. These provided a much appreciated breath of fresh air, but there remained a big problem that ran me into some trouble. The women writing their accounts (yes, they had to be women, or else I wouldn't have been able to identify even *this* much) were brilliant, yes, but they were nothing like *me*. These were women who were already living adult lives, whose experiences were **very** different from mine, who had external encouragement and direction from real Medicine Women, priestesses, and books literally flying off of shelves and into their hands. They had careers, sometimes children, and almost always husbands. They were *grown up*, for goodness' sake. I was a 20 year old pageant queen, working her way through college, studying for hours on end to make a perfect GPA so as to end up with a good career and avoid the poverty that I'd lived in during my childhood and adolescence. A poverty that was so artfully hidden that I'm sure a person or two reading this, who knew me during those years, will raise their eyebrows in surprise as they discover in these words the actual truth that I starved my way through high school, eating nothing but tea and toast and an orange or two for days at a time.

The books I read were helpful, but, as I've said, not *that* helpful. Not when I could find loads and loads of literature telling me that my age often marked the onset of illnesses like adult schizophrenia and multiple personality disorder. Great. The voices I heard in my head from time to time certainly didn't make me feel at all better about *that* possibility.

Only years **later** would I learn that my age then was also the time during which our brains have their last great growth spurt – similar to the language growth spurt that happens at about three years old and the reasoning and social growth spurt at seven years – except that this later one is located in the frontal lobes, which control inhibition and impulses and *psychic activity*. More on that later.

Had I been able to take a book in my hands (or read it on my phone, for that matter,) that described a person who was young, reasonably normal, driven, and previously unconcerned with spirituality (even a full-out agnostic bordering on atheism,) who then had a spiritual awakening hit her in the head like a baseball bat coming from the *inside* – however, without any books flying off shelves and no Medicine Women showing me the way (at least, not at first) and really nothing external happening at all, but rather receiving internal directions and explosions and visions and experiences that were impossible to ignore because of their intensity. Now *that* would have been truly helpful.

And I'm aware of the teenagers today, and how out of place they feel in this world that not only can't see the things that they can and do see, but that tells them they're either imagining things or flat out lying. I think that there are a lot of people the age that I was, right smack in the middle between adolescence and adulthood, who are likely, as I was, sitting in libraries, furtively visiting the spirituality section, "just for a minute," or doing internet searches in the middle of insomniac nights, trying to figure out what the heck is happening to them. I've spoken to people like this who KNOW that there is more inside of them, like those visions and knowings that they've read about or seen in movies, that their hearts are *crying out for* but that they have no clue how to really **access**.

This book is for those guys and girls – and all of those people at various walks of life, waking up to these same feelings – to tell them that yes, this is **real**. It's real, but more importantly, it's *okay*. This is something that is a deep and eternal part of Human experience, and it's been happening to Humans since we've been Human at all. Now is the time that it's happening more than maybe ever before – and certainly more than has ever happened in our currently accepted (and ridiculously incorrect, mind you) official history books. I'm writing my experience so you guys can know that you're fine – and that, in fact, once you get a hang of what you can do (which will be different for everyone, as much as the noses on our faces are all different,) this is when thing will get *really* interesting. I should also warn you now that I won't be explaining everything that has happened. To be more specific, I won't be explaining much at *all*. Things are hardly ever as they seem, and from past experience I've learned that if you try to put a rigid definition on just about anything, you'll be eating your words sooner or later. I'm just going to take you through what I experienced as I experienced it, offering up the ways I've put it all together and am continuing to do so. I learn more every single day, and that holds true for these experiences. Also, it's important to say that I'm not including every experience I've ever had, or even that occurred it the time frames I'll be discussing. If I did, this book would instantly transform into a volume so large that no one would ever read it...no matter *how* interesting things became.

Speaking of getting interesting, I guess I'd better start at some semblance of the beginning.

2: Library Aisles

I blinked hard as I picked my head up and looked around me. Well, this was just starting to be embarrassing. What if someone I knew walked by? How would I explain what I was doing?

There I was, *again*, on the floor of my university's library. Again, I'd come here to do research for some paper or another, and again, after doing whatever research I needed to cross off of my "To Do List," I'd wound up here, in the 100's of the Dewy Decimal delineated spirituality section, sitting on the floor, with a circle of opened books around me.

Sometimes they were on Edgar Cayce or Atlantis or Alchemy. Often they were about Wicca and Earth Religions. Shamanism came up, and so did other indigenous spiritual practices. I couldn't predict what titles would jump out at me, calling to my awareness as strongly as if there were flashing neon signs there on the books' spines rather than ordinary lettering, but many books always did. No matter how rushed I was or how strongly I told myself that *this* time I'd leave the library as soon as I finished my research, I'd end up here, somewhere along these familiar two aisles. Somehow my steps would veer away from my intended path and I'd assure myself that I'd just spend a minute or two looking around, just to see what was there...and before I knew it, I was voraciously tearing book after book off of the shelf, fanning the pages with my thumb, skimming three or four of them, then setting the book down on the floor next to me, lying open to whatever page I'd ended on as another book caught my eye and I reached for it instead. I invariably found myself surrounded by opened volumes, with no idea what I actually wanted to check out and take home with me.

I never checked any of them out. I would gently close each one, finding its place on the shelf and returning it gently but quickly, as if the off-limits subject would scorch my fingertips if I held the book for too long.

None of this stuff was *real*, anyway. I was wasting my time. Everyone knew that these were just stories and made-up practices that were as silly as they were ancient. And yet...there was a tugging that always brought me here, and then a passion that took me more firmly than anything I'd ever felt before.

That winter, I called a college friend who I shared a microphone with during drunken karaoke, went to toga parties with, and occasionally took tests with using more, er, "collaborative" methods than were encouraged by the powers-that-be, and I told her in a shaking voice that I thought I was psychic, or crazy, waiting for laughter that never came. Rather, there was a silence, not an unkind one – just a feeling of confusion and a compassionate lack of anything to say in return.

Months later I would find my first teacher, a Reiki instructor named Susannah, who, after two classes and many late-night discussions, I'd never be able to find again, although I had visited her house many times and exchanged countless calls and emails with her while she was teaching me.

Years later I would learn while studying for a PhD. in Transpersonal Psychology that the brain's final growth spurt that I mentioned above, similar to the language and logic growth spurts that come during earlier years, was an explosion in the frontal lobe's number and complexity of neural connections. This is a time, recognized across continents and centuries (until Western culture blotted out the old knowledge of such things,) as the period of rites of passage and spiritual awakening. It happens at the end of adolescence and the beginning of true adulthood, at roughly two decades into a human life. When I found myself sitting in the 100's section of the library, I was 20 years old.

Trying to find an actual event that began the whole spiral is a useless task. I end up winding through labyrinthine memories, wondering if *this* or *that* was the beginning, always deciding that it was. A moment later I'll suddenly land on another time, sometimes before, sometimes after, always making me wonder if there was ever a beginning.

Probably not, I decide, after I've let myself wonder about it for seconds, or minutes, or longer. And I make another decision, nested in the first one, that I won't ask again. I always do ask again, sooner or later.

I suppose as good a place to start as any is during one of what I call my "previews" - events that shook me, not enough to actually crack the rigid world that had been built around me by dogma and fear-based beliefs, but enough to serve as a funny thing to talk about, an exception shining in my mind like some faraway star.

I was driving home, late on a school night, after spending hours debating the existence of God with Amanda, my best friend. We were seniors, a state of mind which comes with a certain cockiness to begin with. Add to that a love of psychology and a fascination with analyzing everyone and everything around us, and you get a sum of many late night conversations, discussing what we thought were the mysteries of life, but what now, after the fact, feels more like our own flavor of teenage angst.

I was already feeling a certain non-verbal dissonance between what I believed to be true in my heart and what I was told from the fundamentalist dogma that was pounded into my mind three times a week. The constant threat of a lightning bolt at any time, in any place, as part of that ever-looming Armageddon, if I *didn't* believe what was being shoved down my throat kept me from ever taking the chance to truly examine these topics without a considerable amount of fear until my teenage years. My family had stopped attending meetings after my parents' divorce when I was 12 years old, and my young philosophical mind was finally left to its own devices from that point on.

After much consideration, I came to the firm conclusion that God must be imaginary. At best, God was a perfect example of wishful thinking created by weak-minded individuals who could not fathom their own responsibility when it came to the more unpleasant aspects of life. At worst,

God was a means of immoral social control. If neither of these things were true, then considering the information I had gathered from my childhood sermons and other people I spoke to throughout the subsequent years, God was nothing short of a sadist. If he could see the future, *and* if he was all powerful, then the fact that horrible Human suffering existed at all (my favorite example was any diseased, starving child, born into poverty just to die from malnutrition before preschool age) was proof that whatever God everyone was worshiping was a jackass. I would have no part of it.

The best I could get from any religious person I had this debate with was the idea that it all came down to "faith."

Uh – huh.

At that point my eyes would glaze over and I'd roll up the windows in my mind, aware now that this individual was as empty-headed and brainwashed as the droves of people wasting their time and energy praying to an empty space (or a terrible creature, watching very real suffering with a cosmically huge bowl of popcorn sitting in his lap.) Unacceptable.

This was one of those nights. I loved Amanda, but when she gave me the faith line after an air-tight argument on my part (according to me of course,) the conversation pretty much ended. Again. This wasn't the first time we'd discussed this. I simply couldn't rectify both things – the logic and the faith. How could anyone have faith in such a monster? But I respected Amanda's opinion more than anyone else's. The whole ordeal was exhausting.

It was getting late anyway. I hopped down from her kitchen counter, where we'd been talking and munching on a chocolate stash. We tucked the plastic bag of goodies back into the cabinet, exchanged a hug, and I walked to my car to start my drive home.

I lived on the outskirts of the small Southern town where I spent much of my life until college. On the way to the house was a long straight stretch down a country road. I regularly used the few minutes of brainless driving it gave me for an opportunity to stargaze – I'd tilt my head to the left, stealing glances at the shining sky with one eye on the road. Thank goodness no deer ever crossed my path – it's unlikely I would have come away from that encounter unscathed, judging by the amount of attention I gave my immediate task on those late, dark nights – which wasn't much.

On this particular evening, as I looked deeply into that network of stars, I **felt** something. An impossibly big, impossibly strong, impossibly intelligent something. Or *someone*, I should say. This presence was so big that measurement was impossible, and the interaction happened so quickly that I had no time to second guess it or question what my experience was. It just happened - there was no argument possible.

First came the pure awareness. It was like someone walking through a doorway and standing in front of you, squarely looking you in the face, silent and full of purpose. The message was pure existence. Only years later would I recognize the similarities that this wordless exchange had with the several Biblical accounts of a certain someone saying the words "I Am."

True to form with the egoic teenager that I was, my non-verbal response was something along the lines of the following:

"Well, fine. If you *do* exist, then explain all of the reasons I gave before," those reasons being poverty, war, suffering, and the like.

The response, also non-verbal, was a calm and completely assured knowledge that, although the order was not clear to me, everything that occurred down to the tiniest, most seemingly insignificant detail was inside of, directed by, and part of a complex balance and clockwork-like orchestration of matter and energy – so no, there were no loose ends. No such thing as meaningless suffering existed. And, just because I, in my limited scope of understanding, could not explain the reason behind every occurrence, this lack of perception in no way served as any real argument against the truth of what **was**.

"*Oh.*"

This happened too quickly, even, for me to be humbled by it. It *just happened.* For that matter, the entire conversation had probably begun and ended within a span of five seconds or less.

And then it was gone.

I tried to explain this to those around me, including Amanda, and while no one ever rejected or laughed at my experience, I could never adequately describe the immensity of what had happened that night. The interchange became one of those funny and odd stories relegated to late-night exchanges of ghost and UFO sightings that are only told after inebriation caused by either chemical or psychological means. Once people get really drunk or really relaxed, the strange stuff comes out. Before then, no one wants to talk about it.

I added the conversation to my list and tucked the list away in a drawer of my mind until two years later, when I was doing my best to make sense of my library experiences. The time span may even have been longer, as I may not have unpacked this particular conversation until I had more of a leg to stand on in my own mind than the one that came with a compulsion to go to the third floor and sit in the middle of the aisles, tearing books off the shelves, reading more quickly than I'd previously thought my comprehension would allow.

3: Beacon

During the fall semester of my second year in college I worked on the weekends at a home decorating shop in the mall. I quite liked the job. We sold beautiful and high quality things that I could actually genuinely recommend because I knew they were good products. I didn't have to sell them in order to make someone else's weekly projections, feeling like an uncomfortable fraud the entire time. Obviously, I'm not the biggest fan of sales nor accumulating possessions just to accumulate them.

Anyway, after the mall would close at night, I would walk through the damp, dark Floridian air to my little green car sitting in the empty parking lot. The nights were usually pretty dark, as the humidity and light pollution where I was working blocked the starlight. Even with those barriers in place, I would feel a presence above me, somewhere far away. From what I could tell, this strange presence I felt didn't seem to be paying much attention to *me*, but I wanted it to so badly! I was lonely and stressed and internally aware somewhere deep down that I was capable of quite more than the multiple choice college tests I was taking and polished wooden accent tables I was selling, no matter *how* beautiful they were. There was *more* to life. And I wanted it.

Of course, I had no clue what the presence I sensed or even this "more" that I longed for would look like, or even feel like. The feelings I got on these short walks never crossed my mind at any other time than during these solitary moments in the empty parking lot, but **during** these times, this desire burned within me with a brightness that I could not ignore, no matter how much I tried to tell myself that I was fine or that I was only imagining things.

So what did I do about it? I released that bright light within me up into the sky above, of course. With no clue of how or why I was doing this, I imagined that this light inside of my chest and upper abdomen burned brightly, exploding out of the top of my head and reaching far into the night sky, a brightly shining beacon, letting *them* find me.

Who were *they?* I had no clue. I have an inkling now, yes, but at the time, this question somehow failed to ever cross my mind. I was alone and I was *feeling* rather than *thinking* for once (which is, since I mentioned it, apparently the next phase in Human evolution, or so I've heard from spiritual literature and scientific research alike.) I didn't take the time to analyze what I was doing because by the time I turned my car key to start the ignition, I would be distracted by whatever song was playing on the radio and I'd totally forget what had just happened.

This went on for months, with me never thinking about it except for when it was actually happening. Only years later did I look at the time line and realize that the *really* strange things that heralded my awakening in earnest began to happen the following spring, *after* I'd been instinctively shining that beacon for a few nights each week.

The first time I tried to meditate was during a visit to see my father in northern Virginia. He'd been studying Taoism for the past year or two. He was also practicing martial arts, and, of course, had a regular meditation practice. We spoke about it while I was there, and after seeing my interest, he offered to guide me through a common meditation he did, involving the ocean, an island, a cave, and a few other things.

I found a comfortable position on the floor and he sat in a chair, slowly speaking to me and describing the feelings and images that relaxed the body and mind and began the meditation. I relaxed well as those initial instructions were given but as he began to describe the experience of swimming through ocean waves toward a bright, sandy beach, I saw nothing of the sort. I did *feel*, however – I felt the size of my hands and feet fluctuating. With my eyes closed, I felt my hands growing larger and larger and larger, as if they were blowing up just like the balloons that clowns create little brightly colored, squeaky animals from. My hands grew big enough to take up the living room, then the whole building, and then they continued to grow larger. In the next breath they would quickly shrink so as to be nearly invisible. Then they would expand again.

I tried to stop it. When that failed, I tried to simply stop paying attention to the strange and uncomfortable feeling, but my attempts were to no avail – this growing and shrinking craziness was *all* I was aware of. The same thing was happening with my feet, and although I knew that my extremities were not literally changing sizes (or else my father surely would have said *something* – and besides, that's impossible,) I was powerless to ignore it.

Eventually I stopped the meditation, sitting up and shaking my head. I felt frustrated and exhausted. I never did reach the beach that day.

Back in Florida, trying to meditate at my apartment, I would close my eyes and focus. Not long afterward, the swelling and shrinking of my hands and feet stopped. I used some of the techniques my father had taught me such as sitting up straight, imagining that each of my vertebrae was a brick – when they were all stacked, each on top of the one below, they would hold me up through balance alone, with no need for muscular activity. This would free my attention so I could focus on each part of my body, one at a time, systematically relaxing myself as I started with my toes and ended up at the top of my head. After that, and after my breathing had steadied, I'd wait.

At first, I saw nothing and heard nothing. Filled with many stories of the amazing things that can happen through meditation, from the kundalini rising up the spine, to visits to and from other people, places, and things, I found myself increasingly disappointed as nothing really **happened**.

Finally, several days in to my 15-minute meditation practice which now consisted of boredom and attempts to clear my mind and avoid counting down the minutes to when the ending alarm would sound, *something happened*. I wasn't talking to anyone or flying through space, which are actually both things that did come in the future and that I do on nearly a daily basis nowadays. Instead, in my mind's eye, I could see that I was sitting on a chair in what felt like the type of ballroom you see in hotels, used for conferences and weddings. The space was large and dimly lit, and there I was, right in the center, all alone. Lining the walls, I noticed, were people. I couldn't see their features, just t heir shadowy shapes They stood shoulder to shoulder, at least one row deep, and maybe more than one. They were all staring at **me**. This was a pretty big room, so there were lots of them there – silent, not unfriendly, but not communicating either.

This continued for days, with me trying to communicate, to speak to them or think *at* them, or just to do whatever I could to get some type of result. Sometimes that version of me sitting in the chair would yell, pleading with them to just **say something**! Talk to me! But they stood there, implacable, silent, still, watching me. Nothing more.

4: Spiral

My meditations became more interesting and informative after I met some kindred spirits that helped show me the way. I also began practicing Reiki. Here's how all of it happened.

During my senior year in college, one of my classes consisted of completing a semester's worth of work-study hours at various locations that corresponded with each student's career aspirations. Because I was interested in child care as well as working with individuals with disabilities (which is what I wound up getting my first master's degree in,) I signed up to be a teacher's aide at a small school just across from the campus I attended. The children who attended this school had mental as well as physical disabilities, so this job kept all of us on our toes. My favorite child there (I know you aren't supposed to pick favorites, but every teacher will tell you that they invariably do – you can't really help it) was a little boy from Russia. He was about 3 years old, with blonde hair and stunningly clear blue eyes. He was also as sharp as a tack, but he couldn't speak and had emotional outbursts as well as tendencies that resembled Autism. He didn't actually have Autism. His symptoms were a result of a lack of stimulation and interaction during his first year of life – he'd been in one of those ridiculously under-staffed orphanages where the most the nurses can do is feed and change each child on a schedule. There was no adult interaction, which meant no emotional regulation and no language skill development from hearing someone speak directly to him, which is what require in order to fully learn how to communicate verbally. I tried to teach him sign language, which he thought was quite funny. Whenever he would actually connect with me over a book or a game, my heart would swell and I would be all the more motivated to help him reach the developmental milestones that would enable him to fully participate in society. I sought out my behavior and learning professor and asked him for recommendations, some of which worked, while some didn't. I came to the teacher I was assisting, Rae, and asked her about how she maintained her emotional center while teaching these children that pulled at one's heart so strongly.

Rae was a beauty, with milky pale, smooth skin, dark hair, and piercing blue eyes that bored right into you in a way that could be quite uncomfortable, if she wanted it to. She was in her early thirties, but looked much younger. As we worked together through the weeks, she told me of her children – a boy and a girl, both of whom had those interesting characteristics that are becoming all the more common with each passing year – the adult-like intelligence and language choices, the childlike impatience, and an emotional, empathetic sixth sense that is difficult to describe.

During a lunch break one day, Rae and I decided to sit outdoors on the grass while we ate. We somehow began debating religious issues, and I started with my "God must not be real, and if he is, he's a jackass and I'm still not signing up" argument. Rae looked at me in her intense way and asked me the following question.

"What if God could be a being full of love, who, rather than punishing you when you made a mistake, would see that the mistake was from an injury that you'd had and who would take you up on His shoulder and comfort you, healing you until you were well?"

As she spoke, her hands physically matched her description and she tenderly brought a tiny imaginary being to her shoulder, holding it closely and patting its back. Her question stopped me in my tracks. I asked her opinion about all of the reasons I had that supported my point of view. She agreed that those were factors to consider, and then she said that the entire picture was probably much, much bigger than anything we could see. This was close enough to my message on the highway that night in high school that I started to pay very close attention to everything Rae said from this point on.

I told her about my recent struggles and lost time in the library, and that while I knew none of this could be *real*, something was happening inside of me that I couldn't ignore. What should I do? Was I losing my mind? She seemed the one to ask, somehow.

In a funny way that I can now recognize as her sensitivity to my lack of knowledge and experience in these matters as well as an attempt to avoid overloading me with information I wouldn't understand, Rae told me to go to The Spiral Circle, a metaphysical bookstore in Orlando. She told me that perhaps, I'd find something there that could help explain things or direct me further.

I went to The Spiral Circle a few days later, once I had worked up enough courage. I drove down winding, tree-lined streets and parked next to the small building, an interesting looking converted house with a purple sign out front, labeling it as the bookstore I was looking for.

I walked up a thin wooden ramp and opened the door. Bells tinkled, announcing the arrival of a customer. As I stepped in, my senses were assaulted by sights, sounds, and smells that I'd never experienced before, but that I quite liked. There was soft, ambient music playing in the background and the smell of warm, subtle incense, which I'd never been exposed to before, made me feel right away as if I were stepping into another world. Beautifully colored tapestries and pictures were covering the walls, and books were everywhere. The same types of books that I found myself lost in during my library episodes. As I slowly walked through the shop, I felt a part of me both relax and *tune in*. I was paying a different kind of attention to the world around me than I had in years, ever since my childhood spent running around in the woods of southern Virginia. During that time I was interacting with plants and animals and swimming in creeks, my best friend and I lying our clothes nicely on rocks and branches nearby so our parents wouldn't know we'd broken the rules and gone into the water.

In the shop, there were great big white singing bowls made of crystal. Someone working there showed me how to use one, running a velvet-wrapped cylindrical piece of wood around and around the bowl's rim, coaxing it into slowly emitting a deep, pure, beautiful sound that I felt my body respond to viscerally, sort of opening up from the inside in a way that I wouldn't be able to describe until I discovered through my Reiki training what chakras actually felt like as they expanded and opened.

I went into the back room of the shop and began to take books that called my attention off of the shelf, each one more intriguing than the last. I handled them as if they were made of precious material. I didn't know that anyone *published* books like this! I had discovered a treasure trove. Finally something was happening. I realized now that perhaps I wasn't crazy. There were people here, on these pages who definitely sounded sane – and yet they were talking about crystals, energy, and angels – maybe there was something to this that didn't lead to insanity or delusions – if not, how were some of these books describing the same experiences I was having?

On the front counter sat an orange calendar with the shop's events printed in black ink. Today, beginning in just a few minutes, a Reiki workshop was being given. I asked a woman standing behind the counter what Reiki was. First she said something about how Reiki had to do with healing and energy – both concepts that earned her a blank stare from me. I had no clue what she meant. I was then told in a friendly and encouraging way that I should go to the presentation out in the meeting room and find out for myself. It was free, and I was there already...alright, I'd go.

I nervously spent the last 15 minutes or so fiddling with various things in the shop, reading a page of a book here and there, flipping through decks of artfully decorated cards which I didn't understand at all, and studying crystals of various colors, sizes, and shapes.

When it was time for the Reiki presentation to start, I walked out to the meeting room that had been pointed out to me earlier. There was only one other person there, a woman sitting across the small room. I felt a bit awkward, still not over the fear that if I talked about anything other than the ordinary small talk that didn't exactly seem appropriate here, I would be treated as if I were a nutcase. So before we had a chance to introduce ourselves, Susannah came in. She was in her fifties and had fiery red hair. She wore glasses and those flowing, brightly colored clothes that are popular in New Age circles. She sat down in front of us and began to talk about Reiki. I quickly discovered, because of the conversation that they made with each other during Susannah's relaxed presentation, that the other woman was not only familiar with this type of practice, but that she had already been trained in Reiki to some extent. I felt significantly out of my league as they talked to each other, but at least no one in this little group would call me crazy.

Reiki, I learned, is a method of healing using pure energy, directed through the practitioner through his or her palms. I didn't really understand this – what did they mean by *energy*? It sounded kind of frou-frou to me. It seemed like it would be easy to fake too, especially because you can't see it. As I was thinking my skeptical thoughts, the other two women were chatting about how Reiki can be used to speed up natural healing and relieve problems like chronic pain, high stress, and basically any type of illnesses, especially those that are commonly accepted as being caused or exacerbated by stress.

When I shared that I hadn't ever tried Reiki before, much less been trained in it, both Susannah and my fellow audience member encouraged me to let them give me a short treatment. I didn't even have to move, they told me. I could sit right where I was. More than a little weirded out, I gave in to my curiosity and consented under the pressure. Susannah pulled her chair around to sit behind me while the other woman sat on my right. They both did something funny with their hands, the woman to my right holding her hands together in a few different formations and Susannah appearing to trace shapes in each palm with the finger of the other hand. After a moment, they each gently laid their hands on me, keeping them still. Susannah touched my shoulders, and the other woman clasped my right hand with hers and laid her other hand on my right elbow.

We sat there for a minute or two, mostly keeping silent. I felt more awkward in that moment than at any other time that I could remember. Then I started to feel a bit *odd*. It was as if I were getting chills, but not any chills that I'd experienced before. Because I am one of those people who becomes uncomfortably cold at relatively high temperatures, compared to most people, I am quite familiar with chills, or those little waves of, well, *energy*, moving through me – but now I wasn't cold at all. In fact, the room was quite warm. The chills also didn't feel like normal cold chills – they were tiny, warm tremors that ran through my arms and legs and made me shudder for just a moment each. These shudders weren't unpleasant, but they were distinct, and they lasted for less time than any cold-based chill I'd ever felt before.

The little energy tremors began to come more and more often, and I, still skeptical, tried my best not to show what was happening. I then began to have a strange emotional reaction. An excitement was rising within me – I felt that happy, blossoming feeling in my torso that you feel on your birthday, or on Christmas morning, or when you've accomplished something that you've worked long and hard to finish and succeed with. Still a skeptic, I tried not to pay attention to this new experience, telling myself that I must be imagining things. At this point, Susannah began to talk.

She spoke to me of my father, describing, with no prompting from me, his recent knee injury, which happened while sparring with his martial arts teacher. She then described that teacher to me – talking about his large ego and how he had been acting more and more irrationally lately, which was absolutely true. She also told me exactly how the knee injury happened and what it was – a torn ACL. This is an important piece of connective tissue inside the knee. My father had been told that the only way to heal this injury would be surgery.

Okay. This was just *weird*. And there was no reasonable explanation for it. Even if Susannah had done extensive research on me (which was a ridiculous concept anyway. I was just a random college student, *and* I'd decided to go to her presentation just a few minutes before it started, which would have given her no time to look me up) there would have been no record, anywhere, of this occurrence – my father's ACL had been torn just a few days before. In order to know this information, Susannah would have had to know my father and spoken to him about it. This was impossible too – the guy lived a thousand miles away. There was no way for me to rationalize this away, no matter *how* skeptical I was.

I was still feeling those little tremors, which I later found out were caused by blockages being cleared in my electrical, or energetic, circulatory system. The emotion was also still building inside of me. By the time my mini Reiki session was over a few minutes later, I was definitely intrigued. The ladies told me to quickly drink the water out of the bottle I had sitting next to my chair on the floor. They told me that after being so close to a Reiki treatment as strong as that one was, apparently the enhanced life force now present in the water would have made any microbes floating around in there go nuts, so the water would have quickly begun to grow whatever algae or scum naturally grows in sitting water as if several days had passed, rather than a few minutes. I followed their directions, and after the other woman left, I talked more to Susannah.

We walked through the bookstore together and she explained what some of these interesting things were. She showed me again how to use the different singing bowls on shelves and tables in the shop and explained how Tibetan bells clear a space of any negative energy. You ring them a few times, making them sound by gently bumping the bells together, holding the cord that binds them to one another and avoiding the actual metal. Between each sound, you wait for the previous one to completely fade away naturally. You never silence the bells while working with them. A few tones in, the sound will come out pure and clear. When the tone is true and unwavering, you know that the space is clear. She demonstrated with the bells, and I did hear a difference after a minute or two. I was surprised. *Something* had certainly happened to the sound the bells made.

We walked over to a table of crystals, and Susannah picked up various kinds one by one, telling me their uses, offering each she chose to me to hold in my hand and "get a feel for." White quartz for general purposes. Rose quartz to soothe the heart. Amethyst for enhancing one's spiritual and psychic abilities. Black tourmaline for healing and protection. I held each crystal she handed me, noticing only a very, very subtle feeling, almost a buzzing, or a pressure, actually *inside* whichever hand was touching the crystal. Sometimes the feeling moved into my wrist and lower arm. After showing me several others, Susannah picked up a small, round, clear crystal with a very subtle brownish tint, and held it up to the light.

"This one is a rutilated citrine."

She turned it in the shaft of sunlight streaming in from a corner window, and I saw tiny, thin filaments in the crystal glint and sparkle as she slowly rotated the crystal in her fingers. Susannah held the crystal, about an inch in diameter, close to her face, adjusting her glasses so she could look deeply into it.

"There is a tree inside. See that?" She held the crystal close to my face now, and yes, I did see that the shining, curving filaments all came from what looked like a central vein that resembled a pine tree.

"It stores information. This one is for *you*."

I didn't really know what to say to that. Of course my mind initially tried to spot some sort of trick, but why would she lie about it? *She* wasn't getting any money from The Spiral Circle's sale of a crystal. The forty dollar price tag made me cringe – my job as an undergraduate adviser in the Psychology Department at my university paid peanuts and I was continually down to my last few bucks – but I felt an odd draw to follow her direction on this. I bought the crystal.

"Carry it with you all the time – do you carry a purse? Keep it in your purse."

I put the crystal in its small black velvet bag and tucked it into one of the inside pockets of my purse, wondering.

After I asked her what felt like a million more questions, Susannah told me that she would love to teach me. She taught all levels of Reiki, she said, and taking it would help me to discover and understand the questions that were tugging at me. She gave me her information, which included the fees for Level 1 Reiki, which cost two hundred dollars. Er. Being a broke college student, I didn't feel that great about spending a couple hundred dollars on something that was odd and cool, but not very practical. I'd have to talk to Noah about it. We had been dating for almost four years and he offered a more grounded viewpoint than mine which helped a lot whenever I had a big decision to make. I thanked her, said I'd be in touch, and started home.

As I drove away, I thought about the strangeness of that afternoon. I did want to learn Reiki, yes, definitely. If I could learn how to do what Susannah could do when she just seemed to somehow see *into* people like that, what a life it would be! On the other hand, I probably shouldn't waste money on such an odd thing. Keeping one hand on the wheel and my eyes on the road, I dug out my crystal and held it in my hand, curling my fingers around its smoothness and rolling it in my palm. Just as Susannah said it would, the crystal warmed quickly, growing so warm that it seemed to surpass my own body heat, which has always been abnormally low. Strange.

Back at home, I told Noah how I felt and he encouraged me to take the class. Why not? If I was that interested in it, he told me, I should see what it was all about.

"Let's stop for today. Do you like cantaloupe?" Susannah laid the papers she'd been holding down on her coffee table as I stretched and took a deep breath, looking around. I blinked hard, feeling as if I'd just woken up. We had just finished an entire day of Reiki lessons, and I was surprised at how dark the room had become. We hadn't noticed the sun going down. Susannah had asked me a few times during the day if I wanted to stop or take a break, but I never did. I didn't want to do anything but keep learning. Everything made *so much sense*. I already knew that much of the body's signaling was electrical, which was what made it was possible for doctors and researchers to stimulate nerves with electricity. Muscular contractions could even be controlled with little bursts of electricity. Reiki was a way of tuning in to the body's energetic circulatory system which governed and channeled this electricity as it naturally occurs. I'd never pondered this subject enough prior to these conversations to realize that the energy moving through us couldn't just be in a homogenous cloud – that certainly wouldn't make any sense – so if there was a system to carry this energy, then how *was* it arranged, anyway?

I was learning about chakras and meridians and the emotional connection to injuries and illnesses, which goes both ways. Emotions can both come as a result of an illness, causing that illness to flare up whenever we feel that type of stress again down the line, or they can cause illnesses directly. As I learned, I was drawing definite connections between my own sources of stress and chronic illnesses I would get. Whenever I visited my home town in rural Virginia, I would get a throat infection. When I was stressed about finances, a particular spot on the left side of my spinal column, just inside my shoulder blade, would ache and grow very tender to the touch. These things happened like clockwork, but I didn't see the connection until I knew enough to be aware of it. Now I was understanding my own health in a completely new way, a way that made me feel much more powerful and less at the mercy of luck or fate, or for that matter, whatever doctor's office I stepped into.

Later, Susannah would tell me that I'd gone through the information with a hunger that she'd never seen in any of her other students, and that no one else had ever opted out of taking any rest or break periods over the course of an entire day. I never wanted a break during any of my Reiki training. At the time, however, she didn't mention it.

The next day, Susannah stopped the lesson in the early afternoon, announcing that we were going to take a break and have something to eat. She got out of her chair and began walk towards her hallway, then invited me to follow her into the kitchen.

Susannah's house was full of interesting things. Beautiful art decorated her shelves, colorful blankets were laid across unique wooden furniture that had been hand made by friends of hers. Musical instruments from Africa and Europe hung on the walls, and crystals were *everywhere*. They were on shelves, tables, and on counter tops. As we walked down the hallway toward the kitchen, I saw that crystals, neatly laid on brightly colored pieces of cloth, were clustered on the floor in the corners and lining the walls of the hallway. I stopped next to a geode with amethyst spikes peeking out of its shadowy center. Susannah told me to hold my left hand over it and she waited to see what I felt.

"The left side is the receptive side of the body, so whenever you are trying to pick up information through your hands, use the left one," she told me.

Nothing much. I tried to discern something more than the incredibly subtle sensations I was having in my left hand and wrist, but I couldn't. I felt a little disappointed. I had expected there to be more bells and whistles to all this. All I could feel was a slight pressure, as if the air over the crystals were somehow *thicker*, as strange as that probably sounds. I told Susannah this and she nodded, then turned and went into the kitchen.

After staying there for another moment or two, trying unsuccessfully to have some type of mind-bending epiphany, I walked into the kitchen and saw a bowl sitting on the table for me, filled with chunks of light orange cantaloupe. A spoon was lying next to the bowl, and Susannah was across the table, sitting down to her matching dish. I do like cantaloupe, but I was surprised when I took the first bite. I asked Susannah what was different. She'd sprinkled the cut pieces with lime juice. Hmm. I wasn't sure if I liked it or not, but I kept eating, to decide whether I did or not. She finished first and walked outside for a moment. As I ate, contemplating the odd taste and texture combination of lime juice on cantaloupe, my attention was drawn to a corner of her kitchen counter, where another collection of crystals sat.

In the center of the collection, up on a thin cushion, sat a large, nearly life-sized human skull carved from white quartz. I did a double-take, turning around in my chair to look, since part of the kitchen counter was nearly behind me because of the direction my chair was facing.

A *skull*? Seriously? Honestly, it kinda freaked me out. I shrugged and went back to my cantaloupe. Before I knew what I was doing, my eyes slid over to the skull again. My attention focused closely on it, though I had no idea why. Yes, it was odd, but other than its strangeness, there didn't seem to be anything remarkable about it.

Back to the food. I decided that yes, I did like the cantaloupe, although I didn't know if I'd pick lime juice again, when having it at home (and in the eight years that have passed since, I haven't used lime on cantaloupe, so there you go.) My mind drifted for a moment, and I came back to myself, staring at the skull *again*. Why? This house was filled with things to look at, so why did I keep going to the skull?

Susannah walked back in, and I told her, a little embarrassed, that for some odd reason, I couldn't stop turning to look at the crystal skull on the counter. On her way through the room and back down the hallway, Susannah nonchalantly nodded.

"Oh yes, she's quite chatty."

We were talking about past lives. As the rest of my conversations, and for that matter, my life in general tends to be, these Reiki lessons were very tangential. We would stray from the topic and visit all sorts of interesting places, eventually coming back around to where we started with a much richer understanding and experience of the subject, as well as of each other.

I was almost completely unfamiliar with this topic, knowing only that past lives were something that crazy, New-Agey people talked about. I assumed that everyone claimed to have been Cleopatra or Nostradamus or someone like that in a previous life, which made the entire thing sound pretty ridiculous. That said, I had the same curiosity about the subject that most people seem to – after all, if the reason that we are alive at all is to learn, and if our souls are immortal, which just about every wisdom tradition says, whether that tradition is religious or not, then it doesn't make much sense to believe that we'd only have about seventy years and one try to get it all done. Then there is all of eternity to sit around and think about what happened during those seventy years, or to pay for it, as the case may be. Besides, what about the people who die when they are young? Is all of eternity based on a life that may have only been a few days long? That didn't seem very fair. It also didn't logically hold up. After I gave myself permission to actually question this process with my reasoning mind, rather than sticking to some dogmatic rule that somebody told me, I realized that something was missing.

Later, I discovered that even the Christian religion used to believe in reincarnation, and that most of the scriptures referring to the subject (and all of the scriptures directly speaking of it) were removed centuries ago during one of the major rewrites of the Bible. However, at the time of this conversation, since I wasn't a huge fan of Christianity anyway, I didn't think much about Biblical references to the subject.

Susannah confirmed that yes, as far as she knew and had learned, life is essentially a big classroom, where our souls have different experiences and learn different things, also interacting with a similar general group of other souls, who we trade roles with throughout our various lives. Some of us have lived many lives, and some have only lived a few times. She also told me that you'd be hard pressed to find anyone living nowadays who is on their very first life.

Well, Susannah seemed pretty sure of herself. And put that way, reincarnation did make more sense than any other explanation I'd heard. I asked her what, to her knowledge, happened after death. Susannah replied that at first, the thing happened that you expected to happen – if you believed in the normal Western idea, for instance, you'd be sitting on a cloud, in a white robe, with little cherubim playing harps all around you. But after a while of that, maybe even a few years, you'd get pretty bored (definitely understandable, I thought – I'd be bored of that after an hour!) and when you finally asked if there was anything more to it, everyone around you would say,

"Yes – glad you asked. Here's what's *really* going on."

The veils would be drawn back and you would have a review of your most recent life (the one you'd just died in,) where your actions would be studied and discussed, the good, the bad, and the in-between. By the way, the "bad" would not be labeled as such by arbitrary rules, but rather by how you affected others, and the world in general – did you bring light, or darkness? Light was encouraging, in some way or another, positive growth for everyone involved. Dark was the opposite. Things are often more complex than this, but even with all of that complexity, there is still choice and you can still break a person's intentions and actions down to one of those two options.

This information would be used to determine what would happen during your next journey in a physical body, and what opportunities you would be given to increase light and to balance out any damage you had done. Susannah told me that whether or not you choose *everything* that happens to you before you are born is a hot topic of debate. She also said that, after a very fatiguing or traumatic life, you may "sleep" for awhile, resting and recharging in peaceful quiet for as long as it takes you to be healed. We also talked for awhile about lost souls – people whose death is so shocking that they get confused, become quite literally *lost*, and can't find their way to the next plane. This, she said, explains hauntings, and also why and how they can be cleared.

Since this conversation, I've learned more about such things, and even experienced first-hand some of what we talked about, which will be included in these pages later. But at this point, I kept my judgment pushed aside. Now, I'm not sure if I believe **everything** she said, but each person finds their own language of Truth, and we are always unfolding and learning more. At the time, it was a step up from what I already knew, and I often wonder if Susannah actually told me *everything*, or if she edited information to put it into a package that I could understand. As I've never been able to locate or contact Susannah since, I would have no way of finding this out. It's funny, how people appear and disappear in life.

I sank back into the couch, pulling my feet up so he wouldn't trip on them as Noah passed me on his way into another room in our apartment during a commercial break. It was the part of the evening where we were winding down, watching some random television program that provided vague stimulation while allowing our minds to go into rest mode for sleep. We would go to bed in the next hour or so. Basically, we were doing the same thing that most households in America do, at least on week nights. Sitting in bed and reading a book would probably work better, but television is pretty addictive. Until you realize that it turns you into a zombie, you can't be expected to know better.

Noah had left the door cracked just a bit, and something caught my attention about the thin column of light shining between the door jam and the edge of the actual door. This was the first time I'd ever "seen" anything, and I was so shocked that I nearly fell off of the couch. Before I describe what I saw, I'd like to tell you about the type of "seeing" that I have, so as not to be misunderstood.

This is not physical sight, using the eyes. Instead, it is as if your mind's eye, or your imagination, places the visual thought of something before you, in the space that you currently occupy. It isn't like a daydream where you are in a different location and situation.

I'll show you. Take a moment to look around the space that you are sitting in as you read these words. Notice the details. Go ahead, I'll wait.

…........

Now, look around again, and just imagine that (no pun intended) there is a small elephant in the room with you. Simply imagine it standing there. See its ears flap, and imagine the details of its body, like the wrinkled knees and long trunk common to every elephant. See its wide toenails and its small, intelligent eyes looking at you.

Okay. *That* is how I "saw" this – I knew that it was not physically present. However, this creature was unlike anything I'd ever seen, and not only was it extremely detailed and specific, it was downright disconcerting (even a little frightening,) and it was moving, and interacting – with **me.**

Over the course of about five seconds, give or take a few, I "saw" long, green, pointed fingers curl around the edge of the door that Noah had left cracked. Then, in the space between the door and the door frame, a face appeared, as if a tall being, about six feet in height, was standing there and peering out at me. The face was green, and wide, and generally similar to a Human face in the *placement* of its features, though the features themselves looked very different. There was also something funny about the entity's head, and although I couldn't get a firm fix on what it was (as I was completely shocked to be seeing this at all – I mean come **on,**) later I had the idea that whoever was looking out at me resembled those cartoon, marketing pictures of "Sea Monkeys," and also the Grinch in that famous Christmas tale.

As I've said, not only was this thing looking out, but he was looking at *me*. Staring right at me, as though he knew me quite well. And this was not at all a kind gaze. It was playful in a way that made me fully aware that whatever game he wanted to play, I would not enjoy it one bit. His eyes stared into mine for a moment, and then he smiled a very slow, very large, *very* unfriendly smile.

In the next few seconds, he faded away and there was just the door again. I realized instantly that he had been in the same room as Noah, so I called in to Noah and hurried him, asking that he return quickly. He did, and we finished watching our television program. Of course I didn't *say* anything – I would have sounded like a crazy person!

(Note: This was one of the experiences after which, in my research, I became very well versed – not to mention nervous about – the onset age of adult mental illnesses, such as adult-onset schizophrenia, where people basically see things that aren't there. This worry stayed near to me for the next several months, until I became very familiar with otherwise quite "sane" people whose "visions" were even more intense than mine. The conversation I was to have with Susannah later helped too.)

Later that evening, Noah and I sat in the guest room. He was playing a computer game and I was reading a book behind him, stretched out on the futon. Over the music coming from the computer's speakers, we heard a knock on our door. A moment later, the knock was repeated. We looked at each other, and at the clock which read about nine thirty pm. Noah got up and walked to the front door as I nervously waited, motionless, on the futon.

I heard Noah talk to someone. Thankfully, I did *not* hear our front door open in response to whatever was said. Soon Noah walked back into the room.

"Who was that?" I asked him as he sat down at the computer again, a mildly confused expression on his face.

"I don't know. They said they wanted to use the phone."

"Use the *phone*?"

"Yeah, apparently their car broke down on the road."

"Well, was it a man or a woman?"

"I couldn't tell," he told me, his attention returning to his game.

"You couldn't *tell*? How can you not tell that?"

"I don't know, the voice sounded weird and I couldn't tell."

"Weird how?"

"I don't know."

"But wait," I said, my blood running cold, "We live in a gated community. If their car broke down, *how did they get in*?"

"I don't know," he replied. "But I told them that there's a gas station a couple of blocks away that they can use."

"And then what? I heard you talk for a couple of minutes."

"Oh – they were trying to convince me to let them in."

"Whoa. I'm glad you said no!"

"Me too." And he went back to his game.

I'm usually not the type to ever refuse someone who needs help, but on this night, after what I'd seen in the bathroom, I didn't want anyone else in my house.

A few days later, at Susannah's house for another lesson, I asked her about what I'd seen. She had me describe the green guy's appearance more than once, and then she sat still, asking me to be quiet so that she could go into a meditation and ask her "guides" for help in figuring out what to do.

After a few minutes, Susannah's eyes opened. She then told me how, hundreds of years ago, maybe even longer, I'd had a run-in with this creature. Back then, she said, where I was located, which had been in Europe (and in a man's body to boot,) people lived more closely with what they call the "Fae." These weren't the cute little winged creatures in today's fairy picture books. They were another species, human-like in some ways, and unlike humans in others. These were the creatures that you'd hear stories about babies being kidnapped by and people spending one night with, awakening the next morning to find that decades had passed during their slumber. These were also the creatures that still gather a healthy respect in many parts of the world today, with construction never being done on "Faery Mounds," because if it is, bad things happen. I read a story not long ago about a power station attempting to put up a pole on top of a Faery Mound for running electrical cables. Apparently the contractor was American, and although his workers, all local men, informed him that building on a Faery Mound was a bad idea, he laughed this advice off and told them to dig and place the pole anyway. The morning after the pole was placed, it was standing quite crooked, making it unusable. According to his orders, the workmen righted it, using all of their best equipment to fix it securely in the ground, and on the next morning the pole was at a slant *again.* This happened at least once more before the contractor gave in and moved the pole off of the mound, where it sat peacefully and perfectly functionally from then on.

This other species, apparently, lives much longer than we do. Long enough that something I did hundreds of years ago was still bothering a particularly tall, green individual.

In her meditation Susannah had discovered that in a past life, I had been male, and since our two species still interacted on a much more common level than nowadays (for you still hear odd stories, even now, on occasion,) I had interactions with some of these people. Susannah said I wasn't at all a nice person during that lifetime, and I'd made a definite faux pas, somehow embarrassing, shaming, or hurting this creature significantly. As a result, he's followed me since, throughout my incarnations (able to track me, of course, since these folks work through soul recognition, not physical appearance,) bothering me and making me pay for the problems I caused him. Usually he would cause trouble that I couldn't see, Susannah told me, but now I was becoming open and able to see and experience more of what is actually *there,* and not only what happens to be visible in the light spectrum that our eyes can ordinarily discern. My mind was beginning to escape the binds of "consensus" reality, including all the things that we are told as children aren't real so that we choose to block information that we do naturally perceive, beginning this block at about age seven and maintaining it for the rest of our lives. I was clearing this block now, which is why I had become consciously aware of his presence.

I felt terrible. First of all, the news that I'd been a jerk and done such damage bothered me to begin with. Now knowing that this thing would be hanging around, causing all sorts of mayhem with intentions to harm me, was downright scary. Susannah meditated again without closing her eyes this time, instead doing the same thing I've seen other psychics do as she stared off into space for a moment, seemingly listening, and then gave me information that she'd received from somewhere *else*. She told me that her "guides" would help her do a spell that would protect me from the mean green guy, keeping him from being able to find me.

This was a tapping spell, Susannah said, and I had to keep my eyes closed while she did it. I closed my eyes, a bit nervous, as she began to tap a wooden walking stick on her stone floor. All of a sudden, I could hear other, smaller taps working in concert with hers, coming from all over the house. They sounded in the room where we now sat, and where there hadn't been time for anyone to run in and make these noises while my eyes had been closed – I *did* wonder about that possibility, because this was just too weird. The sounds came from other rooms close by, and also from the hallway. The tapping came faster and faster, until one loud tap of Susannah's ended the sequence, the silence seeming louder than the noise assaulting my senses over the last couple of minutes. It wasn't that the taps were *loud*, but rather that they were absolutely **real** – these were physical noises, coming from something, somewhere, that I wasn't allowed to see and that wasn't at all human. That was enough to garner all of my attention.

In the silence, Susannah told me that I could open my eyes again. I slowly did, looking around the room, wondering what had happened while my eyes were closed.

"That's it, you should be fine now," she told me simply. Then she changed the subject.

In case you're wondering, no, I've never had the slightest glimpse of that entity since.

We were talking about reincarnation again. I was firing all the questions and arguments at her that I could possibly think of against the possibility of multiple lives. Sure, it made sense on a cosmological level, but then, if we all had past lives, how did it *work*? What about all of the people who said it was nonsense?

As we spoke, Susannah's explanations of the concept easily stood up to every criticism and philosophical loophole that I could come up with. After I'd exhausted every opposing viewpoint, Susannah asked me a question.

"Would you like to know how many lives you've had?"

Well, of *course* I did. I mean, what else can you even **say** to that?

She asked me to stand still and wait for a few moments. I took a deep breath and tried to open up my mind and my energy field, quieting all resistance, becoming empty and loose. I instinctively knew that this would make it easier for her to gather information.

She turned her head a bit, staring off into space and using her method of muscle testing (something I've never been able to do,) where she made a circle out of her left pinky and thumb, and flicked it open with her right forefinger. Some people use another person's arm strength to do a similar thing. Although I understand how it works: your energy field, and therefore your physical strength, becomes more healthy and strong in the presence of truth, or good information, so arms are more difficult to push down or circuits are stronger, and even though I can do it on another person, using their arm, I've never been able to get accurate results using my hands like she did. Although I couldn't do it, I saw Susannah answer questions correctly that she could not have possibly already known using this method. I never saw her give an incorrect answer either, although some things, like what she was testing for right now, there aren't logical nor scientific ways to verify. Susannah counted quietly as she did this over and over, waiting until she reached a few numbers that her fingers stayed closed for.

"Three hundred and thirty seven. That's a lot. You have a long history," she told me.

Okay. It was nice to know, and although I've never been quite sure whether this one is my three hundred and thirty seventh or three hundred and thirty eighth life, something about that initial number gave me a peculiar feeling – somewhere deep within, I knew this was correct information.

Weird.

Susannah tilted her head down slightly and looked at me over the rims of her glasses.

"Would you like to know about some of them?"

Again – what are you going to say to that? I mean, who *wouldn't* want to know?

There was a long silent moment while Susannah focused, her eyes closed, and I tried to steady my breathing, feeling very strongly, down in my core, that something very important was about to happen. When she finally began to speak, it wasn't exactly what I expected.

"I won't be able to see every one of your incarnations, and I don't think you would want me to. Some of them are not easy nor pleasant, and some are downright boring. It's like that for everyone. Each of our lives is connected to certain other lives because we don't often complete every task we set out to do in any given life. Sometimes we even make mistakes and move backwards. Usually there are a few important lives that can give you a good glimpse, at any given time, into any issue you are struggling with now, in this incarnation. We keep trying to learn the same lesson and make the same accomplishment until we get it. One of your biggest lessons, this time, is linked with your being a healer, and having faith in the goodness of life and Mother-Father God. You have usually, if not always, served as a healer in some form or another, and you lost your faith in a very traumatic way. Here's the most important one that I'm seeing right now.

"You were a healer – a man – in Atlantis. Wait. Yes, the *third* age of Atlantis. There were three ages, you know. The shining, technological Atlantis that you see in movies and paintings was only first one of the three. At the end of the first age, the wrong people got their hands on the technology that was used back then, which was based on crystals the way ours is based on electricity. These people wanted to use their power to control and manipulate others rather than to oversee a balanced civilization. Things are hardly ever perfect, but they got progressively worse throughout the three ages.

"The technological systems that were in use broke down after they were utilized for purposes other than those that the systems had been created for. Because of this, as well as other things, each of the three ages ended in a gigantic storm. What started off as a continent was progressively pounded down, by these storms, into a small network of islands. Each age of Atlantis consisted of less and less land mass until the time during which this life of yours happened.

"You were a doctor, although to our cultural viewpoint you would seem more like a medicine man because you used plants and energies to heal. By this point the powers-that-were had grown incredibly corrupt and were doing all sorts of nasty things. Genetic manipulation, for one. Crossing humans and animals – really weird Dr. Moreau type of experiments. You lived on an island where a lot of these creatures that had been mutated and experimented on lived. The experimentation wasn't done in a kind, logical way. A lot of creatures were in a tremendous amount of pain and came to you for help. You helped as much as you could, but there was just too much pain and suffering around you for you to make much of a dent in it. You tried your hardest and you were completely consumed by this effort to heal the damage that you saw, but eventually, all of the agony that surrounded you every day caused a part of your spirit to die. You were alive when the final storm came and destroyed the islands, and you knew it was coming. You knew you would die, and you were glad. During this lifetime, you are a healer again and one of your main tasks is to recover that faith in Good."

As she spoke, I could *remember* things. Wondering at each vision if I was imagining it, I first saw my house – a thatched hut, with many plants and bundled herbs hanging from the low roof. There was a smell in there, too, the smell of potent plant material. Things were always brewing and steaming, the smells of which flavored the air, I supposed. I saw my feet, the brown feet of a man, walking barefoot through a semi-tropical island forest. I heard crying at night, and I felt the despair that she was describing settle around me – a despair caused by fighting, nearly ineffectually, against impossible, malicious odds.

I thought about this for days afterward. Some of my tasks for this lifetime, she'd said, would be to heal others and to regain my faith in Good. As I perfected my Level I Reiki skills, learning to open up my healing channels by creating three shapes using my hands in order to begin each Reiki session. First I held my hands clasped in front of my sternum, my fingers interlaced and forefingers straightened and pressed together, forming a steeple. This position was held until I felt a pulse between my palms – not my heartbeat, because this pulse was much slower and more gentle than that quicker rhythm. I've always had a faster resting heartbeat than what is considered normal. This position "tuned me in," the way a radio tunes into a particular frequency. Susannah taught me that anyone can do Reiki – it's just about being able to tune in to that particular vibration. Next, the forefingers would be interlaced as usual and the middle fingers would be held up and pressed into a steeple. This brought the Reiki energy down into my body. I'd feel a gentle settling around my shoulders that would indicate to me that it was time to move to the third position. This last one was simple, consisting of all the fingers interlaced. During this moment, a person is connected with the Divine, which is why this is the same popular pose taught to every child learning to pray. This time was for asking that, as I worked, I be guided in the best way for whoever I was helping's highest and most beneficial path.

"Sometimes," Susannah told me, "Reiki can be used for a different type of healing. I've used Reiki at death beds before to ease the transition. Always remember that YOU are not the one doing the healing – Reiki has its own intelligence because it comes directly from God. You are just the facilitator. That's why you always ask that you be guided to do what's *actually* best for the person you're working with. Never assume you already know the answer to that question of what is best in any given situation when healing someone else, or even yourself. It'll come to you as you work."

And come to me it did. I learned to feel when a portion of the body had finished receiving Reiki by paying attention to the way that my hands would pulse. I learned, through practice, to be able to "see," with my mind's eye, the golden Reiki energy I was sending into someone travel from one of my hands to another, and when both of my hands pulsed in rhythm, I knew that I'd finished with that spot. I learned to "feel" new and old injuries, and to speak the language of the body, each individual having his or her own specific dialect.

I followed Susannah's direction and gave myself 15 minutes of Reiki each morning, starting with my left foot and moving up the entire left side of my body and down the right side, ending with my right foot. There were specific hand positions commonly used, but I tweaked them to what worked best for me. Like any tradition, Reiki serves as a base for learning, and there comes a time that what Reiki tells you to do becomes automatic guidelines, rather than dogma. This is what I experienced.

Working with energy came naturally to me. I could feel things almost immediately in that slow, subtle, hard to place way that energy evidences as when you are unfamiliar with noticing it. I could manipulate the way in which it moved soon after I began doing Reiki. I could direct it, focus it, and when I didn't already have an intuitive feeling about what should be done, I could send it out freely, trusting it to do its work without my conscious direction.

Once I recognized what this mysterious life force actually was and how it acted, I realized that I'd already been working with it all of my life. When I was a child, I would get headaches often enough in the Kingdom Hall (which is what Jehovah's Witnesses call their church) during meetings. The women in my family were plagued with migraines, and although I never get migraines anymore as an adult, I suppose that I didn't know any better back then, so my body did what those around me were doing. Migraines are also, I've learned since, at least partially created by the shutting down of sixth chakra (a.k.a., third eye or psychic) energy. This makes perfect sense. As I've recovered some foggy memories about how anything psychic I ever may have said or done as a child would have been received by the adults around me, who were themselves conditioned to label anything out of the three dimensional norm to be "demonism" and to be paralyzingly terrified of it, I can understand that I probably, under no circumstances, made those around me aware of what I was doing once I realized that it would be met with that inevitable response. Considering that I was, at heart, someone who only wanted to be cuddled and loved by my parents (I was very physically affectionate compared to others in my family – the only "emotion-brain" in a family of "computer-brains") then it makes sense that I would not only hide these possibilities from others, but that I'd opt to completely shut down anything going on inside of me that I knew could be labeled as "bad" in order to get that much-needed approval.

Whenever a headache would come over me in church, I would begin to isolate it in my brain, feeling the edges where the pain bundle ran into a non-painful area. I would label the pain as a color in my mind, as well as painting the non-painful area with a different color. Slowly, carefully, and with a great amount of focus, I would force the pain color to transform into the non-painful color, with the pain vanishing along with its associated shade. Once all of its color was gone, my headache was gone. No one taught me to do this (that I was consciously aware of, that is.) I just *got it*. Only a decade later, while learning Reiki, did I understand that I was doing energy work on myself.

My sister suffered from poor circulation when we were children, and as our family was too poor to always outfit us with such things as non-holey socks and any gloves at all, when the weather was cold her hands would begin to lose blood flow completely, finger by finger. Mine started to do the same after I'd reached adolescence as well, but as a child, I didn't at all like seeing my big sister's hands turn a deathly white. I would take them between mine, using my will to force her blood to flow back into the chilled area. This would eventually work, and she'd take her hand back and thank me. Eventually she would return later, once it had begun again.

This work stopped mostly during my early adolescence, when my world became boys and makeup and the intrigues of junior high school social politics. Anything particularly esoteric remained on the back burner throughout most of high school. However, during the spring of my senior year, I was driving along a winding country road one sunny afternoon when I hit a butterfly.

Not being one to be particularly squeamish about bugs or small squirming things in general, I still didn't like to kill innocent creatures, especially when they were outside, in their own territory. It wasn't like a spider was hanging out on my ceiling, holding the possibility with it that once the room was dark and I was asleep, it would walk over my still body, leaving painful, itchy bites behind in little rows. Besides, everyone loves butterflies.

The smear of yellow from the monarch's wings on my left on my windshield created such a gnawing, guilty feeling inside of me that I couldn't let it go. I turned down the radio and cried as I drove, bemoaning my speed and the poor butterfly's bad luck.

I could *feel* it behind me, dying on the road. My consciousness locked onto its pained, simpler one, and I slowly and completely *peeled* its life force out of its small, broken body. After the connection was completely severed between whatever glowing, filmy thing I was pulling on with my will and the biological encasement lying on the asphalt, I felt that life force completely evaporate into thin air (and what I didn't recognize then as the Great Force behind all things) as easily and painlessly as a drop of vanilla dissolves in a glass of water. My tears stopped. I'd done something. Although I didn't know what it was, I knew that I'd helped the butterfly.

Only years later did I recognize the connection between this work and the Reiki that I was learning from Susannah. There are many ways to work with energy, and Reiki is but one of them. This knowledge that popped up inside of me every now and then came from *somewhere*. It just never crossed my mind to question *where* that was.

My father visited me later in the summer, after I'd completed my Reiki I course and was practicing on a daily basis. I had a pretty good handle on how to heal injuries and illnesses by this time, although I'd never been faced with more than the flu or a paper cut (both of which healed right up, I might add.)

My father wasn't limping, but I knew that his knee was bothering him.

"No, there's no way to fix it from the outside," he told me sadly when I asked him about treatment options. "The ligament is disconnected. They'll have to go in surgically and reconnect it."

Neither of us liked that idea very much. I asked him if I could try to work on him using my new skill. Being familiar with life force energy from his martial arts training, and because, after all, he was the one who had introduced meditation to me in the first place, he figured that it was worth a shot.

I didn't own a massage table, which would ordinarily be the setting for a Reiki session, so he lay on my living room floor instead. Any bed or a couch that Noah and I had in our apartment would have limited the freedom I had to move all the way around my father during the session, and that movement was very necessary for a full body treatment.

I made him comfortable the way that Susannah had taught me by placing pillows at certain spots under and around his body. I didn't have that many pillows, especially of the various shapes and sizes that Susannah used, so I improvised. A rolled towel went under his neck and a folded one under his head, to provide adequate neck support and a little cushioning for his head. The spine should be kept in as natural a position as possible. Another folded towel went under his lower back, and small throw pillows were set under each forearm and hand. Then a flat pillow under his knees, and another folded and rolled towel combo under his ankles and feet.

"Wow, this is really comfortable. How did you figure out how to do this?"

"I have been learning *some* things, Dad," I said with a laugh.

I gave him a full body treatment, beginning with his left foot and working up to his head, then back down his right side again to his right foot. He relaxed and drifted into and out of a light sleep, his muscles tensing and eyes widening whenever I "pulled" energetic blockages out of his body, using my fingers as though I was actually grabbing something invisible just over wherever the blockage was located, envisioning thin, golden, painless needles coming out of my fingertips and grasping the dark, sticky blockage. In my father, most of these were located around various joints.

"What was *that*?"

"What did it feel like?" I asked him.

"Like you just pulled something out of my body. I felt that come all the way from my foot!" I had just pulled a clump of invisible gunk out of his upper arm.

"That's because I did."

I explained to him how this worked, telling him that energy isn't difficult to manipulate, once you decide to just go ahead and **do** it. Most people don't understand that energy is *real*, and if you just pay attention to it, you can probably figure it out. Most assume that this invisible energy is imaginary, so they never try to work with it, and they aren't able to even feel much from that decision on. The same would be true for walking. If you thought the act of walking upright was imaginary and never actually tried, we'd be a culture very heavily reliant on motor scooters, wouldn't we?

After I'd finished with his normal session, I slid one hand under his knee, my palm up and the other on top of it. I felt for the tear with my newly developed energetic awareness, and I quickly found an empty space that was highlighted in a painful red color in my mind's eye. I asked my father then how a healthy ACL would ordinarily run through the inside of the knee, and he confirmed what I was thinking when he pointed to the diagonal path it takes.

For the next hour, I concentrated, first flooding his knee with unfocused Reiki, which I like to think as the "stem cells" of life force because it will go where it needs to go and do what it needs to do on its own. You don't *have* to direct it. Of course, I do direct it sometimes too, and I did in this case after I filled the area with ordinary Reiki energy. After his knee was saturated with light, I felt for each end of the ligament. They were coiled against the inside workings of his knee, snapped back like a rubber band would be if it had been cut from a stretched position inside a chamber where it was permanently pulled taut. I fed Reiki into each of the two pieces, filling them with the soft, warm, golden energy that Reiki appears as in my mind. Then I ran a cord of golden Reiki energy from one curled piece of ligament to the other, forming a strong bridge of light that replicated what the ligament would look like, feel like, and act like. I set a strong intention with my will that the torn ligament, over time, would use this bridge as a scaffold to slowly stretch over and rebuild itself, connecting when its two pieces met in the middle.

I became lost in the process, screwing my eyes tightly shut and filling my entire world with this task of rebuilding his knee.

"Charis? What are you doing?" His voice sounded confused and a bit frightened.

"Why, what do you feel?"

"Things are moving inside my knee."

"Good. That means it's working."

After I felt like I'd done all I could, I ended the Reiki session, sweeping any remaining energetic pollutants out of his three-layered aura by brushing the air over him with my hands, from head to feet, thrice. In my mind's eye and with my energetic awareness, I willed any debris or blockages still floating around to move the direction I was sweeping them, down and out of his aura. The first pass was only a few inches above his body. The second was about a foot above that, and the final pass was made about two and a half feet from his physical form. Then I had him stand up, as I'd been taught, remembering Susannah's admonitions against forgetting this part, and told him to stand up straight and keep his eyes open. I placed my left hand's first two fingers on the center of his forehead, and swept my right hand up his spine, a couple of inches away from his body, beginning just below his hips and curving my hand over the top of his head, circling the energy around in three small horizontal, clockwise loops over his head and at the end of the third loop, flinging off the extra energy I'd collected during the first sweep upward. I repeated the sweep and the circling process twice more, then removed my fingertips from his forehead.

I fed him a little bit of food and a glass of water then, because it's a good idea to have a light meal or at least a glass of water after a Reiki treatment. This balances you and helps your body to detox via the digestive system.

We repeated his treatments a few more times, scheduling an afternoon session every remaining day of his visit.

My father never had surgery on his knee. I don't know whether he's had any x-rays taken to determine what the ACL is, or is not, connected to. But the following year, he took a bicycle trip from northern Virginia to Maine, and then across the uppermost border of the United States to Portland. His knee never bothered him.

"You're certainly not originally from *here*. Let me see where you first incarnated."

I stood again, holding my breath, clearing my mind, attempting to make myself as easy to read as possible while Susannah used whatever sense she had to look into my soul's past. Actually, she didn't do much of the looking herself, she's recently told me – what she was really doing in those moments where she either closed her eyes or stared off into space was listening to her "guides." *They* did the actual looking, and then reported back to her. At least, that's what ordinarily happened, when she was doing purposeful research. Sometimes knowings came upon her unbidden, and that was a different story.

As I stood there, not really understanding at all how this worked yet, I also knew without a doubt that she was *not* lying. As my own extrasensory senses have developed over the years, and even before then, I've been able to spot lies, most of the time. I've certainly been tricked as much as the next person by letting myself go into denial about half truths and complete non-truths that I would rather have believed, but basically whenever I wasn't in a romantic snare, my natural lie detection ability has always been uncanny. I'm not a mind reader – I can't see what the truth *actually* is, but something about lies stand out to me. Because I've tried many times to and have never been able to put a finger on exactly what happens in these moments, I think that there is a disturbance in a person's energetic or electronic field that happens when they knowingly tell a lie that I can somehow pick up on. Of course, having studied things like subtle body language and micro facial expressions doesn't hurt either.

I've digressed again. Let's get back to that late Floridian night where I learned about my original soul heritage.

"You were one of the Crystal People."

"Crystal People? What were they?" My mind was still. I didn't even want to give my imagination time to come up with something on that. Who knows where it would have gone.

"Well, they were tall and very thin. They looked generally human, except for that thinness. But you're pretty thin now, so perhaps that held over. These people looked almost stretched, from what our perspective of a normal body type would be. They had very long, slender fingers. And their skin was a light blueish color, and very delicate looking, kind of translucent in a way. They were actually quite beautiful. Very gentle, too, dignified, and they worked with crystals. Your first incarnations were as one of them."

And that was all there was to that story. Hmm. I didn't really know what to say. It was interesting, I supposed, but I really had no container for this sort of thing. The idea that we are alone in this infinite universe is just silly to me, and to think that another civilization could exist with reasonably humanoid inhabitants was believable enough, considering that this could have been a very, very long time ago, and according to Susannah, it *had* been extremely long ago. Okay, whatever. I didn't dwell too long on the times that I've joked about how I look like someone took a normal body type and *stretched* it, or on the way that the length and thinness of my hands has been commented on a great many times throughout my life. Maybe it was just a coincidence. Maybe Susannah was just perceptive and had noticed my hands. But if that was true, then what about her remark about looking stretched? She couldn't have known that.

As my ability to meditate progressed and I put myself through a shamanistic training course outlined in the book entitled *By Oak, Ash, and Thorn: Modern Celtic Shamanism* by D. J. Conway, I decided to go back and revisit an odd encounter from when I was a child. It, like other similar events, had been relegated to the "wow, that was weird" drawer in my mind, only to be taken out and reviewed during those conversations about all things strange and unexplainable that are only had late at night or on road trips, or both – you know the ones I mean.

When I was ten years old, my sister and I shared a bedroom at the head of the stairs. The end of my bed faced the doorway. When the bedroom door was open (which it was, on this night,) I could see the small wooden globe that sat atop the upper end of the staircase banister. It ran up the stairs, and then along the wall, edging a small hallway that led to the upstairs bedrooms. Our parents' room was next to ours, followed by my little brother's room at the opposite end of the hall.

I slept relatively soundly during my childhood. I had the normal amount of nightmares when I was younger, but by the time I was ten, they had basically dried up. I hadn't gone into my parents' room for reassurance in a long while – maybe even years – so this evening's events came as quite a surprise to them.

It was in the wee hours of the morning, and I awoke and looked around, my eyes naturally going to the brighter doorway. During the night the hallway light remained on to help all of us avoid stubbed toes while sleepily making our way to the bathroom. Standing there just under the overhead light, her hand resting on the brown wooden ball at the top of the stairs, was a woman. She had dark, smooth hair which was parted on the side in a perfectly arranged style. Part of her bangs covered the outer edge of one of her eyes. Her face was serious and intent (stern and foreboding, it seemed to me at the time, although in retrospect I've realized that she was simply serious, and that the following bit was what scared me the most,) and she was staring directly at *me*. Right into my eyes.

This was no glimpse of a filmy white ghost disappearing around a corner, off in some eternal replay of a walk from one room to the next. This was a freaking *person*. Three dimensional. Fleshed out. In color. Standing there, as plainly as any person I'd ever seen, and focused directly on me.

I screamed. Of course I screamed! Who *wouldn't* scream? She **didn't belong there.** I didn't recognize her. And this was not my imagination. This was no dream. She was *there*.

My father ran into the room, darting over to my bed to see what the matter was. I covered my face with fistfuls of sheet, my words jumbling into some sort of frightened description of what I was seeing. Later my father told me that I wasn't making enough sense for him to be sure of *what* I saw, just that whatever it was, it was outside my doorway.

"There's nothing there. Charis, there's nothing there. You're fine. Look for yourself. Go ahead, take a look."

I slowly removed my hands from my eyes, hopefully squinting in that direction.

*She was **still there**.*

I think it's pretty easy for you to imagine what happened next – a full fledged, ten year old **freak out**. He couldn't see her, but *I could*. Did that mean he couldn't protect me? It seemed to. And if he, my all powerful father, couldn't make her go away, then to put it mildly, I was pretty much screwed. I sat frozen and as tense as a stone for a very, very long time until my father convinced me to look again.

This time she was gone.

Years later, during my self-training as a shaman of the Celtic tradition, which felt *right* to me in a strange way, I discovered different levels of reality that I could visit and glean information from during my meditative travels. One was the World Tree.

After the grounding and descending processes that I'll explain later, I began each meditation by picturing myself sitting on a grassy slope with a small stone well directly to my right. Far in the distance before me was a mountainous horizon, and in the valley below and nearer to where I was sitting grew a great, ancient tree.

I would dig my toes into the fresh-smelling grass and turn my face up to the sun, seeing its orange brilliance through my closed eyelids. Little sensory tricks like this help to make the meditation more solid. Then I would stand up, turn right, and take the few steps to the little stone well, drawing items out of my pocket that represented any stress or worry that was plaguing me in my three dimensional life at the time. If I was worried about money, I would pull out a dollar bill. If I was having interpersonal problems, there would be a picture or a little doll that resembled the person I was struggling with. If I was stressed about my grades, I would find a piece of paper with an "A+" written on it in bright red marker. Then, one by one (there were usually about three or four items) I would drop them into the clear water, watching them twist and turn, glinting in the distorted light, until they vanished into depths of the gray-blue water. Once all of my worries had been dropped into the well, I would be free to take my journey. If I left this step out, I wouldn't be able to properly focus on the task at hand.

When I visited the World Tree, I would walk down the hill towards it after my trip to the well. Sometimes I would take giant leaps for fun, sometimes I'd swiftly glide over the tall, soft grass. In a few seconds I would reach the huge tree at the bottom of the slope where I'd begun my meditation. There was a door in the massive trunk. I would open it and walk inside. I could turn to my right, which took me to a small platform overlooking a swiftly flowing, dark river, or I could ascend a spiral staircase in front of me and slightly to my left. The staircase took me to visit the Upperworld, which, for some reason, appeared to me as a great, bright room with walls made of windows. Dust was floating in the shafts of sunlight in that dreamy way that it does, and the room was filled with drafting tables. These tables were covered with paper, writing utensils, and instruments that reminded me both of my middle school geometry class and the navigational tools used by old world sea captains. The odd thing about the Upperworld, during my visits, was that it was always utterly empty. No one was ever there. Because of this, I'd often get bored quickly and go somewhere else. In retrospect, I don't know why I wouldn't ever choose to read the maps and diagrams on the drafting tables... Perhaps one of these days I'll take another trip and see what they've been working on up there.

The Underworld was a place I visited more often, and that I'll come back to in a moment. It was much more variable and populated. Many interesting things happened there. That wasn't accessed through the tree at all, however. It used a different visualization entirely that I'd do after I dropped my worries into the well. The well was an integral part of my shamanistic journeys because my worries would distract me if I didn't tell my subconscious that I'd shed them first. After the meditation had ended, I would always have those concerns again, although they often seemed smaller and less scary. This could have been simply because meditation is a natural stress-reliever, or the explanation could have been more mysterious. I never much worried about it.

The river in the World Tree was a way to travel through time. I could choose a place and time to visit, and I would be able to get impressions of the chosen destination. I never developed this visualization very far beyond what I desired to see for novelty or entertainment, or verification. Early in my journeys I wanted to make sure I wasn't imagining things, so I would pick places and times that I knew nothing about, researching them after I took a glimpse to check and make sure my subconscious wasn't making up something random. What I saw was *always* verified by my subsequent research. For some reason, I didn't feel any particular desire to keep doing this after I was sure it worked. Simple voyeurism has never much appealed to me. The experience I had after I decided to take a look at Victorian times in Europe may have been what turned me off to the entertainment provided by my river views. The stench alone drove me away. They didn't bathe too often back then, you know. The room I saw, decorated with lots of shiny gold paint and pastels, smelled like strong perfume, sweat, and unwashed bodies. Gross. Of course, that was normal for the time. Either way, it got rid of that pastime for me.

My visits to the Underworld were different than may perhaps be expected, given the preconceptions that surround the term in our culture. In Celtic tradition, the Underworld wasn't negative at all, but rather a realm where more types of creatures existed than just humans and animals, which is basically all we have here on the three dimensional surface world. It was also a place where the laws of physics worked differently, and where all types of things were possible. Shamans did much of their work there, according to what I was learning at the time.

I visited the Underworld by going through my normal routines to begin a meditative journey – relaxation, cleansing energetically and placing protection around myself in the form of a pure white light, and then dropping my worries into the small well. Next, I traveled downward, through a private entrance (everyone has their own) to find a door that led into the Underworld. The first time you visit, you are only supposed to look in and see what is beyond the door. When I did this, I saw an outdoor area during what seemed like the afternoon. There was grass, shrubbery and trees growing in a way that suggested a kind of natural park. The area seemed easy to spend time in and not full of undergrowth and brush, though not officially tended or landscaped. I didn't see anyone there, but in subsequent visits I met interesting people, or people-like entities that is, such as a fawn in the "Pan" or "Dionysus" fashion with little horns on his human head, curly hair, and two legs representing his namesake. I was supposed to be met with a guide for each visit, and originally the fawn guided me. In a subsequent visit, I sat on my familiar rock just beyond my entrance to the Underworld, waiting for my guide to appear. Up walked a beautiful, tall woman with dark golden hair coiled in an elaborate style held in place by golden circlets. She wore a long white robe reminiscent of a toga. She had a serious, no-nonsense demeanor, although she wasn't unkind at all. When I asked her name, she told me that she was Diana, but she pronounced it "dee-AH-nah," rather than the normal way we often say it here and now in the West. After she told me her name, I knew that she was one and the same with the Greek Goddess. As a child, I had a short-lived but very intense interest in Greek mythology, and I learned quite a lot. I never expected that, as an adult, I'd meet any of these people in the not-quite-flesh, whether it was my subconscious creating that meeting, as some would surely argue, or not.

Diana, one of my most resonant Goddesses, as it has turned out over the years since, also appeared to me before this Underworld journey during an automatic writing experiment I tried early into my awakening process. One does this by clearing the mind, holding a pen still, with its tip pressing against paper, so it would simply have to move to create a line. One then asks questions and moves the hand in whatever strange ways it wants to go. You never *feel* like you're writing anything besides random scribbles – at least, that's how it was for me. And yet, when you open your eyes and look down at the paper, there are definite words there. Messy, but legible. And when, during this experiment (I didn't continue automatic writing much, it seemed more difficult than some other practices I took to more easily,) I asked who I was speaking to, the name "Diana" was written on the paper through me.

The funny thing is that she never even stood out to me that strongly when I was a child, reading about her and her relatives' adventures. It was a bit of a surprise at first when she was the one I had the most contact with.

One of my most interesting and easily verifiable experiences in the Underworld came one day during a visit that hadn't been rigorously laid out for me in my training book. I had finished whatever task I had to do that day, so I was free to roam around and explore.

After a bit of walking, I rounded a bend and found myself in front of a huge stone cauldron that reached easily up to my neck. I looked into it, first finding it cold and empty, then noticing movement at the edge of my vision. I raised my head to look. On the other side of the cauldron stood an extremely tall woman. She was at least twelve feet or so in height, and possibly taller. It was hard to tell so suddenly. She was literally shining and glowing brightly. I tried to see her face, but it kept changing so quickly that I couldn't get a firm fix on her features. Her hair was also sometimes light, and sometimes dark, but she was always stunningly beautiful, although her facial features continually shifted. She smiled down at me serenely and benevolently, and then she dipped her thumb into the cauldron, now filled with a shining golden liquid. She pressed the thumb into the space between and a bit above my eyebrows, and I was instantly hurtling through space, my sense of time and self completely dissolved. I saw great celestial bodies moving and spinning. I saw galactic alignments and dissolutions – the dances of stars and planets walking along their preordained paths, directed by the unseen hand that we talk about the effect of but so seldom question itself because,

.

after all, what would be the point? I saw colors I have no words for, and all of this in an instant. In less than an instant, even. But it felt longer than any eternity I know how to describe.

Slowly, gently, like a leaf falling through a soft, breezy afternoon, I floated back into my body. I was out of the underworld, and still sitting, in the same position and the same room that I'd begun my meditation in. *What the heck was that?* I wondered. But there was no way to know. I'd never heard of anything like this before.

A few chapters later, my shamanistic training book said that occasionally, a person may meet one or more of The Shining Ones. These were labeled as Gods or Goddesses who may speak or give you instructions, and who usually had a glow about them. I later heard that Cerridwen, the great Celtic mother goddess, would sometimes appear with a cauldron and with it or its contents, perform a ceremony of initiation and that this was never to be taken lightly. When all of these bits of information coalesced into a blurry understanding of what had happened, I was shocked. Before, everything that had happened in the Underworld could have been explained by my own subconscious. But I'd known nothing about this "initiation" that was possible, via the Celtic Goddess Cerridwen, with a *cauldron*. Those are too many coincidences to ignore. I was sure, now, that I wasn't journeying only in my own mind, I was going somewhere **else.**

This was neither the first nor the last time that I meditated or "downloaded" something that was explained to me in the three dimensional world afterward. I like it when this happens, because it provides me with a nice validation for experiences that are unique and often difficult to describe (not to mention, to *prove*.) However, at this point I'll admit that proving anything is leaving my realm of concern. My job in these pages is simply to describe what happened, in exactly the way that it happened. No embellishments.

Once I'd mastered the general process of traveling here and there via my mind and willpower using the shamanistic methods I was learning, I decided to experiment with other things that caught my attention and sounded like fun. The first was remote viewing.

This is how it worked. I would sit still, slowing my breath into a steady rhythm, relaxing my body piece by piece until I was floating in a no-place kind of numb comfort. Then I would imagine that there was another version of me, finer in consistency, made out of something akin to mist, or light, but that was really neither of these things. This version looked like my physical body does and it is always around, but is usually seamlessly "stuck" to my physical body. Essentially it's a similar principle as Peter Pan's shadow. This is the part that thinks and feels and actually experiences everything I use my physical vehicle to experience. I would let it would rise up out of my physical body, where it was able to fly around without any need to combat gravity or wind, or use things like doors and hallways. Then, I could go wherever I wanted.

At first, I decided to test this to see whether it worked. I decided to go see Amanda, my best friend from high school who I used to discuss philosophical matters with over chocolate. We spoke regularly and I kept her pretty much in the loop about the strangeness of my life. Unlike others (it could get pretty dicey at times,) Amanda was always as cool as a cucumber, encouraging me and never once calling me crazy. She told me later that she'd always known I would end up somewhere near here, although she couldn't have predicted where that place would realistically be. I've gotten that from other friends too. Funny, that I was so worried about hiding my true self from everyone, when most people knew anyway.

When I tried to remote view Amanda, it was on a week day, at roughly two o'clock in the afternoon. I flew up and out of my body, getting a sense of direction both from what I could see and what I already knew from the position I'd been lying in, down below. I traveled north, and slightly east, using the feel of my friend's personality as a magnet. This type of searching, using someone's essence, is a difficult thing to describe, but once you get the hang of it, the process is very simple. You can recognize a person by how they *feel*, especially if you have an emotional bond already, like good friends or family members do.

Anyway, I used this method, which works in some ways like a compass, to find her. I saw that she was sitting in a classroom, paying attention to whatever the instructor was saying and taking notes. She was wearing orange shorts and a ponytail. I returned to my body soon afterward.

I called Amanda later that afternoon.

"Let me ask you something random," I said. "At about two o'clock today, were you in class?"

"Yeah. Why?"

"Were you wearing orange shorts and a ponytail?"

"Yes...How did you know??"

Luckily for me, Amanda did not get completely freaked out by that conversation like some people would have. She thought it was cool. But in the future, just to be safe, I asked my family members and friends to give me good times to check in on them so I could hone this skill. I didn't ask what they'd be doing, I wanted to find that out myself. I simply told them what I was working on and asked if they would help me experiment. Again, luckily for me, they either assumed that nothing would come of it, or they tallied it in the "Charis is a weirdo, just go with it" category. Either way, I got in some great practice that way.

After I was finally emotionally prepared to find out more from my terrifying childhood encounter with the lady at the head of the stairs, I sent myself into a deep trance, beginning by relaxing my body and then descending those five steps that brought me into the deepest type of relaxation, where I did my heavy duty work. The number "5" was carved on the top stone step clearly and the following numbers became more crude and faint until, on the last step, the number "1" was made out of some sort of embedded wire that glowed blue and that had decorative scroll work embedded around it in the same fashion. I didn't understand what it meant, but I didn't pay much attention to it. I figured that it was either something popping up from my subconscious, an ancient memory, or both. In any event, the only notice I took of it was to think that the effect was pretty. Whatever.

I went to my grassy slope, dumped images and figures representing my current worries into the small well, and bounded down the hill to the World Tree in its little valley. I went into the trunk as usual, and turned right to see the dark river. Once I was leaning over the water, I sent the intention down into it that I travel to that night when the woman stood in my hallway. After a moment, an image of my bedroom door and the bookshelf behind it was clearly superimposed on the flowing water. I jumped in.

I stood next to my opened bedroom door, noticing the thick layers of white paint peeling around the door's outer edges and the full-length mirror nailed onto the back of it. Not wanting to be seen, just in case I could be, which I doubted, I crouched in the darkness behind the opened door, sitting next to the messy bookshelf that I spent so much time rifling through back then. I could see my ten year old self in bed, still sleeping quietly, but I couldn't see into the hallway. The open door blocked my view.

I saw the girl in bed stir and sit up, looking toward the light in the hallway. I saw her eyes widen in surprise and her hands fly up to her face as she started to scream. I heard my parents rustle in their room and then my father's bare feet thumping down the hallway and into the room. I saw his back as he ran over to the bed, and I listened to the conversation between the two, hearing his reassurance, her second fright, and then his reassurance again. After she looked up for the second time and saw no one there, I quickly slipped out of the door and onto the top of the landing myself, to see what I could discover. I saw the back of the woman with dark hair descending the steps in front of me. I took a few steps downward, and called after her.

She turned around. As I'd thought, her hair was parted on the side and fell down smoothly, partially obscuring one of her eyes. This was a very similar hairstyle to one I've worn in recent years. What I'd wondered about was true. She was identical to me, now, as an adult. I looked much different as a child, so I couldn't see the similarities back then. In my memories and when talking to others about that strange story, I had recounted her features over and over and wondered if this strange explanation, which didn't actually explain *anything* (and confused me more than ever,) could be the case. Sure enough, it was.

"Who *are* you?" I asked, in shock. She was staring into me with those same serious, intent, slightly stern eyes.

"I'm you." This was said with a nonchalance that implied that I should understand this paradox, which of course I didn't. But I also had a feeling that our time was limited. Answering the question I was asking in my mind, she then told me, very firmly and seriously and allowing no argument with her tone,

"You need to *go back*."

Then she turned and walked down the stairwell and out of my sight. I knew the conversation was over.

Go back **where**? What the heck was she talking about? Back to my childhood home? That didn't make sense. As the scene faded and I returned to myself, coming out of the meditation, I sat still, lost in confusion. What did this *mean*? I thought about her cryptic words obsessively for a day or two, and then gave up trying to figure it out. If I was supposed to know what she meant, I would know, sooner or later.

My cell phone rang. I looked at its screen to see who was calling me. Rae's cell.

"Hi, what's up?" I asked.

"Can you come up? Robin needs us to exorcise her house," Rae said, her nonchalance covering obvious excitement. I could tell that she thought this was going to be fun.

"Number one, yes, and number two, you're definitely going to have to give me more details on that one."

As it turned out, Robin, a friend of Rae's with long golden ringlets fit for an angel, had been having a problem with her three year old son's playroom.

"He won't play in there for longer than a half hour," she'd told Rae earlier.

After about a half hour of spending time in the room, the little boy would run up to his mother and say that he didn't want to stay in there, "with that mean man."

Robin asked him about the mean man, and always received similar details.

"I don't know who he is. He just stands in the corner and looks at me like this." At that point he crossed his arms and looked at his mother with a dark, scowling face.

Well geez, I thought to myself as Rae told me what he'd said to his mother. *I wouldn't want to play in there either.*

The problem had been going on for awhile, and the disturbances weren't only due to these conversations. Something in that room kept tripping the house's security system. It had gotten so bad, Robin told us, that her husband had to reprogram the system so that the perimeter of protected area did *not* include that room. The family would never sleep through an entire night if they hadn't taken the room out of the system, she explained.

Okay. Well. Obviously we'd never exorcised a house before, but we were the only ones she knew who could even *begin* to be capable of such a thing, and we certainly didn't know anyone else to refer her to. Rae and I each meditated on our own, asking our guides to be present and help us clear any negative entities out of the house. The issue was time-sensitive. Robin was pregnant with her second child so this room would soon be converted into her first son's bedroom.

That Saturday afternoon, Rae and I drove over to Robin's house together, meeting eyes and laughing nervously as we rang the doorbell. Robin opened the door, looking calm enough – she was always calm – but a little tense. I could understand why. Although she didn't feel anything other than a faint uneasiness in the playroom, she certainly didn't want her son sleeping in there if he couldn't even spend an afternoon with his toys in peace.

The three of us chatted for a few minutes, Rae and I each quietly getting our bearings and building up our courage for a completely novel experience that we didn't have the option of taking very lightly. If we failed, what would Robin do? She didn't have any other options. There isn't exactly a section in the phone book for this sort of thing. We asked to see the room. Robin led us around the corner and down the hallway to the closed playroom door.

It was wooden and painted white, and had a shiny brass doorknob. The entire thing seemed laughably ordinary, but I could tell that when we opened that ordinary door, strange things would happen. I took a deep breath, strengthening my personal shields, which are different for every person (mine tend to be white with various colors accenting them, depending on whatever task I'm doing and of a more or less complex design, depending upon the same thing.) I looked over at Rae. I could tell she was strengthening hers too.

We opened the door and walked into the room. It looked like the play room of any small child. Multicolored plastic toys lay on the floor. The white walls were mostly bare. The room had two windows. There was a closed closet with white sliding doors.

Although it looked like one, the room didn't *feel* like any child's play room. Children's rooms tend to feel emotionally lived in and comfortable. Kids put more attention on their environment than adults do, and since they are regularly focusing on and interacting with objects in the room such as toys and games, remnants of their happy "playing energy" always stick around.

This room didn't feel that way at all. It felt dark, and serious, and silently sinister. I could tell that it was *always* silent in here, even when the small boy was trying to play with his toys, ignoring the man in the corner.

Speaking of the corner...I asked Robin what corner the man usually stood in. She pointed to the one on my right, across from the door. Sure enough, an emotional coldness was coming from there. I could feel it with my emotions the same way you can put your fingers into the mist falling off of a block of dry ice and feel the liquid-like chill permeating your skin. He was **there**, and he was watching us. He also wasn't happy about our presence.

Robin left the room after Rae and I asked to be alone, wishing the two of us luck and closing the door behind her. We started to say words of clearing and protection. They weren't quite mantras, nor prayers, but ended up serving as something in the middle. We spoke, using our words to consciously direct our own personal energy and to invoke our guides and non-physical friends to our aide. We used colored, glowing energy (which anyone can direct, using attention and will) that would clear out negative gunk from the place. We both felt that cold feeling expand and become more intense.

He was not happy with what we were doing, and he wasn't being shy about it. So far, none of our methods were working on him.

"He's laughing at us," Rae said.

"Yeah. It's okay, we'll get him out," I replied, not wanting doubt to infect my focus.

We increased our own intentions and strength of will, visualizing clearing and cleansing energy more clearly and more intensely, swirling it around the room like a giant washing machine. We used the energy of our own physical and energetic bodies to get rid of anything in there that could be remotely harmful or problematic to a little boy's health and growth.

After a few more minutes of this, we felt a change in the air. He was going. He wasn't happy about it, but the secret that few people know about non-physical entities is that, since we are present in the physical world and they aren't, we are **automatically** more powerful. We have to *know* this however, in order to effectively clear away unwanted energies and entities. There are also pure cosmic rules. For instance, you can't enslave or boss around any sort of entity, not if your goal is to create a greater peaceful and loving integration of all things, which is the goal of any Lightworker worth her, or his, salt. However, if something is hanging around and causing trouble, bringing negative energies and creating negative events, you can always tell it to leave. You simply have to be more sure of yourself than it is sure of itself. This is done with focus, intention, and sometimes, a little help. Sometimes with a *lot* of help. Occasionally you'll find a very powerful entity that doesn't listen at all and does whatever the heck it wants to do, either until it's convinced to do otherwise, or until someone more powerful makes it leave. Luckily for me, I've never come up against one of these guys. I've always been able to get rid of nasty energies, so either I haven't faced any big bad ones, or I've just been more powerful, somehow, than any I've come across, even if they were stubborn. From time to time it has taken me longer to clear a space than I would have preferred. Because this playroom clearing was my first real time at this, I think Rae had more of the energetic clout than I did. Either way, the guy was eventually gone. The room felt clean and open, as if you could breathe easily for the first time since we'd walked in, about twenty minutes before.

We looked at each other and smiled. We'd done it! He was gone. Then, as if on cue, both of our eyes went to the closed closet doors.

Children are often afraid of closets, believing that things come out of them at night. Adults often reflect the same fears. Even many horror movies have unpleasant entities hanging out in closets. This is based in truth. For some reason, closets can be reasonably hospitable places for yucky energies of many types. I think it's because energy doesn't flow much in closets, especially in the back of closets. They are usually shut off and able to stagnate. I'm not sure if this is the reason why they end up serving as portals or not, but it's the only link I've been able to make so far. This closet was no exception. Something was *in* there.

"Rae, open the closet door."

"I'm not opening the closet door. *You* open the closet door."

One of us was going to have to open that door. I steeled myself and walked over to it, looking at Rae to signal her that I was about to move, and then flinging it open, taking a step backward at the same time.

Slowly, with a fluidity and an emotionally unclean feeling that turned my stomach, in my mind's eye I saw strange, long, malicious tentacles begin to work their way out of the closet. Rae and I directed all of our energy at whatever was at the base of those tentacles, bathing it in the brightest Light we could conjure up through our intention, banishing it with our will and asking our guides to help us get it out of there directly.

This only took a moment. Either it looked and felt scarier than it actually was, or Rae and I packed a bigger punch than we realized. Either way, it was gone nearly as quickly as I'd opened the door.

We each sighed with relief. We met eyes and started to laugh.

The entire string of events may sound anticlimactic, but this was a very intense afternoon. After we set protective energies in and around the room and the entire house and then emerged, we ate lunch with Robin in her dining room, recounting the "battle." Her son ran into and out of the playroom, grabbing toys and exchanging them for others in the course of his little story as young children do.

As far as I know, Robin's family never had another problem with that room.

5: Weather

It came to my attention one day via some book I was reading and can't remotely recall the name nor the author of, that a person, especially one with a natural or consciously developed affinity for it could control the weather.

Hmm. I thought about this for about a minute and decided to try it immediately. Why not? Besides, I'd had conversations with non-physical stuff before. Why couldn't I persuade a little rainstorm or two, as long as my intentions were benign?

Considering that I lived in Orlando, Florida, I couldn't have picked a more suitable place to explore this particular trick. When I first moved to the area in 2001 as a college freshman, I was shocked to discover that it rained every day at about three or four o'clock. I found out later that this was only true for late summer and most of autumn. During the warmer months where afternoon showers came like clockwork, the rain would suddenly appear out of nowhere. It would continue for an hour or less, then, just as suddenly, the sky would miraculously clear and the sun would shine brightly again.

Pondering this after more than a few drenched walks to and from class, I figured that these afternoon showers were probably a result of the amount of groundwater in Florida and the heat of the sun. I guessed that each day, water evaporated until some saturation point was reached overhead. Then the skies would empty of all that accumulated moisture and the process would start again, culminating in another shower the next afternoon.

During the other seasons of the year, however, rain was less predictable where I lived. The morning sky would shine beautifully clear and by late afternoon, thunderstorms would roll in and cancel all of the plans made earlier to spend that evening outside. The opposite would happen as well, with dark mornings fading into beautiful afternoons. The air was constantly humid enough to dampen your shirt before you had spent ten minutes outside. Rain would fall in the front yard of a home and the back yard would be dry. More than once, I had to carry an umbrella and wear sunglasses at the same time.

I learned quite a few things as I experimented and felt my way through working with the weather. First of all, not *all* weather can be manipulated. It depends on your consciousness and the consciousness of what you're dealing with. Luckily, whenever I've put my mind to it, I've always been able to mold the series of events of weather patterns at least a little bit, but of course this could just be coincidence. Besides, I don't do this very much. Usually the weather doesn't bother me. Getting rained on every now and then is fun, and it makes you feel more alive. Think about the last time you got caught out in a thunderstorm. It's exhilarating. All of that information that water carries, along with the bits of electricity it brings from the activity that each droplet was just swirling around in overhead are absorbed into your skin and enliven your nervous system.

I also discovered other rules, through trial and error as well as "downloads," which is a name that Rae taught me to describe those packets of knowledge about a subject being understood, completely, in a nanosecond, as if the information was literally downloaded into my brain in an instant. When this happens, I hadn't the slightest idea about this subject a moment beforehand, and all of a sudden, my mind turns over on itself and expands, and I now have an understanding of the workings of something or another that I can often go and research in order to verify. So far, this knowledge has always been spot on.

One of the things I learned was that it isn't effective to try to change the weather experience of everyone around you. For instance, if I was driving to some destination and would rather not get soaked on my way into the building, I would very firmly *intend* that the rain would let up just for that ten seconds or so that it took me to trot from door to door.

This inability to change others' experiences of weather, it seemed to me, was because every person is always manifesting necessary happenings for her or himself. If the person in the office with me needs to get squelchy shoes in order to learn some life lesson or have some very important experience in their personal scheme of things, who am I to take that away from them? You never know, and I don't like to mess around with such things. So if I make sure the rain stops for those few seconds during, and *only* during, the time in which I'd like it to, then my coworker would probably forget something at his desk, or need to make a bathroom stop on the way out the door, or there would be some other sort of delay so that he would not leave the building at the same time I did. That way, I could have my break in the deluge, and he could also have his lesson. If it didn't matter to his sequence of necessary life events whether he was caught in the rain or not, then we could certainly just happen to walk to our cars at the same time, staying dry along the way.

There is an intelligence to the Universe that is smarter than any of us, because it literally consists of all intelligence, everywhere, in *everything*, combined into one cohesive, interacting, symphonic, and extremely sentient whole. It knows what it's doing. So, in the same vein, if I really need to have squelchy shoes myself and my weather manipulation doesn't work, then I don't complain too much. Instead, I perk up and look for whatever it is that I'm supposed to learn and experience. Something is being specially delivered, and I want to receive it.

This rule about how far your weather intentions can reach, by the way, may be different in today's world, where the weather is going so far out of whack that it defies prediction and many people are dying from the intensity of it. In fact, just a few days before writing this, tornadoes came through the town where I was staying in the mountains of Pennsylvania. Tornadoes don't come *here.* When I heard that there was a tornado warning, I affirmed, without interacting much at all with the weather system but rather within my own consciousness and acceptance of what *is*, that the tornadoes wouldn't cause harm anywhere nearby. I did some searching the next morning and discovered that although there were several tornadoes in the nearby counties, no one was injured. Weeks ago, hundreds of deaths occurred in another part of the country after more tornadoes were seen in the same few days than had been recorded in decades. Was it coincidence? Or was all that damage a reflection of the belief that we can't impact the weather and that it is out of our control? I wonder what would have happened if the people living in those areas had done the same affirmations that I did, with the same confidence. I can't say, but maybe one day this idea will spread far enough that we can test it and find out.

The same principle, by the way, works with gridlocked traffic. Years after my Floridian raindrop escapades, my sister and I drove on Los Angeles highways, headed to the drop zone where she skydives on the weekends. She was driving, switching radio stations in order to hear a traffic report. The road that we were on, we heard, was about to be solidly backed up. Our delay, would be significant – of at least an hour or two. We would hit the blocked area in just a couple of minutes. I wondered if I could do anything about that, so I told my sister that I was going to give it a try and asked her to stay quiet while I concentrated. I reclined my seat, closed my eyes, and pictured the great highway system as a big vein, or artery, with a clog in it. I dissipated the clog with my willpower, also affirming (aloud, for my sister's information since I knew she was likely to ask me later) that if the person next to us needed to experience shoddy traffic, they could. But for everyone who could benefit, the roads were clear, everything moved like clockwork starting *now*, and there would be no more congestion. We never did run into that horrible knot the radio report had warned us about.

That's the thing about weather and traffic, and probably other things that I haven't linked up yet. As I said, you shouldn't manipulate someone else's experience. But for your own experience? If it is harmless and will bring you more fun and joy? Go nuts. Go right ahead. Imagine what you want, see it as clearly in your mind as you can and set it there as firmly as if it were carved in stone with your willpower (I would, for instance, picture myself walking across a dry parking lot, or something similar,) fill it with a positive emotion (the mental image is the vehicle, and the emotion is the gas, when it comes to manifestation,) and then let it go. Let the Universe do its work, and see what happens. Often more interesting things come about than you would have predicted anyway, especially when you don't get too specific and just go for the broad strokes of what you would *really* love.

It was wonderful that Susannah was teaching me so much, yes. However, my ordinary life hadn't changed drastically. I was still an ex-beauty queen with a boyfriend who was the president of his fraternity. I was still zipping through school, studying every night to ace every test. I was on a fast track to an early graduation, planning to zip similarly through graduate school so I could become a top notch school psychologist. My grandest dream at the time was to help children thrive in school. Of course, this was before I realized what a tragically broken system our current educational paradigm is. Back then, I still wanted nothing more in life than to drive a nice car and push papers all day in designer shoes. But I could feel a strange stirring that told me things were about to change.

6: Burning Bush

I'd finished my daily cleaning routine after returning home from my morning at work followed by classes until early afternoon. The day was growing late and I had some time to kill before I needed to start dinner in order to have it ready when Noah returned home from work. Especially with the new things I was learning, this was a generally happy time for me. Life was relatively simple and I had discovered how *easy* it was to excel scholastically. If I'd only know the benefits of actually *studying* when I was in high school, I probably could have ranked higher in my class than I did, which was at the tenth percentile or so. I could have scored higher on college admittance exams, and likely wouldn't have had to pay for college at all. I only slightly beat myself up after that realization. Oh well. Hindsight.

On this particular day, everything was up to date. I didn't have any papers to work on or studying to do. I'd been starting off my mornings with a quarter hour of self-administered

Reiki, which gave me plenty of energy for the remainder of the day's activities, so my mind was alert although I didn't have much to set it on.

Even though I wasn't much of a television person, I was also quite bored, so I went ahead and turned on our set to see if there was anything worth watching for an hour or so. Right away I discovered a special program airing that discussed events from the Bible's Old Testament scriptures. This edition revolved around Moses and his experiences.

Ordinarily, I would have dropped that channel like a hot poker, switching the television to another program as soon as I heard the "B" word. I'd had more than my fill of Bible study as a child sitting through goodness knows how many hours in the Kingdom Hall, listening to someone drone on about this scripture or that, invoking only guilt or fear in my impressionable mind. However, on this particular day, for some strange reason, the subject interested me.

I watched the program about Moses, experiencing a strange and building emotional sensation as the show progressed. Something about what I was seeing, although it was only the relatively straightforward story that most of us are familiar with about Moses's early life, was evoking strong feelings inside of me that were both unfamiliar and completely impossible to ignore. When the part of Moses's story that centered around his conversation with a burning bush was discussed, I actually slid from the couch to the floor, my eyes glued to the screen.

Something within me *knew* that I was **supposed** to be right here, right now, watching this and hearing these particular words. I'd never felt this way before. It was neither a pleasant nor unpleasant sensation, but it was an incredibly intense one. A deep and unimaginably huge knowledge tickled the edges of my mind – something within me was reflecting, of all people, *Moses*. Was I supposed to do something? Was **I** meant for something greater than a life of polishing table legs, cooking dinner, and sitting behind a desk while filling out forms as a school psychologist? Surely *I* couldn't have a purpose so great, and besides, what would it even *be*? And yet...there was no arguing with this. It was a knowledge – not a reasoning, not even a belief. It was as true and as real as the clothes you are wearing as you read this. There they are, simply in existence. You can't argue away your shirt. It simply *is*. And so was this.

As I finally relaxed into the possibility of the truth that I was being exposed to, no matter how strange and unrealistic it felt, I heard a voice speaking in my mind.

I am *not* (or rather, I *was* not, because this thing happens all the time nowadays) the type to hear odd voices – and this "hearing" didn't happen in the way that you may imagine. It was not auditory at all, like it would be, had I heard something in the room or outside in the parking lot below. It was more like hearing one of my own thoughts. If I were to tell you to read out loud, in your mind, the words "purple pig," you'd just hear them, right? You would silently "hear" the two words in your own mental voice, which probably doesn't sound all that much like what you hear in recordings of your actual, physical voice.

Well, this was *mostly* like you hearing the words "purple pig." The main difference was that these words spoken in my mind were **not** in my own mental voice.

What did it sound like? Well, it didn't *sound* like anything – it wasn't audible. But just as surely as you can hear "purple pig," I heard this statement. I also felt a presence behind it, and there was no chance of me having the remotest idea that this could have been me. It was **not** me.

The voice said:

"If you are to walk this path, you cannot have him."

Unacceptable. I knew instantly who the "him" was, it was Noah! My love – the person who I'd pined over in high school and proudly shown off, and been shown off by, in college. The one who'd saved me from a town full of racist jerks, and who wrote me poems and held me at night. We were beyond just in love, we were permanent fixtures in each other's lives. We'd been all but legally married for years now – and I had to choose? I had to *choose?* No! I wouldn't! I wouldn't do that to us, not to him, and not to me.

And yet...

The most heartbreaking part of the next hour, which I spent crying and pleading and pacing the floors of our apartment, trying to reason with whomever had just given me that tidbit of knowledge, that impossible choice to make, was that I knew what my choice would be.

I knew what my choice **had** to be.

Once you glimpse eternity, once you're aware of the possibility that something within you can serve as a great tool to help countless other people if you allow it to simply come *through* you and do what it has always been meant to do, once you see that there is so much more to living on this Earth than any amount of beautiful jewelry or nice cars or manicured lawns can even attempt to bring to your experience of life, *how **can** you say no*?

So I begged. And I reasoned. I threw a heck of a temper tantrum, but there it still was, the implacable, immovable voice in my head that represented the truth of the matter -

*"If you are to walk this path, you **cannot have him**."*

"Fine!" I sobbed. I was lying on the floor by now. "But if this future is taken from me, I will NOT break his heart. He is a wonderful man who deserves the best. If this has to end in order for me to walk where I should, then he has to feel it too! Don't make it just be me, please don't make it just be me..." I lowered my forehead to the carpet, repeating those words over and over in a shaking voice, pleading that this shift in our future bring blessings for *both* of us.

I didn't know how I could do it. This relationship had served as the hub of my entire life for years. *Noah* had served as the hub of my entire life for years. How could I change that? How could I walk another path and live another life?

But the other question remained – how could I choose *not* to do these things, once I'd seen a glimpse of what sat behind that door?

Once I had spent my tears, I pulled myself up off the floor, dried my face, touched up my makeup, and made dinner for Noah.

During the same summer that I began to learn and practice Reiki, I took a Child Psychopathology course at my university. Because this was a subject that really interested me, I kept up with the textbook reading assignments we were given. That's more than I can say for many other classes I've taken throughout my long and tedious academic career.

Textbooks today all have a similar layout. There are chapters which are further divided into sections, and every now and then, a little text box is inserted onto a page, often in a different color that marks the text box as being an addition. The paragraph or two included in the box is not written in the same dry, intellectual style as the rest of the chapter. It is usually made up of a personal experience or an example of something specific that illustrates what is being discussed in a way that is easier for the reader to relate to. These boxes, therefore, are the best parts of the book. I have to wonder if more students would complete the reading assignments that were given if the book's proportions were reversed so that the real-life, personal information took up the majority of the text and the dry, academic-speak was put into those little boxes!

Anyway, I've since forgotten the subject of whatever chapter I'd been assigned to read (so there you go,) but no matter – the point here is what happened after I read what was inside of one of those little text boxes. This one spoke of two brothers. They were eight and five years old.

The brothers were walking home from school one day when they were overtaken by a group of slightly older bullies. The bullies wanted to take money from the older brother. Somehow the kids all ended up in an abandoned building with the bullies holding the younger brother out a high window – four stories up, perhaps? Six stories maybe? It was high enough, in any event, for the following to happen. The younger brother was dropped out of the window and the older brother ran down the stairs, hoping that he could catch him. He was obviously wrong, and the younger brother died.

That was all the text box said. And yet, *something* happened to me so that even typing about it now gives me a sinking feeling. For **days** afterward, I would have small, silent, unpredictable panic attacks thinking about this event. My mind's eye could see what had happened clearly, and with details added that weren't given in the book – the sight of the younger brother who had trusted his older brother to take care of him slipping from the bullies' grasp and falling. The older brother, who *had* always taken care of the smaller boy, racing down the stairs, holding onto the metal banister as he swung around the corner of each set of stairs, descending flight after flight. I could *feel* his breath panting, his heart racing, and his sneakers pounding against the stairs as he ran, faster and faster, repeating the same words in his head.

Please. Please. I can make it. Hurry up. Please....

And then his loud explosion out of a heavy door, and the sight-

There I can't stay with the vision anymore because it is as if a bomb goes off in my mind. There's a tearing, a rending, and a wordless, soundless anguish that is all-encompassing and beyond true verbal explanation.

This anguish would hit me walking across campus and getting out of my car at the grocery store. Sitting at my desk in the office where I worked, my mind would slide to the side, feeling my heart beginning to race and hearing those words passionately whispered words repeated in my head.

Was I imagining this?

*Why **would** I imagine this?*

It wasn't as if I could just **stop** – the flash of memory and emotion would overtake me at completely unexpected times, rendering me speechless and sticking in my mind like a thorn, so deeply and painfully that I was unable to think clearly about anything else.

I went to my Reiki teacher and asked her what was happening. Susannah told me about a time when she had initially begun to practice Reiki, many years ago. She told me that she hadn't gotten her "screens" up enough so that she could be protected against literally *feeling* others' pain while she worked on them. One woman, I was told, had been tortured. One by one, many of the bones in her body were broken, slowly and deliberately. As Susannah gave Reiki to this woman, she could both see *and feel* the trauma until she was exhausted, in deep physical and psychological pain.

Susannah told me that she'd spoken to her guides when this feeling overwhelmed her until she had difficulty functioning. She asked that screens be put up in front of her so she could see and feel only what she needed to in order to perform a good healing, but not so clearly and deeply that she would be injured or debilitated by helping someone who'd had bad things happen. After she learned how to set up her screens, she said, she had never needed to deal with that effect again. She suggested that I try the same thing.

It didn't exactly work for me.

It took me a few years to be able to both witness another's pain and not be paralyzed by it. For me, I don't accomplish this using screens. I remind myself consciously that yes, suffering happens, it happens every day, it's happening right now, but ME feeling this suffering does not make it stop. In fact, if I *did* feel everyone's suffering, I wouldn't be able to get out of bed in the morning. The way that I **can** help, however, is to yes, see and witness the suffering (and sometimes even feel it,) but keep myself divided enough so that I can still hold enough strength and health within me to actually be a beneficial presence. Sometimes a word or a touch is needed to help another person, but sometimes all I'm supposed to do is be there, pumping in as much light as I can to whatever area I find myself in.

Once I realized that keeping myself a little bit closed off was actually *helping* others, it was an easier thing to do. Nowadays, I still experience things deeply – for instance, while writing about the brothers, I felt those old sinking and despairing feelings that so impacted me before – but I can also swim up out of it without leaving part of myself behind. *Hurting oneself does **not** make another person's pain less.* If we can remember that, then we'll **all** find our way, once we figure out what works best for us.

Things between Noah and me began to change now. True, we were both workaholics who only interacted once in a while over interests that were probably just shifting naturally as we both reached adulthood, but we'd also been in love for so long that these little differences mostly went unnoticed before this. As I went deeper and deeper into a life driven by intuition, however, Noah and I argued more often and grew farther apart with each passing week.

One day, during a Reiki lesson, Susannah told me that one shouldn't give Reiki to a person who didn't want it, or who strongly believed that it wouldn't work.

"This doesn't help anyone," she told me, "and besides, you'll feel it. It will be like a toothache going up your arm."

Although I hadn't much of a clue about what an arm toothache would feel like, it didn't sound very pleasant. I asked her for a clearer description but she couldn't really give me one, replying that I'd know if and when I felt it.

I'm sure you can see where this is going.

I would come home from my Reiki lessons all but vibrating with excitement. I was learning things that I picked up faster and more completely, and that made more sense to me, than anything I'd learned in my life, other than some psychological theories I was currently being exposed to. These theories were, as it turned out, actually quite closely related to this other realm of information, if you know how to look at it. I *loved* the feeling of learning so much and just **getting** it. I would bubble out pieces of what I learned to Noah, and he would look at me with a calm and loving, but very condescending expression on his face.

"I believe that *you* believe it," he'd tell me after long debates over the validity of my new understanding of the world.

I don't know whether you've ever had anyone say that to you – but if not, take my word for it – the statement is *infuriating*. Not being a person who deals much in fury, I would instead try to explain things in a different way, getting the same response, or a similar translation of it, until I finally begged him for the umpteenth time to let me just give him Reiki so he could feel it himself.

Eventually he agreed to let me try. I stood next to him as he sat on the arm of our couch, holding his hand in one of my hands and laying my other hand on his shoulder, intending to show him the awesomeness of the warm little chills and feelings of exhilaration paired with relaxation that Reiki gives you.

Then I felt it. A cold, needle-like ache was moving slowly through my palms and up my arms. I let go of him and shook out my hands, replacing them after a moment and trying again. *This* time he'd see.

Again, that same pain, which was dull and sharp at the same time, moved upward toward my body, strengthening accordingly as I pushed the Reiki energy out through my palms more forcefully.

"I don't feel anything," he said in a way that told me he thought he was wasting his time.

Well, *I* certainly felt something. It had to be the toothache feeling. Surely, I realized with a deep and piercing sadness, this is what she'd meant. And this is what the voice had meant as well that spoke to me as I watched Moses's story.

I stopped trying to give Noah Reiki, although I still didn't really accept that we would have to end our relationship. A few months later, we had our first big, stupid fight at a party, shouting at each other in an upstairs room as music thumped up through the floor. Three days later, we broke up in a long, calm, tearful conversation that took most of the day. Although it was a horrible heartbreak for both of us, we both also felt a sense of relief afterward.

I sat at our kitchen table later that week when I knew I had a couple hours to myself, crying from this new loneliness I felt. Noah came home early and walked in on me accidentally. He came to where I was sitting and kneeled next to my chair, leaning his forehead against mine, asking me softly what the matter was.

"You know what it is," I said, trying to keep my voice as steady as I could.

"Then *why* are we doing this?"

"Really? You don't know? You don't think that, if we stopped now and just forgot about it, this wouldn't happen again, and worse the next time?" I asked these questions sadly and a bit angrily, feeling my heart breaking all over again. Although it hurt terribly, we both knew that we were no longer compatible as a couple. We each knew that this was true because of reasons that neither of us could describe but that both of us felt as strongly as the love that we had for each other – love that was changing by the moment into a deep friendship, totally absent of romantic feelings.

Noah stood up, hung his head, and slowly walked away, going into the bedroom that we used to share and that was now his room after I'd moved my things into the guest room. He closed the door behind him.

That was the last time we had a conversation like that. Noah and I have remained best friends to this day. We attended each other's weddings, that happened within a year of each other to wonderful people that fit both of us better than we ever fit each other. Our children will probably play together one day. Over the years since, when our friends have asked us why we *really* broke up, since we seemed so "perfect," we've never known what to say other than that we both knew that it was right. The truth is, and I don't know whether he'll agree with me on this or not, Noah could no longer be with me because I was turning into a fringe crazy person. I could no longer be with Noah because he couldn't come with me into crazy awesome fringe-ness (even though "fringe-ness" is not an actual word. You know what I mean.) It was tragic, and wonderful, and I have a quiet theory that Noah and I were meant to be sibling-like friends the entire time, which is what we've turned into in the years since. Perhaps our relationship, half of which was spent a thousand miles apart anyway while he was in college, only happened at all so that we could have this great friendship.

That winter, a friend gave me a copy of Dr. Brian Weiss's book *Many Lives, Many Masters* as a Christmas present. Because we hadn't spoken much about this particular aspect of spirituality before, although we'd brushed up against related topics every now and then, the subject of the book surprised me. It surprised *her* that I hadn't heard of the book already.

The day that she gave me the book was one of the last times I'd ever see that particular friend, and I have to wonder, now, in retrospect, if the point of our entire relationship may have been for her to impart the knowledge and information that was contained in that book to me. Of course, there was probably more to it. There tends to be more to it when a friendship serves as a "flash in the pan" like that: very intense at first and then gone in a moment, leaving shock waves in its wake. I'll probably never know.

In any event, finding out about the book was well worth the heartache I suffered afterward. Reading about Weiss' experience cracked me open in a completely new way. Here was someone I could *understand* and identify with. An educated psychiatrist who had no interest in esoteric subjects until things began happening before his very eyes that there was no logical way to explain.

That book remains as one of my all-time favorites and also a book that I recommend to others on a regular basis. Understanding how such things as finding out about reincarnation worked for others helped me to unlock in unexpected and much needed ways.

7: New Life I

I graduated from college that winter and moved home to Virginia for much of the next year. My experiences came less often while I lived there. All told, this was a pretty quiet time, however there are a couple of situations that are worth noting.

When I arrived in the city, I followed the directions my mother had given me to her new apartment. I hadn't been home since she moved there several months before, so I'd be staying in an unknown place. When I pulled up to the house, I noticed a curious funny feeling in the pit of my stomach. I grabbed my bags and walked up the front steps. My mother answered the door, we shared a hug, and then as she led me up to the room where I'd be sleeping, I couldn't believe what I was seeing.

"Mom," I asked, "do you realize that this house is built with *exactly* the same floor plan that our white house on Carroll Street had?

"It is? Oh, yes, I guess it is. Huh. I hadn't noticed that before," she replied, not thinking much of it.

We went up to the landing and turned left. My mother opened the first door and showed me my room. In front of the opposite window was a bed. The left side of the bed faced the doorway where I stood. My mother went into the kitchen then, and I very slowly walked over to the bed. I turned around and sat, staring at the doorway, out onto the landing where I could see the top of the banister. This one had a wooden square rather than a globe, but aside from that detail it was just the same. That other version of myself I'd seen standing there a decade ago had told me a couple of months before that I had to *go back*. I was now sitting in just the same spot, looking in just the same direction, in just the same room that I had been in when I first saw her. It was a different house, and in a different city, but it was still the same. Another paradox. I was back.

Throughout the following months, I understood the direction that I'd been given through that initially confusing statement. The explanation wasn't esoteric or spiritual in a direct sense, but the months I spent in this place healed a rift in my mother's and my relationship that probably could not have healed in any other way. I was glad that I "went "back.""

Richmond, Virginia, let me just say, is *quite* a haunted place. This is understandable, considering the amount of emotional upheaval and traumatic deaths that have happened there over the past several hundred years. For this reason, I would have had to be much more naive than I was to believe that I wouldn't have seen *anything*. Whenever I actually did see things, they were pretty anti-climactic, so I didn't ever have the shock or fear that I'd suffered from in some of my previous experiences. My bedroom had three doors. One led to my mother's room, one led to the hallway and the stairwell, and the third led to a sitting room. The thing about the sitting room door was that it never stayed closed. First I assumed that this was due a problem with the weight of the door. Or maybe the door jam was warped. Yes, there was a little shoving necessary when you wanted to completely close the door. However, the door would never open when you stood next to it, no matter how long you stood there. But a few seconds after you took a couple of steps backward, it would slowly open just far enough to reveal a few inches of space leading into the sitting room.

Just after I'd moved in, I was sitting on my bed one evening just after I'd come home from work, reading. The bed faced that same doorway. I happened to look up and saw a shadow move in the sitting room, quickly, as if someone had passed just in front of the door. I figured that it had been my mother and I went back to my book. A moment later, my mother called to me from her bedroom. I did a slight double take and asked her if she'd just been in the sitting room. Three guesses to what her answer was. It was a ridiculous question anyway. I would have heard her if she'd walked back to her room from the one on the other side of the doorway. Whomever it was continued to walk just past the door, and the door refused to stay closed, until I stopped paying close attention anymore. Nothing remotely menacing ever happened in relation to that, so I suppose I was correct in my assumption that some spirits simply hang around, not caring to interact much with the "room mates" who are sharing their space.

The apartment where we lived was in the upstairs portion of a converted house. The staircase we descended each morning when leaving for work passed under our kitchen and down to the lower level of the house. On this lower level, there was a small hallway to the right, with doors leading into rooms on this floor. A sweet elderly woman lived downstairs, and we didn't see her very much. One morning, as I descended first, with my mother a step or two behind me, I was looking straight ahead, at the wall that separated our kitchen from the hallway and landing. Out of the corner of my eye, I saw someone walk down the hall below, moving toward the door. Once he or she reached where our stairs ended at the floor below, the person turned to face the stairwell, looking up at us. This wasn't far into my peripheral vision, and in fact, I was nearly looking right at whoever it was, standing just a few feet away. I thought that it was our downstairs neighbor, and as I started to greet her, I moved my eyes to fix them upon her face.

No one was there. As soon as I looked directly at the person I'd seen standing there a second before, he or she vanished as if no one had ever been standing there.

Not wanting to be rude, I whispered to my mother that I had something to tell her once we were outside. After I shared what I'd seen, she shrugged her shoulders in that implacable way that she usually does when I bring up such things, basically saying that it happened, and it's over, and we're fine, so what else is there to say? Very logical, my mother.

When I spent those very lonely eight months or so in Richmond before I went back to Florida to earn my first master's degree, my main way of remaining internally peaceful and sane was to make weekly visits to Maymont Park. This collection of gardens remains one of my very favorite places in the whole world. It was built initially by a philanthropic couple in the early twentieth century. When you walk the grounds, moving over cobblestone pathways, around winding brooks, and into the arms of giant magnolia trees that create cathedral-like "rooms," you can strongly feel the love that went into creating the place and the compassion and true affection that keeps it beautiful now, a century after the buildings and gardens were originally built and planted.

I visited Maymont each Saturday morning during that early spring, carrying a cup of sweetened coffee in one hand and my books in the other. I was studying for the Graduate Record Exam that would not only allow me to attend graduate school, but that would also serve as the deciding factor as to whether I would be able to afford to go at all. On my first day at the park to study, after I'd toured the Japanese and Italian gardens, standing at the edge of a stone wall that overlooked the nearby river and feathery, still-naked tree tops, I went searching for a place to sit and read. The park was pretty empty those days because of the cool temperatures. It was chilly enough for me to leave my gloves on during my entire morning study session. I didn't mind. I couldn't think as clearly anywhere else. No matter the weather, this was where I wanted to be.

I tried out a couple of gazebos, none of them being exactly *right* They were drafty and too close to the walking paths. Whenever people walked by, which happened regularly enough, I was distracted by their voices. It would take me minutes to focus again, and after awhile, I became exasperated by the entire process. Finally I began to aimlessly walk again, allowing my intuition to guide me in a seemingly random path towards the back corner of the park, close to the railroad tracks that sat just outside Maymont's border fence.

From the top of a hill near the white stone mausoleum that held Maymont's creators, I looked down to my left and saw the uppermost dark green curve of a relatively small magnolia. When I say "relatively small" I'm still talking the size of a small house. Compared to some of the other ancient magnolias on the property, with branches several feet in diameter growing under, then back above ground in great, living, spiraling formations, this one seemed like barely an adolescent.

Something about that tree drew me. I crunched my way down the hill, walking through a shell-thin icy layer of snow, avoiding any misstep because I didn't want to end up with coffee all over my books. In a few moments, I reached the tree. Its branches grew low enough to the ground that the ones nearest me could be stepped over, and there was a place on one long, low branch were lightning had struck long ago, leaving a scar that hollowed out the top portion of the branch, creating a shallow trough a few feet long. A knothole created a flat place between this branch and another one to its right. This second branch was a bit higher than the first and much more textured, with the undulating bark creating varying levels all within a few feet of each other. I walked up to the trunk and circled it, stepping over low branches and bending under higher ones, getting a feel for the tree. I've always loved trees, ever since I climbed them as a little girl and was soothed by the kaleidoscope of greens, blues, and whites that would lull me into a sleepy trance on warm afternoons.

I *liked* this tree. The week before had been an especially trying one and I was heart sore, needing a place of refuge and rest. I completed my circle around the tree's trunk and came back to where I'd begun, at the knot between those two low, horizontal branches.

*Wait a second...*I thought to myself as I looked at the space in front of me with new eyes. Then I turned around and sat down on the knot, which was the perfect size and height to create a little chair. I looked at the dark trough on the branch to my right and then straightened out my leg along its flat bottom. The hollowed out area ended about an inch below where the sole of my shoe sat. It was as if that branch had been molded for my leg. I looked at the higher branch to my left. It was just the right height to sit my study books, and there was even a flat indention where I could *rest my coffee cup*. This was insane.

I leaned back, tilting my head up and letting my eyes be dazzled by the sunlight shining off of the magnolia's large, shiny, curving leaves overhead. I let my energy mingle with the tree's, which was soft and welcoming.

*Will you be **my** tree?* I asked it. I felt a warm, gentle, almost maternal wave of subtle emotion wash over me. Tears stung my eyes as I thanked it, then felt my worries being literally *pulled* out of me, leaving me relaxed, content, and comfortable.

I spent every Saturday until my GRE exam sitting in that tree. Once summer came and the magnolia's leaves filled in I could sit there in a private little hiding place, far enough away from any nearby path that no one would walk over, but close enough for the voices of laughing children to cheer me as I read a book or wrote in my journal. To this day, whenever I visit Maymont Park, the first place I go is to visit "my" tree, which still stands alone on the far side of that hill, below the mausoleum.

I parked my truck and got out, resting one foot at a time on the back fender while I tightened my shoe laces. This would be my last visit to Maymont. I was leaving in a few days for Florida, and the park would close in a half hour. I was about to take a run across the grounds. Actually, that was my excuse. I'd really come to say goodbye.

I started to jog slowly, warming up as I passed families headed to their parked cars with blankets, strollers, picnic baskets and sleeping babies. I wanted to cover as much ground as I could before the gates were locked. I ran up and down hills, avoiding paths and running over soft grass, splashing through hidden puddles from time to time. I didn't mind. If you can't get dirty when you run, then when *can* you get dirty? Besides, I spent the rest of my days buttoned up so tightly at my hospital secretary job that getting a little mud on my socks was a nice bit of rebellion against my other, "grown up" self, who never had a hair out of place and maintained perfectly manicured nails at all times.

I ran past the park's aviaries, then around the great big magnolia that has entire little ecosystems in its branches alone. I skirted the mausoleum, running up to my magnolia tree and laying my hands on her trunk, thanking her for her help and wishing her lovely tree times without me, whatever those may be. She was a tree, and who knows what trees enjoy? So I left it open.

As I ran through the Italian garden and down uneven stone steps winding through a small bamboo forest below, I thought about the upcoming changes in my life. I was about to move a thousand miles away, to a place where I knew no one. Not that this would be different. I hardly knew anyone in Richmond, either. The downside to graduating early was that all of my friends were still in school, and I was working all the time, unable to visit them very much. There wasn't much social interaction in my life, which was the main reason for my loneliness. The other reasons, of course, included that the few friends that I did have, and barely ever saw, would probably have gotten so freaked out if they knew what was *actually* going on with me that, directly after telling them the truth, I'd soon have no friends at all. Holding secrets as interesting and consuming as the ones I kept quiet takes a toll on a person, and I was ready for a change.

I ran through the Japanese garden, saying goodbye to the land I loved with each step as I passed a waterfall, ran over a little bridge and hopped across stepping stones that wound through a glassy pond populated with big, friendly, golden and white koi fish.

I stopped to rest in a little wooden shelter built on the edge of the koi pond and at the bottom of a great hill covered by gnarled old trees with decades' worth of love notes carved into their trunks and roots. This always made me sad, but what can you do, once the damage is done, except lie your hand across the scar and send love and healing energy to the tree? I did that whenever I passed, but the thought of the selfish, thoughtless harm done by carving letters into trees was bothersome in general.

I didn't see the trees today, I just sat in the shelter and waited for my breathing to slow, enjoying my solitude in this part of the park that was usually a favored spot for families and lovers alike. I sent my love out to the entire place in waves, alternately tearing up as I thought that I wouldn't be able to come back here for a long time. I don't visit home very often when I'm away, and I knew that it may be a year or more before I could come back to this place, and to my family across town.

As I sat on the built-in wooden bench, I heard what I thought was a steady wind moving toward me, coming from my right. I couldn't see out of that side of the shelter, but when the sound of the wind didn't alter in frequency or tone, I realized that it wasn't wind at all. Rain was coming. I stood up and walked to the edge of the shelter, standing just under the eaves of its slanting Japanese-style roof. I watched the army of small, warm raindrops move as thickly as a solid curtain across the pond. Foot by foot, the surface went from a glassy stillness to a blurring, jumping, dancing cacophony of sound and movement until the rain reached the near bank and covered the shelter. A cool, refreshing breeze blew before it, drying the tears in my eyes. Now, standing just beyond the water pouring down in soft, gray sheets, I thought about how lovely it was going to be to run back across the park in this refreshing, warm downpour. I tightened my shoelaces again and left the shelter at a slow, gliding jog, sending back another wave of love and gratitude to the beautiful land behind me.

This time I ran up the twisting path of carved stone block steps that brought me to the Italian garden. This is one of the most beautiful and famous parts of Maymont park. It consists of that gorgeous lookout and an intricately built waterfall that falls down the slope below, ending in the Japanese garden I'd just come up from. Just above the waterfall is an intricately paved, constantly replanted geometric flower garden and a beautiful pergola that ends in a circular domed area which produces an interesting echo that can be heard far across the garden. The stone pillars and white, open wooden slats roofing the pergola's long path has been covered with meticulously trained wisteria vines. It is a perfect place to be married, and I'd always imagined getting married there. In more recent years, I had imagined marrying Noah there. I started under the dome after emerging from the Japanese garden below and walked down the long, wet, gorgeous pergola. At the end of the pergola, under the "Via Florum" inscription meaning "flowering way," I turned and looked back up the picturesque length of it.

Suddenly, in my mind's eye, superimposed over the quiet view before me, stood people flanking the aisle, looking down toward where I stood. The sun shone above, and there at the end stood Noah. I'd pictured this scene **so many times**. It had been my dream. But as I looked, I could feel with a bittersweet certainty that the girl who stood alone at the edge of the flowering way was not, anymore, the same girl who had dreamed that dream. I thanked the people, and Noah, for providing me with such beautiful dreams for so long. Then, after a final wave of goodbye coming from my heart and flowing over the vista before my eyes, transforming it back into the empty, wet Italian garden on the edge of a rainy sunset, I spun on my heel and jogged away, feeling, with each breath, that I was letting go of the old version of myself and coming into a new version, one with bigger dreams.

As I ran over cobblestone walkways and through slippery grass, I found myself wondering about the time to come in Florida. Who would I meet? What friends would I make? What lovers would I have? What would my days be like?

I started up the last hill before the grassy plateau ended at the edge of the parking lot I'd parked my truck in, slowing to a walk in order to cool my body down and not feel uncomfortably overheated during my half-hour drive home. I began talking lightly in my mind to *someone*, the same someone that I'd known had been with me throughout this entire poignant evening. I asked with a silent laugh whether or not I'd be able to control the rain again in Florida. It wasn't that

I minded this afternoon, of course, but since I'd come to Richmond, the weather hadn't obeyed my wishes anymore. It didn't occur to me in the moment, however, that I hadn't been putting nearly the amount of focus and intention on adjusting my weather experience that I had while in Florida. In any event, I stood still for a moment, thinking about this past year and all of its changes, as well as the great unknown before me.

I took a deep breath and almost began to walk again when I noticed that I wasn't being rained on anymore. There were none of the tiny, soft patterings on my skin that there had been a couple of moments before. When had it stopped? I couldn't say. Sometime in my brief reverie, the rain had dried up.

But wait – I could still *hear* rain. And I could still see it too – falling onto the slender, drooping leaves of grass, about five feet in front of me. I watched it there, making the grass dance subtly. Still no drops on me. I turned around. There it was – making splashes in puddles going down the hill several feet behind me. The border wasn't moving. I was seeing it, and hearing it, but I *wasn't* being rained on.

I turned around, amazed, and slowly began to walk towards my truck. The rain continued to fall around me as I crossed the fifty or more feet to the parking lot, then the seventy five (at least) feet to where my truck was parked. I retrieved my key from where it was tied at the drawstring to my shorts, unlocked my truck, and stood there for a moment again. Not a drop. I got into the truck, turning the key in the ignition and starting my windshield wipers to clear away the small drops steadily falling against the glass there.

I guess that answers my question, I thought with a smile.

8: Hurricane Ribbons

Rae and I lay on the trampoline in her back yard, side by side, faces turned up to a blue sky dotted with fluffy little marshmallow clouds. A big hurricane was brewing in the Atlantic, and the television news stations were all aflutter about the damage it was capable of doing. Surely we could do *something*, we'd decided, so we laid there, breathing deeply, clearing our minds and sending our thoughts skyward as we discussed quietly how to do this. Going off of intuitive in-the-moment inspiration, we closed our eyes and took random turns directing each other up and out of our bodies, then over through the skies in a southeast direction. Here, we became quiet, each doing her own work.

My consciousness hovered high in the atmosphere, looking down at a giant, swirling mass of clouds that appeared to be moving slowly, although I knew better. Rae and I had discussed storms earlier that day, Rae saying that each storm had a consciousness and a life of its own, me disagreeing and of the opinion that storms are a part of the larger atmosphere, which has one big, all-inclusive consciousness.

As I looked down, I could "see" the streams of energy that made up the flat, swirling vortex of clouds and winds below me. It was almost as if each ribbon was colored, or lit, in a unique way. I could even see into the tiny spaces between them. Slowly, carefully, using my full concentration, as I knew that anything else would have been ineffective, I began to lift these streams of destructive energy out of their spinning circuit, where they dissipated once they were removed from the ordered, swirling mass below. Make no mistake – this mass *was* ordered. Hurricanes are not at all random winds blowing in a circle, there is a science and a formula behind them. I don't know what it is, and perhaps this is documented, perhaps not, but my experience that day convinced me fully of their precision and deliberate formation.

I continued to remove more ribbons of energy until I was mentally exhausted. Hoping that I had done enough, I allowed my consciousness to return to my prone body on the still black fabric of the trampoline, my skin warmed by the sun and caressed by a soft, humid, Floridian breeze. I let my breathing deepen and quicken, feeling my heart beat and wiggling my fingers and toes until I felt grounded enough to be sure that opening my eyes and sitting up wouldn't make me nauseous, which can happen if you return to your body too quickly after a good meditation – this is similar to how you feel when awakened out of a really deep, dreaming sleep too abruptly.

I opened my eyes and looked over at Rae, who was just beginning to move as well. The world looked bright and clear, and as I sat up, Rae did too, opening her eyes. They were electric blue, and glowing with an inner light that shocked me with its intensity. I'd never seen anything like it, and I looked into Rae's eyes all the time.

Just at that moment, she spoke.

"Charis," she said, "your eyes look so green, they're almost glowing."

...By the way, the hurricane didn't do nearly as much damage as the weather-knowers-that-be had predicted. A coincidence? There's no way of knowing for sure.

Back in Gainesville at school, a large hurricane was on its way. Noah was in town and he, Kate, and I were all spending the weekend at Kate's house, which was the most suitable for housing three people. As I was trying to set the two of them up anyway (they did end up dating for nearly two years,) we figured that Kate's place would be better than mine, which was chilly and sparse. She had more secure windows and her movie collection was better than mine anyway.

A few blocks away, my apartment sat empty. The news had told us that this hurricane was going to bring trouble with it, and sitting in Kate's apartment with a stack of DVDs to watch and a kitchen stocked with non-perishable snacks, I thought back to the trampoline work that Rae and I had done weeks earlier. I figured that I'd try a little experiment, just to see what would happen, and told Noah and Kate that I was going outside and would be back in a couple of minutes. I was going to talk to the storm.

Rae and I had debated over whether each storm had a consciousness of its own. I was about to test this theory. I stood on Kate's tiny concrete patio and sent my consciousness upward, searching for the source of the winds that whipped tree limbs around me into a frenzied dance. As I connected with a certain *something* that certainly didn't feel like a blue sky would, or even like stormy skies usually did, the wind around me quieted.

Into the stillness, I sent the following thought.

*You **cannot** harm my home.*

I sent a detailed and emotion-filled mental picture of my apartment, complete with its slatted fiberglass windows, wooden door, stone tile floors, and even the tree that stood out front.

This is my home. You have no right to destroy it or disrupt it in any way.

All of a sudden a forceful, angry blast of air whipped the trees around me and sent strands of my hair flying.

*No. I can't speak for other spaces, but that is **my** home and I am telling you, you can **not** harm it.*

Another blast of wind. This one, however, seemed more emotional and less forceful, if I can say that and make any sense. I know it's an odd thing to describe, but that was what I felt.

Thank you. Do you want anything in return? Can I give you an offering?

The largest blast of swirling wind answered me here, and I got the message loud and clear. No. The only thing that this force wanted was to destroy whatever it could. Destruction was in its nature. No offering would placate it.

I'd gotten my point across. I shrugged, not worried since I'd been willing to give something back but nothing was requested. I went back inside.

We stayed at Kate's place for the next day and a half. There was a short power outage the next afternoon that only lasted for a few hours.

Over the course of the next week, my boss told me about the giant tree branch that had crushed his front porch and ruined his living room. He showed me pictures and shared his plans for rebuilding his place bigger and better than it was before the storm. My students told me about broken limbs crashing into their windows, ruining their furniture and frying their computers.

When I finally returned home after the storm had passed that Sunday, my neighbors told me that the power had been out for about half a day and had come back on a couple of hours before. As I was walking up my front path, I noticed that a few leaves and small branches had fallen off of the big tree and landed in the yard in front of my apartment. I also noticed that a wooden rake that had been leaning against the border between two of my front shutters ever since I first moved in *hadn't even fallen over*. I walked up to it and took hold of the handle, having the strange thought that perhaps it was nailed to the wall – because seriously, how in the world did it not even get blown down? The rake came away into my hand. No, it was just leaning there. I guess my little conversation on Kate's patio worked.

9: Ekriem

While living in Gainesville, I rented a hidden apartment on the edge of town. I say that it was hidden because on the weekend before I moved in, there was a small kitchen fire in one of the other units. There was no damage, but a fire engine came to the address anyway, along with a police officer who was on duty in that part of the city. I was chatting with the officer at the grocery store on my corner a few days after I moved in, and he told me that although he'd worked in the precinct for twenty years, he had never been aware that my small complex existed. It only had six units, and inside each there were floors made of stone tile, large kitchens, and those sweet old-fashioned windows made of fiberglass shutters that you open and close by turning a little metal handle. I loved it.

There was one problem with this place, however. I found it initially through serendipitous means and knew I wanted it as soon as I saw the advertisement. I also knew that my finding this place to live was no coincidence in the grand scheme of things. I realize why I'd found it a couple weeks after moving in.

I started to have "visitors." The first ones came just as I was just falling asleep after a long day of school and work. I was earning my master's degree in health at the time, along with teaching undergraduate fitness classes, so I split my time between exercising with my students during the first several hours of each day and attending my own classes in the afternoons. I was a busy girl and welcomed my early bedtime, although I was sleeping on an air mattress because my furniture hadn't yet arrived.

My air mattress was the size of a small double bed and it sat on the floor. My feet faced a large window in the room, facing a big back yard, and my head was roughly in the center of the stone floor. One night, as I was in that drifting space between sleep and wakefulness, sliding gently into dreaming, something odd happened that had never happened before. I saw myself clearly as if I were standing a few feet away, looking down at my sleeping body. Standing on each side of my little mattress were two very tall beings – so tall, in fact that their heads nearly brushed against the ceiling. Their skin was a smooth silvery gray color and they had extremely long necks, large, oval-shaped heads, and short, squat bodies near the floor, at the bottom of those sinuous necks. They reminded me, after the fact, roughly of pictures of what the Loch Ness monster might look like.

They were both looking at me intently, their heads tilting down and placed almost directly over mine. Then, in an instant and with a very, *very* quick motion, one of them sent its head down towards my sleeping face, craning its long neck down in a lightning-fast move.

This shocked and terrified me completely awake. I was all of a sudden back in my body, and I instantly called on every protective tool, force, and entity that I could think of. I said prayers. I sent my energy out coursing through the room, swirling around, clearing out anything at all that shouldn't be there. I put a dome of completely impenetrable light around my bed and called on any personal guardians I had to stand sentinel all around me throughout the night. Finally, I felt safe enough to fall back asleep, and there were no more events — that night.

A month later I was lying in my new bed. It cost more than my rent, but it was *so* worth it. The four poster, canopy bed frame was made of metal and artfully arranged into what looked like vines and leaves, curling and twisting around each other to make the head board and foot board, and twining up around each of the columns holding up the canopy portion of the bed. I'd bought a used mattress set, but outfitted them with a thick feather bed and a plush mattress pad, high thread count sheets, and a down comforter along with down pillows, both wrapped in their own silky linens. I *loved* my bed.

On weekend mornings I would lie in bed as long as I could stand it. I've always been a morning person, popping up, bright eyed, either before the sun's arrival or with the first birdsong as it rises. On Saturdays I would spend a few morning hours at the lake owned by the university I attended, paddling around in a rented kayak, looking at the alligators that sat in the swamp land at the edge of the large body of water, who were calmly looking back at me too.

Before the sun was high enough to provide me the warmth I so loved while I paddled around on Lake Alice, I would lie in bed for hours, feeling the smooth sheets against my skin, drinking tea and writing in my journal, feeling joyously decadent. On this particular morning, the sky was cloudy and I was contemplating whether or not to keep my kayaking date. I closed my eyes, snuggling deeper into my soft bedding and pulling my comforter up around my face. I relaxed my body and my mind, allowing my awareness to become a cloud around me, not focusing on any particular thought, just delighting in the pure blissful *being* of this morning.

That's when I "saw" him standing just outside my window. I say "him" because this being had a decidedly masculine energy. Rather than this "sight" coming from across the room as it did when I was falling asleep, I "saw" this entity the same way that I "saw" the green guy in my bathroom, or the way I "saw" the octopus-like tentacles of the nasty creature in the playroom closet during that exorcism Rae and I did a couple of years before. It was as if I were imagining him, seeing him in my mind's eye through the window blinds, only I wasn't looking at the window blinds. And I'd never seen anything like this before.

He was very tall, probably about seven or eight feet in height, and extremely broad. Thicker in stature than any human. More bear-like than human-like, actually. He had long, dark "fur" that disguised the specific lines of his appearance, and he was staring down at me with angry, glowing red eyes. It was like a peeping Tom from a nightmare.

I instantly started my clearing process, protecting myself and banishing anything negative from my vicinity. I repeated this a few times until I felt safe, and then I stretched out my consciousness again, tentatively. He was gone.

I asked Rae for her take on what the heck was going on at my house. Her initial response was to suggest that perhaps negative entities found me in order to be sent on their way – sometimes this is reported by people who are aware of such things, especially during the first couple of years after they start to "wake up." I can understand this – I mean, negative or no, if ninety percent of people I met on the street completely ignored me, consciously *or* unconsciously, I'd probably hang out around those people who knew I was there too.

But this explanation didn't feel quite right. If that was all there was to it, then why hadn't this *always* happened? Stuff was at my house all the time now. I smudged the entire place with white sage every night to even feel *normal* at all. Each night just after I came home I would light my white sage bundle, walking through my rooms one at a time, choosing the rooms in the same order each night so that my entire tour was in a counter-clockwise motion (to clear out unwanted energies) and through each of those rooms making a counter-clockwise pattern inside the room as well, making sure to send the sweet-smelling, white smoke all over the windows and back into corners. Then I would repeat the process, this time moving in a clockwise motion through the house as well as through each room, consciously placing the energies that I *did* want to be there, like protection, healing, safety, and Light.

But this kept happening. I'd long complained to my few metaphysical friends that I wanted to actually see things with my *eyes*. This "mind's eye" seeing was great and all, but if something were actually there, I just wanted to see it, plain and simple. Of course, like any off-the-cuff request, I didn't think this through enough to put smart limitations on how it may present itself when the opportunity to actually see something arose.

One night, as I was headed to bed, a noise came from my living room. It was a tap here, then a tap there. Taps that I didn't often hear. Taps that meant someone, or some*thing*, was in there, rattling around, trying to get my attention.

This *something* did not feel good at all. It felt large, and powerful, and **dark**. I could sense somehow that if I crossed from my bedroom into my living room, I would see it – yes, with my actual, physical eyes. It would appear as a man, standing there, looking at me. But there would most certainly *not* be an actual man there in my living room. It would be something *else*. And I didn't want to actually see **that**. No thanks.

I stood on the other side of the doorway, my forehead leaning against the wall, trying to build my courage up enough to walk into the next room. I never did. I didn't want to actually *see* him. I was afraid. So I stood there, head bowed, concentrating fully, and sent him away in the same way that I sent all of my unwelcome visitors away. And when I was sure he'd gone, I smudged. Again. By then, there was no one in the living room.

I went back to Rae. Why in the world was this *happening*? We brainstormed over the next couple of days about why my current home would be such a hotbed of activity. I told her about the surrounding area. I was on the edge of town, and my small complex was behind a shop, hidden from the road. Across the street were businesses and houses, and we were one lot away from a busy intersection with a health foods store across the street.

We kept running through reasons for what the link may be and eventually I mentioned the lot next to me, between the apartments I lived in and the intersection. It was undeveloped. In the middle of a reasonably busy city, this one lot was still filled with very tall, old trees and thick underbrush.

"A vortex," Rae told me after no hesitation at all.

"A *what*?"

Sure, I'd heard the word before. But I never knew what it actually meant, and I'd certainly never seen one! One that I knew of, that is.

As Rae explained it to me, a vortex was a place where, for any of a number of reasons, there was an opening between our three dimensional physical reality and other places, or dimensions, or planes of reality. There are plenty of names out there for basically the same things.

There are many of these places, with conflicting views on just how many. Vortexes can be opened to two places, or between more than two. This one, it seemed, was at least open to a place that allowed folks that weren't very nice to come through. Due to my opened and aware-of-these-things nature, my house probably shone like a beacon.

I told my father later of the experience with the two tall beings over my bed, and he asked me whether they felt scary or malicious. I had to admit that they didn't, and he suggested that they may have been explorers of some type.

"If someone is looking for information," he said, "and they come across you, a decidedly unique member of a species that doesn't have a pretty important – to them – piece of, um, let's call it *machinery*, then it makes sense that they'd be checking you out."

I had to agree with the premise. Of course, that didn't explain the dark furry thing in my back yard or the scary guy in my living room, but it explained at least a piece of the puzzle. And when I remembered the event logically, not clouded by the fear of that moment, I also realized that no, even the lightening-quick dip of the head didn't *feel* harmful. It just felt like he or she or it wanted a closer look at me. Okay. That, I got.

But what about the rest of it? Dad couldn't help me there. But Rae suggested that I ask for a guardian.

"How?!" I was intrigued and excited by the idea.

"Just go into a meditation and ask your guides that you have a protector hang around. Be as specific as you like. Ask for exactly what you want, and you'll get it."

So I did. I sent myself deeply into meditation that very day and asked my "powers that be" to send me a protector who was strong, and smart, and, well, large. Size mattered to me in this case. Couldn't hurt.

A couple of days later, during my daily meditation, I became very aware of what felt like a warm, golden-colored presence outside of my apartment. I rose out of my physical body (it really is as easy as that, but it takes some practice) and went outside to look.

There he stood – a big (at least four feet tall at the shoulder, and I had the idea that he was in his "small" version at the time so as not to be more intimidating than he had to,) golden, *Griffin*. Let me be more specific – he didn't look exactly as illustrations of Griffins usually do, but that is the closest thing that comes to mind when trying to describe his appearance. The Spinx of Giza also resembles him, minus the headdress. His body was that of a lion, and his short, smooth fur was the golden color of a lion's. He also had a lion's tail. His face, through framed by a lion's mane, was that of a man's, or something more like a man's than anything else, and his eyes were iridescent and glowing. They actually reminded me of the shine that comes from a disco ball, as funny as that may sound. He also had wings that I never did see outstretched, but I knew that they were beautiful and deep shades of red with a little blue. They reminded me of fire. He was *extremely* strong, completely fearless, and stunningly intelligent – much smarter than me, but then again, he was obviously of a different species and probably much, much older, so you really can't compare, I suppose.

I looked at him and he looked at me. I greeted him in the way that seemed the most natural. I bowed. He slightly inclined his head toward me. Although we never talked in anything much like English words, we formed a friendship over the following year.

Soon after I met him, I told my father about getting a new guardian. He humored me as he usually did, and also as he usually did, he told me that this was probably just a piece of my own personality or unconscious that I was anthropomorphizing and seeing out of context.

This same old argument of his was somewhat frustrating, but I didn't argue much – who am I to say? Some people would certainly say that I was having repeated hallucinations and that I should probably be committed. And here I was, with a day job teaching the young adults of America how to keep themselves healthy. Go figure.

Dad came to visit me that Christmas, and as we neared my driveway, I told him that I would try to call my guardian in so that Dad could see him. Skeptical, he agreed – I guess there was nothing much to say other than to agree – why not? I hadn't told my father many of the details of my protector's appearance, other than that he didn't look human and that, since he'd been around, there hadn't been any dicey and unwanted visitors in or around my apartment.

My truck crunched over gravel as I parked under the outstretched arm of the tree growing next to my front walk. I turned off the engine and asked my father to take some slow, deep breaths as I tried to call the guardian.

I concentrated as much as I possibly could, sending out a mental request that my guardian come and show himself so my father could see him. Once I couldn't ask any more without growing repetitive (and probably annoying,) I felt his presence. I opened my eyes and asked my father to do the same. He did, and then, looking through the windshield, his eyes widened and he completely froze.

"Charis....?"

"What do you see, Dad?"

There was no answer. He was staring at *something*. I remained quiet, trying not to appear smug. After a few more seconds, my father shuddered and seemed to "thaw" out as he turned his head to look at me.

"I saw something."

After I asked him to be as specific as he could, he told me that he'd seen a creature come up to the front of the truck. He said that it looked like a Griffin, with a golden body, wings, and the face of a man with glowing, iridescent eyes. He said that the shoulder of this creature came up level with the hood of the truck, and that after he brushed against the truck, as though in greeting or affection and much the same way that a cat does, the entity dissolved into a golden cloud and swirled around the entire truck for a moment before quickly disappearing.

"That was him," I said.

Months later my sister told me that during a conversation she had that weekend with our father, he'd told her what happened in the truck.

"Charis describes stuff, and I don't believe her, then I visit her and see things that shouldn't *be* there."

A couple of days into his visit, my father told me that during the previous night he'd suffered from nightmares. These were a normal occurrence for him. He hadn't gone more than a week without nightmares since he was a little boy. He'd had a rough childhood and pieces of it remained. The nightmares were one of those pieces.

He told me that it had been between two and three o'clock when he'd woken up with a start, unsettled and in a cold sweat. Sitting even with his head, he saw two great big shining, golden eyes, *staring at him*. It was my guardian. He was visible enough that although my father could make him out in detail, the opposite wall of the room was also clear through the guardian's head and body. The guardian's body was so big that, when crouched down like that, the curve of his back was still so tall that it nearly brushed the ceiling. My father looked at the eyes, and the eyes looked at him, and then slowly and smoothly, the guardian stepped *onto* and *through* my father, as well as the futon he was sleeping on. Then the guardian lied down, the way that a cat or a dog does, resting on the ground and also on all four paws, with his head upright. He was positioned so that my father and his bed were literally *inside* the guardian's body. Instantly, my father felt better. Then he fell asleep without a hint of a nightmare for the rest of the night. Before this, he told me, my father had never been able to go back to sleep after being awoken by these dreams. On this night, he slept like a baby.

As it turned out, Dad didn't have nightmares any more for a long time. Soon after he returned home, I asked him, now that he had acquainted himself with my guardian, if he could do me a favor. He agreed. I asked if, during his next meditation, he could ask what my guardian's name was. I really wanted to know, but for some reason I couldn't find that information anywhere, on this plane or any other one, no matter how many times I tried.

Dad reported back to me within a couple of days.

"Ekriem."

"What?"

"Ekriem. Like the word "requiem", but with no "r" and with a "k" in the middle.

"Ekriem, okay. Thank you!"

Every now and then, even now, in his own meditations, my father will go and visit Ekriem. They don't have conversations in English either, but they do have conversations.

After a particularly hard day, I would, as I was drifting off to sleep, step up out of my body and go outside to visit Ekriem. He would sit up, straightening his front legs and sitting on his back haunches, and I would sit down in front of him, leaning into his furry chest, finding comfort there. Even though he wasn't at all the sentimental type, I got the feeling that he liked this, although he'd never admit it openly – not in any way that I'd recognize, at least.

Once, at a healing circle of women that I visited semi-regularly during the next year or so, I inserted Ekriem's name into the healing and blessing chanting we did. About fifteen women were chanting Ekriem's name all at the same time, intending that he be healed and blessed.

Afterward, I asked Rae what she thought Ekriem's feelings were about that move. She'd been aware of Ekriem for awhile, and sure enough, she had felt his energy while saying his name.

"He was surprised, and touched that you would think of him. He liked it." That was all she said.

In the years since, Ekriem hasn't followed me to my other homes, at least, not in the same degree as before. He doesn't just hang out outside, but he will come and help me when I call him. For that, I'm very grateful. He's quite a guy to have on your team.

10: New Life II

This chapter is going to be all about romance and partnership, along with its tangled connection to my awakening process. After going back and forth, undecided about whether to include this information, I've decided to just go ahead and do it. Leaving these things out would be omitting big and very important parts of the overall arc of my story.

Many other people I've talked to about this subject have agreed that finding a trustworthy romantic partner is an incredibly difficult thing to do in any case, and exponentially more troublesome when a unique spiritual life is thrown into the mix. Because it made such a difference to my journey, I'm sharing much of what I experienced in the following pages.

However, as of now I've officially warned you, so if this type of thing is going to bore you, then feel free to skip ahead to the next chapter.

I was sleeping on my couch in the morning. I'd graduated and moved back to Orlando. On this day, I had woken up as usual, come into the living room, and somehow fallen into a sudden deep sleep. I didn't usually fall asleep there, as the couch wasn't all that comfortable. I could have just gone to bed in my room.

Knowing what I know now, and also remembering that this little nap was extremely out of character for me, I've since found a new explanation of this event that would have never, ever occurred to me before.

I was lying on my back, my head toward the kitchen, when my mind slowly began to float up out of the depths of a deep, unusual sleep I'd fallen abruptly into. I was relaxed and still, in that place where you are aware of what's going on around you but not thinking much.

I heard footsteps.

No one else was home. The floor was made of stone tile, and I could hear quick, purposeful footsteps coming down the hallway toward me. Whoever it was circled around me and stood to my right, nearly even with my head.

I was completely weirded out, and even more so when I realized that I **could not move**. Not a *muscle*! I couldn't even flutter my eyelids.

Down the hallway came another pair of shoes. That person took up a position next to the first, judging by where their steps seemed to end.

And another! Same thing – down the hallway, stopped, this time, just behind my head. And I couldn't even make a sound. My body tensed. I was trying to move, but I simply *couldn't*.

With every ounce of willpower I had, I began to turn my head. My eyes still wouldn't open yet. And then a wave of sleepiness came over me that it was impossible to fight. I fell asleep again.

Later I told people about this, and I got the predictable response that I must have been dreaming. That I probably had sleep paralysis because the reticular activating system in my brain (the bit that keeps you from flailing around in an intense dream and breaking things) hadn't come online yet. Sure. I didn't believe that for a second. I never heard any other decent explanations though, not until years later.   .

I reached over and turned my CD player off. I'd just finished listening to the audio version of Sylvia Browne's book *Past Lives, Future Healing*, which ended with instructions on an exercise in recovering one's own significant past life experiences. I had been taking notes and I read over them again, fixing the meditation process firmly in my mind. It seemed easy enough, and certainly not more difficult than some of the shamanistic journeys I'd taken in the path. I was excited to see what would happen.

Something had to give. I was absolutely miserable. I'd moved out to California with Peter, thinking that this change in location would give us a better relationship and give me a new chance at life. All I'd gotten, however, were different struggles, more isolation, and a similarly hostile environment. I found myself in tears at least once every day, and Peter was as crass as always.

He'd completely convinced me that I deserved his horrible treatment. At this particular moment I was sitting in my room on an air mattress while he played a video game in the living room. I knew that this was a terrible situation and that I was worth more than I was getting in this awful relationship. But I also had no idea of how to get out of it. Our lease wasn't up for another eight months, and I couldn't afford to buy it out on my secretary's salary. Besides, where would I go? I couldn't afford to live by myself either. Things seemed hopeless.

My spiritual practice was just beginning to take shape again after a year of quiet, listless depression and relationship drama. Although I'd recently been praying constantly and affirming over and over that if there were *any* way to get out of this situation, I'd gladly run through that open door, no solution was apparent yet.

I closed my eyes and laid back on the bed, blocking out the beeps and muted shouts coming from Peter's violent game. I relaxed my body, piece by piece, and counted myself down into a slower pattern of thinking.

Floating in relaxed emptiness, I asked what century the life I was about to visit had taken place during, and waited for an answer. I waited longer than I would have liked to, but after a few moments, the image of the number "1300" floated into my awareness, quite clearly. Okay. It was in the 1300's.

Then I pictured myself standing in front of a map of the Earth's surface area, large enough to cover an entire wall. Where *was* I in this particular life, one that would hold the keys to unlocking my current struggle? I stood unsteadily for a moment, feeling a little bit forlorn as nothing happened, and then my finger rose and pointed to an area on the unmarked map that was generally where Greece is now located.

I allowed the map and the room to fade. Then I directed my mind to see my general life conditions during that incarnation. Where did I live? What did I do?

I felt my bare feet walking on a hard packed, earthen floor. The floor was clean and dry, and the walls were covered with an earthen plaster as well. They were also clean, and the size of the house, a few windows, and reasonably expensive decorations here and there showed me that this was the house of a wealthy family for the time. I looked down at myself. I saw that I looked generally the same as I do now, with tanned skin and dark, wavy hair. At the time of this vision, I was a young woman, a teenager of about seventeen years old.

I asked to see other details of my life. Was there anyone in that life who I currently know in this one? My sister was around, I realized, but I didn't know what our relationship was in that time. Noah was also there, I knew. In fact, he was my brother – either my twin brother, or we were very close in age. We were also very close in spirit, almost two halves of a whole, really, the way that siblings sometimes are and the way that twins connect more often than siblings do.

I saw that I wore a plain white tunic, undecorated, but clean and in good repair. I was a servant in the house, and my life was generally happy. I had friends and a good family, and I liked my employers.

Then I told myself to go to the event which corresponded with what I wanted to know.

Nothing happened. Deep in the recesses of my mind, I could hear myself pleading.

*No. I don't want to go. **Please** don't make me go there. Don't make me.*

I was surprised by this – Sylvia Browne hadn't mentioned that **this** could happen. Now my curiosity was aroused, but so was some trepidation. If it was that bad, did I really want to go and see what had happened?

A moment later, I pulled myself together. Of course I wanted to see. I reassured that part of myself that was pleading with me that this wasn't real and that I was completely safe. I didn't have to relive it in every way, I just had to see what had happened.

Heat. Heavy sunlight beating down on my head and shoulders, and rough sand in my eyes. My hair had come down and was blowing across my face, tangled in knots, obscuring my vision. I didn't care. I was sitting on the ground, my previously white tunic torn and dirty. Blood ran down the inside of both of my thighs. I could feel hot tears leaving tracks through the dust on my cheeks. My heart was absolutely broken and my body was sore.

The more lucid part of me realized what had happened – I'd been raped. Not only that, but humiliated, out in the open, in front of other people. As if the rape wasn't bad enough. Who had done this?

I looked up and through my tears and blowing curtain of hair, I saw a tall man with pale skin standing there, facing away from me. He was wearing some type of military uniform of the time. He turned toward me, and I recognized Peter. He looked very similar to his physical form in my current life as well – how could this be? I understood my own looks. Sometimes even now, people mistake me for having Greek heritage. But his skin was so pale. How could he have looked the same in this other time?

He gazed down at me with what would have been contempt, if he'd had cared enough to hate me, which he didn't.

I was less than nothing to him, even though he had just utterly ruined my life. He laughed to his fellow soldiers, standing nearby, and walked away from me. I'd never see him again.

I gratefully floated up and out of that particular scene, shaken, asking myself what had happened with the rest of that lifetime. I'd been engaged to be married, I saw, but after this disgrace the engagement was dissolved. I may or may not have born a child from the rape, but either way, my life was spent in misery and I died an old woman (though not as old as my face would make it seem,) tired of life that had started out brightly but been ruined completely by this one terrible injustice.

I brought myself out of my meditation, breaking the surface of my waking consciousness as if I were swimming up out of deep water, gasping for air, my eyes opening widely and staring at the ceiling as I laid there, shaking, coming back to myself and recovering from what I'd seen and experienced.

Now I understand, I thought to myself. *He raped me and ruined my life. Now he's still raping me – not in body, but in spirit. If I let him, he'll ruin my life again.*

I knew so many things about Peter. I knew that his crassness and his maltreatment of women resulted from seeing things as a young child that no young child should see – abuse of his mother, maltreatment of his family, all of the things that can come from being conceived and born into a family full of abuse. I knew that he truly did love me, in the best way that he **could** love, but I also knew that this love, combined with his glee in breaking rules and hearts, could never be enough for what I needed, and deserved, to have from a partner.

I stood up and opened the door that led to the living room.

"Peter?"

"Yeah?" He didn't look away from the game.

"I have a question from when you taught history. What was happening in Greece in the 1300's?"

"I have no idea," he said scornfully. "Nothing. The 1300's were the dark ages."

"So *nothing* was happening then?"

"No, not that I know of." He hadn't even turned to look at me. Hell, he hadn't even paused the game.

The conversation was over. He went back to the game and I closed the door. Then I promptly did an internet search to discover what was happening in Greece in the 1300's. It's true that my high school history classes didn't teach me much about this time period in any country that wasn't England, France, or Italy, but I couldn't help but doubt his assertion that nothing at **all** was happening in Greece during an entire century.

I searched for less than five minutes. As it turned out, since the "1300" image in my mind hadn't specified whether it was B.C. or A.D., I searched for 1300 B.C. as well. That was when I hit my jackpot of relevant information. During 1300 B.C,, the Dorians were invading Greece.

The Dorians were from the North, which would have explained Peter's pale skin. They also wore, I discovered next, the same style clothing which I had seen him wear in that horribly clear memory – and that, at the time, had seemed so out of place and foreign to that version of me as I sat in the dirt.

I did try to tell Peter what I'd seen, later on. Of course he blew me off. I can halfway understand why. It wasn't the most flattering thought. However, this was just another nail in the already sealed coffin that held the remains of our relationship.

Within a few weeks, things in my world did shift and transform in unexpected ways so I could leave that place. On the night I left to move into a new apartment with my sister, I forgot the plugs to my air mattress, having left them on the windowsill of my old bedroom. Peter slept in the bed we'd shared before our breakup. I called Peter, who hadn't been home when I originally left, to tell him that I was on my way to pick up the plugs. When I arrived, he was sitting alone in the newly empty bedroom I'd just left, leaning against the wall, hanging his head, crying. I walked to the window, picked up what I'd come for, and stood there awkwardly. What was there to do or say to help? I certainly didn't want to hug him. He had this awkward habit of not letting me go when we hugged. I couldn't say I was sorry for leaving because I wasn't sorry. He'd been a monster to me, and he knew it. But I also hated the idea of anyone, no matter how monstrous they'd acted, sitting in an empty room like that, crying, all alone. I felt that way even with the full awareness that he was doing it for maximum dramatic and pity-inducing value. Peter had known I was on my way because of my phone call. He'd arranged himself there to seem like he'd been discovered while mourning my departure.

Half of me was exasperated, and the other half felt compassion for him. Even with all of his flaws, he had loved me. When love ends in such a painful way all around, how can you not feel compassion?

So I tried to comfort him with my words. Within ten minutes, of course, I was enmeshed in a nonsensical argument with him where he tried to blame me for his infidelity and abuse. As soon as I realized what he was doing, I was done. No longer would I make myself an emotional punching bag in order to earn some sort of nebulous approval or affection that would be just as unhealthy if it ever did come, which it never would.

I told him again that I was sorry that it had to end this way, but that it was over. I left him there shouting after me as I walked out of the front door. With each step I took towards my car, I felt the filaments of that prison of a relationship float off of my body and out of my aura. I looked up at the stars gratefully, breathing air that hadn't smelled this sweet in months.

That night, in my new home, on my uncomfortable air mattress, I slept like a baby.

After my break up with Peter, I spent the following months casually dating for the first time in my life. After a few humorous but disastrous encounters, I decided that I was sick of the whole darned thing. There were no more good men left in the world, or at least not any that were available. I couldn't think of one *real* gentleman who both treated women the way that we should be treated and who was under the age of fifty five. I completely believed that quality men were extinct, and that belief was reflected back to me by experiences I had more than enough times to set my opinion in stone.

It took me about a year to go through a complete mourning process after I'd resigned myself to a solitary future. I accepted that I must not have been one of those people who fall in love and are able to go through life in the company of a partner that they can trust, share things with, and be truly *themselves* around.

After all, I was living in Los Angeles. I could find a *guy* anywhere. There were lots of them. And there was a collection of some of the most beautiful people in the country available to me. My sister and I went out dancing each weekend, flirting with bartenders, picking dance partners for the evening, and neatly vanishing before any of them could ask for our numbers unless we wanted them to, which we seldom did.

I gave my more reserved sister the following pep talk nearly every night, as we made the final touches to our wardrobe or makeup before we went out on the town:

"Don't worry. Make your primary focus the goal of having a *good time*. Listen – boys aren't **real people**! They're toys. And don't think you're going to hurt anyone's feelings – they *like* it when you treat them that way! Everyone ends up happy. So there is no reason in the world to doubt yourself. Just go with whatever happens. You be the boss of your interactions with anyone and everyone, and let's have a fabulous time."

That speech grew longer or shorter depending on the evening, but you get the main points. I'd decided that true romance was a lie. The few times in my life that I *had* believed in it, things had ended up badly. Not the least of my problems was my "in the closet" status regarding spirituality. Telling any guy I dated that I wasn't "like *other* girls" proved to be a very volatile thing.

My history showed a clear picture. My initial spiritual awakening resulted, at least in part, in the complete demolition of a beautiful relationship I'd thought would be my first and last love during this lifetime. In graduate school, one boyfriend erupted into screams when, after a difficult night on the phone with his parents (who threatened to remove him from the family will unless he stopped dating me because of the particular, ahem, bronze tint that my skin has,) I laid behind him in bed, my hand between his shoulder blades, unconsciously feeding healing energy into his heart chakra. I could feel his aching and sorrow over the rift growing in his family. He jumped up out of bed, turning on me and shouted that I'd violated his personal space, that I was an immoral, manipulative person, and that I could never *ever* do that to him again.

Hmm. Considering the fact that I wasn't really aware that I was doing it in the first place, I knew then and there that this connection wouldn't last for too long.

Next came a friendly and sweet young man whose company I definitely enjoyed – enough, in fact, to open up to him fairly quickly in our short relationship that I coined a "summer fling" from the very beginning, since he'd be graduating and moving away in a couple of months.

He came over the morning after I'd told him the truth about my *unique* history. He was a little jittery and awkward, telling me that he'd repeated the conversation that we had to his room mates, who, of course, made fun of him for it. They told him something along the lines of never making me angry, since I'd put a hex on him because I was a witch.

Ridiculous! I couldn't help but laugh at that one. It never ceases to amaze me how incorrectly people assume that this stuff works.

He laughed too, nervously. Then the question came that I was learning to expect.

"Um, you're *not* a witch, are you?"

Crap. Hmm. How to answer that. Well, honestly, considering what the true nature of that word is, after removing all of the incorrect assumptions that have been put on it through negative media and smear campaigns designed to increase fear and smash any true knowledge of our species' own, completely natural, non-physical talents, then I suppose the answer is yes. Yes I am.

(Of course I didn't tell *him* that. I laughed it off, sorrowfully realizing at that moment that this relationship would never work.)

The problems I had after telling people the truth weren't limited to men I had relationships with. I had a falling out with a good friend during the same period time frame. She came to me a few weeks later, telling me that she'd gained five pounds and asking if I had put a spell on her .

"**Oh my gosh.** You *do* realize that, considering how these things *actually* work, I would have to pull energy through me to send it out anywhere. In order for you to gain five pounds I'd have to gain five times as much. Probably more. Besides, I wouldn't **do** that!"

As you can understand, talking about these things didn't prove to be something I looked forward to. And combine that with a general distrust of all men, as a result of what I'd experienced and what I saw every day (I won't go into details about my anger every time that a husband and father would check me out at the mall – your kid is *right there!* Get a little respect and appreciation for that beautiful woman walking next to you and take your gross eyes off of me! Ew!) I was done with the entire process.

I figured that I would wait about ten years. Once I'd reached my mid thirties and become successful enough at whatever career I'd chosen that I could go into temporary retirement, I would be artificially inseminated and bear a child all my own. Then I would raise her (or him, but my gut feeling had always told me that my first child would be female) and when she hit school age, I'd go back to work. Piece of cake.

Who needs an untrustworthy man? They were undoubtedly more trouble than they were worth.

I enjoyed going out on the town with my sister, anyway. I made a fabulous "wing man" and loved setting her up with people. Overall, my life seemed just fine on the surface. I worked hard during the week and numbed myself into a happy stupor on the weekend, drinking and dancing until the sun came up each night and spending the days shopping and visiting the beautiful gardens in and around the city, trying to regain some semblance of internal balance. I dropped my spiritual practice again for a while, then slowly picking it up again by starting to hold solitary bi-monthly rituals at the Full and New Moons.

One night, soon after I'd begun to meditate semi-regularly again, my sister and I were playing a game of darts when a man walked up to me and quietly told me that I'd better win this game because he had a couple of hundred dollars riding on it. Although I wasn't remotely interested in dating, the timing and delivery somehow made this a great line. For the rest of the evening, my sister and I played darts with him and his friends.

One of those friends dated my sister for a month or two. This instantly made me the third wheel, which I didn't really mind. Eventually the subject of my romantic life, or lack thereof, arose one evening while the three of us were out together. I had no problem telling him that I was completely done with dating. I now approached the entire romantic arena just like a male would, I explained. I was only after fun, with no emotions involved, and certainly no commitment. Everything was simpler that way. In response, he only nodded thoughtfully. I could tell that he had a different opinion about what I actually wanted, but I didn't care. I'd spent a year figuring this out, and I was completely, totally, and in all ways *done*.

A week later, one of my oldest and closest friends was visiting me from the other side of the country. Of course we decided to take her into the city for the evening. My sister's boyfriend came, and he brought a friend of his along. Terry was a polite, quiet, friendly young man, who had beautiful dark eyes and a comfort in himself that made him immediately likeable. It didn't hurt that he was gorgeous either. As we all sat at the french restaurant in Santa Monica where we met, drinking wine and eating dessert crepes, I also discovered that Terry was two years younger than me and studying acting – two strikes that translated into three, considering my no dating, no emotion policy. Although I was sticking to my guns, Terry was easy to talk to, so the conversation flowed easily for everyone around the table.

I asked him what he'd been up to that day. He'd been reading, he said. Of course I asked the obvious question, and discovered that he'd been reading about transcendental meditation. I told him that I used to teach meditation during my days as a semester yoga teacher in Gainesville. He looked at me strangely then, but the conversation quickly moved forward and I forgot about it.

Later, we all went dancing, joining up with more friends and eventually returning to Terry's apartment. He and his room mate made the double mistake of buying toilet paper in extreme bulk and making a pyramid out of the unused rolls in their bathroom. An epic toilet paper battle took place for much of the night. Legend has it that rolls were found weeks and months later in uncommon places such as the back of the refrigerator. The last roll wasn't recovered until the day that the two of them moved out of the apartment.

After everyone fell asleep on couches and floors, Terry and I stayed up talking all night. We laughed as the sunrise brightened the sky outside his window, and the next afternoon the entire group of us went to the beach together. Terry and I kept subtly pressing against each other, hand to hand or shoulder to shoulder as we walked, knee to knee as we sat. One of us would begin, and the other person would laugh quietly and return the pressure, neither of us had any idea why this was so funny, but we both went with it anyway. A couple of years later we finally thought to question what we were actually *doing*. We came to the conclusion that it had to do with our energy. We were magnetized to each other in an odd way.

That same explanation is what we've used to explain why, over the course of the next weeks we would regularly drop any words in the middle of a conversation, sitting or lying face to face, silent, still, staring into each others' eyes. We did this for **hours**.

"We're calibrating," I'd say with a laugh.

As it turned out, that was true.

Three days after we met, Terry told me he loved me. When he said that, his gorgeous eyes looking into mine, full of excitement and vulnerability, the louder and more logical part of my brain threw up multicolored, glittering, flashing flags. This was *not* normal. But the part of my brain that allowed my intuition to have a say in decisions I made and that knew things on a deeper level had to admit that yes, I loved him too.

A few days later he told me he wanted to marry me.

Two weeks after that I sat on my bathroom counter, talking to my sister as I applied my makeup for the evening that we'd be spending with the boys.

"I don't know. In the beginning, everyone puts on pretty faces. But if he actually *is* who he *seems to be*, I never want to be with anyone else." I was as shocked to say it as she was to hear it. *Me?* Even beginning to consider the possibility of settling down?? It was totally out of character. But I couldn't fight it. Something about us just *fit* in a way I'd never felt before.

In six months, Terry moved in with me. A year after our first meeting, he sang his marriage proposal to me on a Southern California beach at sunset, our friends sneaking up behind us with a guitar and cameras to provide accompaniment and documentation.

Terry knew everything about me. He thought my "weirdness" was not something to be afraid of, but something magical to love. He adored my cultural heritage. He not only tolerated the pieces of me that I'd been taught through experience to hide, but he loved me because of them.

Sometimes, it seems, in order to get a prize, you have to stop wanting it and just live your life. And forewarning shouldn't be ignored, either. In Gainesville, I made a silent moonlit night each walk from my office to the parking garage after my long days of work and school. On one of these walks, as I wondered about my future, I understood clearly and completely, all in a moment (one of those downloads again) that I would meet my husband in California and that he would be better than I could imagine. This was before I had even considered a move to the west coast.

I conveniently forgot this piece of information I'd been given as I was in the midst of my other relationships. I even moved to California with someone else, sure that the future I'd been told of on that quiet night was no longer mine, on the rare occurrences where I thought about it at all. It's true, sometimes the paths we're walking on do change. I could have easily been correct when I thought that the download I got that evening was not for me anymore. But sometimes those paths don't change. There may be no way to know – you just have to wait and see, learning your lessons and being true to yourself as you go. In retrospect, I'm not sorry that I closed myself off and cut romance out of my life for awhile. Being able to look back on the sequence of events, I think I needed that. Many women in this culture are under the impression that they must be in a romantic relationship in order to be whole. This not only isn't true, it's a crippling belief. The truth is that we must be whole already, *in order* to have a good relationship. If we don't even know who we are yet, which many of don't, how can we agree to join our lives with someone else who probably doesn't know who he or she is either? It doesn't make much sense when we look at it that way. Romance is not something you can force. It has to arise naturally, and in its proper time. The best way that I've seen to handle the entire process is to give it the attention it deserves. Decide what you want, and let it go, enjoying your life as it *currently* is until whatever you wanted shows up on your doorstep. Or in a French restaurant.

11: All Roads Lead to Aliens

Just in case the disclaimers that I've already put forth in this book didn't catch your attention, here's another one – this is where things get *really* weird. I've read books and heard accounts of people interacting with spirits and non-physical entities and ghosts and more, and yet when the subject of Extra Terrestrials is breached, that tends to be when people's eyes glaze over and one moves from the label of "eccentric" to "bat guano bonkers crazy." Also, as I've said before, I don't expect anyone to take anything I say on faith – each person's experience is different and everyone should always have a healthy, balanced curiosity of just about everything, as free of biases and prejudices in either direction as possible. This has been my experience, and my experience alone.

Onward.

Hmm, where to start...I guess a year or so ago is as good a spot as any, although I'll warn you that there will be definite jumping around in this chapter – forwards and backwards and forwards again. This is because I want you to experience things the way I did, and the way I still do, which is not at all linear.

The day that Rae and I laid on her back yard trampoline together, helping to diffuse whatever hurricane was headed toward us at the time, we also watched bright, fluffy, clouds quickly pass by overhead. She told me that she'd heard that visiting aliens (or ETs, extra terrestrials) use cloud cover to shield their ships as they pass by.

Mm-hmm. Sure. I didn't have much to say to that. Whatever. I was open to anything, unwilling to shut out any possibility simply because I hadn't heard of it before. I also certainly believed in some UFO sightings I'd heard about, I guessed. Other than that, I hadn't thought much about it.

The two of us went back to talking about hurricanes, past lives, and current projects. The subject of UFOs didn't come up again for me until almost ten years later. I was on a road trip with my soon-to-be husband, going from Pennsylvania to Texas to stay for a few months before our wedding.

We were on a highway that ran across the plains of the middle United States, a place with rolling hills and barely a tree to be seen, much less any buildings. There were a few fences and a house here and there, but mostly all we saw for hours was the road, the grass, and a lot of sky. I'd driven through the night and was taking a grateful nap while Terry took over. Just after I'd snuggled down into a comfortable snooze with a black t-shirt over my eyes, Terry spoke.

"Charis? You might want to see this."

That remark was certainly enough to make me emerge from my car blanket cocoon. I looked through the windshield and focused on one of the strangest things I'd ever seen. In front of us, stretching in a disk-shaped edge from one side of the horizon to the other, filling up that entire section of sky and disappearing over the far horizon, was a gargantuan, dark, solid-as-a-rock anvil cloud.

If you've never seen a anvil cloud, as I hadn't, they come as quit a shock. This was quite a way to become familiar with the phenomenon, stuck in the car with no shelter anywhere nearby, driving on a road that went directly underneath the mass into a blurry darkness.

Anvil clouds are BIG, dark, and extremely opaque, appearing so solid that, if your arm were long enough to reach up there, you could knock right against the edge of it. This one came was sitting so low and near to the ground that the road ahead disappeared quite suddenly under it. We had a mile or so to go until we we too went under this huge thing, and I *didn't like it*. That was **not** a normal cloud. I've been a sky watcher all of my life, so much so that my high school friends laughed at me for my constant exclamations about the beauty of sunsets or stars overhead, and never had I seen anything that looked, or *felt*, like this did.

I told Terry that I had a strange, and not very pleasant, feeling about this thing in front of us as we drove closer and closer to it, unable to avoid going directly beneath it – after all, we were on the only road around, what other option was there? We could sit on the side of the road and wait, where it would eventually cross over us anyway. That wasn't any better. At least this way, we would be moving. Besides, maybe I was just imagining things and the trepidation I felt was all in my head. You'd think that I would have learned to trust my intuition by now. Apparently not.

Seeing what was under the cloud was impossible. Its lighter gray, curved bottom lip that stood only stories above the ground curved downward as well as upward, obstructing any view as to what was going on under there. I wondered about the other cars on the road and what their drivers thought of this. A second later I realized (as I would many times in the future) that in all likelihood, no one else noticed a thing and were probably only turning up their music and readying their windshield wipers.

As we neared the threshold, my heart rate steadily increased and my breathing became more and more shallow. I wanted to see what was on the bottom side of the cloud with the curiosity of a researcher. I felt the same feeling as when I wanted to see what was in my Gainesville living room and what was in the playroom closet, but there was an added sensation now that I couldn't remember ever feeling before.

A cold, slow, purely physiological, primordial fear was coursing through my body. I couldn't explain it and I couldn't control it. As our car drove beneath the leading edge of the cloud, I looked up at the multi-hued gray and white folds above us. They reminded me, strangely enough, of what the bottom of a jelly fish looks like. I told Terry that I felt like a mouse under a hawk. I could barely speak. I didn't want to look up, but I couldn't look away from the hypnotic undulations overhead. I had no idea what was happening to me.

At that moment, another realization gripped me. Just as I was watching, I was *being watched*. This sensation is difficult to describe, and all I can say is that someone else was there, with me, or more accurately, *in* me. At that moment, cutting clearly through my gut-wrenching fear, I heard an intent, very calm, but *very* serious and somewhat stern voice in my mind.

Again, this wasn't an auditory **hearing**. As I've said before, it was like the voice you hear when you think, but it *wasn't my voice.* It didn't feel like me at all, and what it said to me was *certainly* not coming from within.

Remain calm. As calm as you are, so too will we be.

With that came the implication that if I *wasn't* calm, they wouldn't be either, whoever "they" were.

I didn't need to be told twice. I told Terry that I was going to meditate to stop myself from freaking out. He was slightly freaking out himself from the winds buffeting the car and threatening to blow us either off of the road or into the massive trucks that shared the highway with us, so he nodded, tightened his hands on the wheel, and leaned forward. I immediately adjusted my seat to a slightly reclined position and settled back into it, closing my eyes and slowing my breathing to nearly a standstill. I talked myself down into a light trance.

Exhale slowly, smoothly, until my abdomen is curved up and in, hugging the bottom line of my ribs. Hold it. Inhale smoothly, slowly – slower, slower, until my lungs are full to bursting. Hold it. Exhale. Slow down. Slow down. Keep going.

And this continued as the minutes stretched, our small line of cars driving in near darkness for easily ten minutes without a drop of rain. All at once, the rain finally appeared in fat, heavy rain drops and all of Terry's attention was directed toward simply staying on the road. I kept myself plastered to the seat, breathing and only letting myself think about breathing, pushing every terror-ridden thought having to do with anything other than that physiological process and sensation out of my head.

After another fifteen to twenty minutes, the rain slowed and quickly stopped. Realizing that things would now be fine, I slowly unwound from my emotionally rigid coil and began to look around. The cloud wasn't any thinner, but the rain had stopped, and up ahead, I could see a small sliver of blue sky peeking over at the horizon.

Minutes later, we emerged. The dark cloud cover ended in a line not quite as solid as the leading edge, but still too solid to be truly natural. After the dark mass passed, the sky was filled with normal looking clouds of the average various density, height, and color, that you would see in any given morning sky.

We stopped for gas and I went into the service station, breathlessly asking a woman at the counter whether they have "storms" like this often. She looked at me, confused.

"Um, sure, I guess so."

She'd been inside, of course. Hadn't noticed a thing. I thanked her and we left.

On the same road trip, Terry and I stopped for a night in Chicago to visit his cousins and enjoy an actual bed. Simple pleasures like this often aren't appreciated as they should be until you've spent a day or two sleeping for no more than a few hours at a time on a reclining passenger seat. We spent the day visiting the local library and downloading audio books for the drive. To clarify, I delete them after I listen to the books once – who listens to an audio book more than once, anyway? If you've ever taken a lot of road trips then you probably already know the invaluable nature of a really good audio book when it comes to compressing hours of boring highway driving into time spent enjoying a story being read aloud to you.

While waiting for my computer to slowly upload the CDs I'd chosen, I aimlessly walked around the library. Whenever I have the time, I tend to head for the 100's. It's habit, I suppose. If nothing jumps out at me, I then slowly wind my way through nearby aisles, letting my intuition lead me, which usually feels identical to aimless wandering, until I come upon something that catches my eye. On this particular day and in this particular Chicago public library, I happened upon the book *Chariots of the Gods* by Erich Von Daniken. Something about the style of the book snagged my attention, so I slid it down from the shelf and proceeded to spend the next twenty minutes reading ravenously, flipping pages and shocked, not to mention *thrilled,* by what I discovered. This made so much sense! I hadn't felt so excited since my Reiki classes with Susannah seven years before. The one thing I'll say for my religious upbringing is that I learned the Bible backwards and forwards during all those years of boring lectures and memorization. Already being well versed in scriptures that he quoted and Biblical situations he described, everything Von Daniken said rang true to me. He didn't make many actual assertions in the book at all, opting instead to mostly compare interesting complementary facts and ask questions about their connections.

This approach to the subject of Ancient Astronaut theory seemed like the perfect way to introduce such a shift in paradigm. I discovered later that there were many people who were quite angry about this book when it was published, calling the author all sorts of names and discounting the logic in his pages as being ridiculous. I didn't think it was at all ridiculous. I thought it was brilliant. Needless to say, I checked out that book and spend the remainder of the day reading it, blind and deaf to anything around me as I absorbed this new way of looking at things that were, previously, so boring and familiar to me.

I guess this is as good a place as any to say that yes, I've been reading the Bible again recently and there are many more connections that support Ancient Astronaut theory throughout the Old Testament than were mentioned in Von Daniken's book. Besides, the Bible is a downright fascinating book to read. Lately, I've spoken to a decent number of people who consider themselves devout Christians, and it shocks me how many of them have never read the Bible. When I mention that I've been reading it and try to have a conversation about some interesting part, they usually shake their heads and tell me that not only have they never read it, but that they have no clue what I'm talking about. How odd, that someone can go an entire life not reading the single solitary book that their faith and understanding of the way the Cosmos work is based on. If it were me swearing by this faith that is based on a single book, I'd certainly understand the Bible on my own, not according to the interpretation of a political structure that is, as all things are, faulty sometimes. No matter what faith you belong to, all of the current major Christian religions I know of have political aims. It seems to me that knowing your own stuff would automatically be an assumed part of any religion, *especially* when those who translate and interpret it for you have been so fallible in recent years. If it is true that we are all Divine beings and, as Jesus said, we are capable of doing everything he did *and more*, then wouldn't we want to read the guide book on how to accomplish these things? After all, Christ does seem to be the example of what the Human race is evolving into. I'd want to get on that train as fast as I could.

I've digressed. I do that a lot. Back to the point. After reading as much of the book as I could that day, we drove away in the wee hours of the next morning. I babbled to Terry for hours about my amazing discoveries, wanting to learn more about what was out there and that I'd never heard of. The fact that this book, and Von Daniken's subsequent ones as well, came out decades ago and that *everyone* didn't already know about them floored me.

When we arrived in Texas, some sort of dam broke and I found myself searching the internet and the home library of our friends, who had rooms upon rooms of books on just about any subject you can think of. I was looking for information about anything having to do with UFOs. I recognized myself as, in spurts, one of those crazy obsessed people you see in movies, staying up all hours of the night, talking about ridiculous theories that their friends and family members can neither explain nor remotely identify with. Usually in these movies, however, these characters are male, growing their stubble into beards, and wearing dressing robes around, trailing a tattered belt behind them. I didn't have scruff to grow and I opted for yoga pants, but the similarities in interest were definitely there.

This wasn't a constant state though, it came on and off. Sometimes I would go for days without thinking much about it, my fancy taken by something else, like natural building methods (I absolutely want to sculpt my own cob house one day,) ancient and modern sustainable agricultural practices (Terry and I are planting a permaculture garden as I type this,) and, of course, as always, spiritual research (I reached new heights during this period in understanding much concerning my own Soul's history, some of which I rejected at first because of the magnitude of it.) Eventually, however, I would be inextricably drawn back to UFOs for another few days and sleepless nights of frenzied research.

One evening, as Terry and I (he often humored me with this, thank goodness) searched user-generated videos, being led from one to another in the way that has been common since the inception of the huge artificial Collective Unconscious that we call the internet, we came across what seemed to be a school project video based on Vimanas, or ancient flying machines recorded in ancient Vedic scriptures.

We were absolutely shocked, and watched the video repeatedly, slowly absorbing the strange and unexpected evidence we were seeing. These pictures, taken directly from ancient holy texts, were detailed, labeled, schematics of airplanes! They weren't airplanes that fly like ours do, going in a straight line with a curved wing on each side providing enough air disturbance to create a lifting action. Vimanas moved in a different way that was accomplished using a round craft. The fact that the crafts were round and would therefore defy all of our currently understood methods of flight bothered me for a short while, until I reminded myself that our current standards of flight aren't even one century old, and these scripts were written thousands of years ago. Even then, they were probably copied from much older texts. Who was I to say that our current state of the art is all that is possible in flight? It would be unfortunate for future generations if we've already discovered everything that can be discovered, and although in every recent scientific age, this has been claimed, new technologies and ways of doing things continually emerge. All things considered, the fact that the craft was round couldn't serve as a deal breaker for me. Not when the plans I was seeing included details about what specific materials to build with, precise measurements for the craft, and even directions for fueling systems that were used. This was no vision from a mountain top. These were directions drawn up by someone who knew what he or she was talking about. I have to wonder now, especially considering all I've learned about Ancient Astronaut theory, if there were any mountain top visions at all. Perhaps they were relatively simple conversations.

But what did it *mean*? Many of the UFOs that people report seeing today are round, and ancient plans of flying machines that seemed pretty usable and that were probably once in use, which would explain the detailed blueprints, were also round. Was this pure coincidence? I was losing my belief in such things as coincidence.

At this point, articles I'd read years ago and filed away under "stuff I didn't understand so I'd let it be" started to surface in my mind. Something about hieroglyphs and ancient pottery showing pictures of what looked just like the pictures drawn by modern-day people who have claimed to have encounters with ETs.

Researching UFO phenomena and ETs stopped being an occasional obsession and smoothed into an off-and-on hobby for me. Okay, who am I kidding? It was mostly on. While I wouldn't blow off other duties to travel down the winding search paths I made on the internet or in libraries about such things, if I had an hour or two to spare, there wasn't much of a question about what I would be doing.

After our few months staying in Texas, Terry and I moved back to the East Coast to prepare for our wedding. This time was filled with to-do lists and planning, so my hobby was moved to the back burner. We had a lovely garden wedding and went on our honeymoon, all without major significant events where this topic is concerned (the visions and "downloads" I experienced during those times are in a different category entirely, and non-pertinent information won't be discussed. This book would be entirely too long if I included *everything*.)

Our honeymoon was a relaxed, warm, sunny, glorious week of laziness that held opportunities to both enjoy each other, which had been lacking during the wedding festivities and bustle surrounding them, and to spend time in solitude, reconnecting with our respective selves.

On the first day after we arrived, we went shopping to pick up some essentials that we would need for the trip. We bought sandals for him, a new swimsuit for me, and other similar little things. As we walked through the outlet mall that we'd happened to stumble upon, I noticed a discount book store. Always one to spend hours and hours flipping through interesting books, I, of course, wanted to go in. We left an hour or so later, each with an armful of new books, one of mine entitled *Anam Cara Wisdom: Spiritual Guidance from Your Personal Celtic Angel*, and written by Donald McKinney. The book claimed to "introduce" you to your own "Guardian Angel" through a series of guided meditations. Something about it stood out to me. Besides, I do love a good guided meditation. Once we were in the car, I tore through the first several pages as Terry drove. I stopped reading once I reached the first meditation. At the moment, I was also serving as a co-pilot and navigator through the unfamiliar countryside, I couldn't exactly zone out in a meditation. *Anam Cara Wisdom* joined the stack of books in the backseat of our rental car and I promised myself I'd start the meditations as soon as I had a quiet moment.

A day or two later, I had the chance to start the *Anam Cara Wisdom* meditations. I started a hybrid meditation, halfway using my own methods, and also following directions given by the book.

I was at the entrance of my "safe place" that I formed years ago in my shamanistic training. I occasionally visit, more or less often depending on how much need I have of the place's particular rejuvenation effects. I stood in shadow, just beyond the tree line. As I always do, I wiggled my toes in the deep moss covering the ancient forest's floor and reached out my right hand to touch the rough bark of a tree that stands at the edge of my little clearing. Then, as I always do, I walked into the sunlight of the clearing, approaching the water's edge where a small river emerges from a beautiful waterfall about fifty feet high. After enjoying the sun's tingling on my skin, I turned around and walked to my white marble gazebo. Sometimes it holds a palette for me to rest in, and sometimes there is only the bare white marble to sit on, warmed to a comfortable temperature by the sun. I stepped up into the large circular structure and sat down at the edge of a bench that circles the inside edge of the gazebo's pillars. I was facing the river, waiting for my new friend. Whenever I have visitors in my safe place meditations, they come from that direction. I only had to wait a moment before I saw her.

There she was, walking toward me. She'd appeared out of nowhere, but had also done it in such a gentle way that I didn't feel startled at all, just interested. She came up to me and we shared a friendly gaze.

My Anam Cara was beautiful. She stood quite tall, compared with most women, with wavy, rippling hair of a deep auburn color. Her eyes were what captured my attention the most. They were exotically shaped, quite large and of a very beautiful rich purple color. They were quite clear, and her gaze was intelligent, benevolent, and extremely focused. This was the type of gaze that one finds very difficult to break.

I asked her questions, and she answered them. Her presence was steady and felt very safe, and over the course of the week, I visited her on an almost daily basis. She gave me advice and offered explanations during each of our meetings. I quite enjoyed our time together. After the honeymoon, however, the necessities of life came back into full focus and my *Anam Cara* book has been gathering dust on a shelf ever since. As I would find out later, however, I'd had enough contact with this particular new friend to greatly point me in the right direction in just a few months.

One of the interesting tidbits of information I picked up while we were spending our honeymoon week relaxing and enjoying each others' company was how to heal a wound using your will and attention. This was described in Lynn V. Andrews book *The Woman of Wyrrd,* which I picked up from that same discount bookstore. Lynn V. Andrews spoke of an experience where her finger was deliberately pricked and she was taught to heal it. As I read her account of what happened, deep stirrings within my unconscious that grabbed my attention signaled to me that there was definite truth to this method. It was also reminiscent of my headache cure when I was a child.

Here's how it works. Take any injury or pain you have. It's best to start with small ones. My first try was on a toothache, then I attempted to fix an injured finger. It always works, and I've used this method many more times since I learned it. Just a couple of days ago, I tried the process on a stubborn blemish and had fantastic results.

Focus very intently on that part of your body. You have to be able to literally *feel* the pain there. It may pulse, or it may not, but it is important that you be able to feel the *edges* of the pain, where your body feels normal and is pain free.

You'll notice then that a part of you is trying to pull itself away from the pain, retreating from the area. You'll think that reversing this and sending your attention completely *into* the pain will hurt more, but you'll see that when you actually do it, the pain doesn't become more bothersome. If anything, it lightens up a bit.

Once you are **in** the pain, find the exact, specific pinpoint of space where the pain is originating. Find the source. Just identify it, down to the tiniest spot. As soon as you find it, the spot will move. You'll have to chase it around a bit. But after a few moments of this, if you keep your attention focused on the exercise, then all in an instant the pain will blossom into nothing. It won't hurt anymore. And when you open your eyes and look at the injury, you'll see that it has at least partially healed in a way that is nothing short of miraculous.

Try this the next time that you get a bump, a bruise, or a cut. It works. You'll see.

A couple of months after our wedding and after much soul-searching, my new husband and I found ourselves back where we had started, in Santa Monica, California, living in a sweet little cottage about seven blocks from the beach. I busied myself with domestic duties, setting up our first home and preparing the delicious raw cuisine that we'd learned to love in Texas, when after experimenting with it for a month, we lost almost twenty pounds each, our teeth whitened, our eyes changed colors, becoming brighter and more iridescent, and our body structure, including the bone structure of our faces, began to shift. We laugh now when looking at old photos, very aware of how different we look. When our diet returns in part to what it used to be, the ordinary Western diet which clogs body organs and energy meridians alike, we begin to return to these old selves. Once we return to more fresh, living foods, the opposite happens.

It is true that our bodies are not only made of what we eat and shaped by our commonplace activities, but they are formed by our mental habits – our moods, our worries, our stresses, and our hopes. And if the human body completely remakes itself, cell by cell, every year or so, then why wouldn't we be able to heal literally *anything*? I know that some people will disagree with that. But so far, I've found it to be true. Decide for yourself. Preferably, after a little experimentation with eating good quality, fresh, nutrient-rich foods so that you can judge off of more information than the food addictions you have. We all have them, and we can all overcome them. The challenge is well worth it. Things can happen to a person's physical health that they never thought were possible, once the body is actually nourished and toxins are no longer poured into it. Fortunately, this information is becoming more mainstream every day. There are many books and documentaries available on the healing properties of food, as well as the beneficial effects of a diet consisting mostly of raw, organic produce.

On the morning of Tuesday, September 23, 2010, I sat down on our sofa with my computer and a cup of tea. I'd finished my morning cleaning routine, which I considered one of the simple joys of domestic life (strange but true,) and Terry had just left to attend a morning class. With the cottage to myself, I decided to check in on the world before getting to work on my current projects. I opened my email and after I'd finished whatever correspondence was waiting, I decided to do a short internet search on some areas of interest before I buckled down for the day.

I never did buckle down that day. Instead, I stumbled across a couple of audio and video files that "cracked me wide open," according to my journal. These included audio directions for energy work and self-balancing which I've since incorporated into my daily meditation practice, as well as a channeling from the Divine that left me shaken, tear-stained, emotionally raw, and grateful. For the rest of the day, I felt odd internal shifting deep inside of my energetic body. The day before this one had been the Fall Equinox and the Full Moon, so the electromagnetic and spiritual energies in the air were high. This, I'm sure, contributed to the strength of effects on me from the information I'd just discovered as well as the following events.

The next morning, I emerged from the shower into our foggy bathroom and began to apply oil to my arms and legs. I use coconut oil instead of lotion and find that it works much more effectively in keeping the skin soft and smooth. It's also nice to apply after a few hours spent in the sun, and it heals sunburn in record time.

Anyway, as I was standing there, I happened to glance up into the foggy mirror. I did a double take.

What was *that*?!

I turned my head to the right, and to the left. This couldn't be happening. What did it even mean? How could it be possible?!

At the bottom of the mirror, where the fog was already beginning to evaporate, I'd seen, where my eyes were supposed to be, two lights, multicolored, with rings around each of them and dark centers. I straightened to see what this would look like if my face was completely obscured by fog. The lights and rainbow rings brightened and intensified while the rest of me disappeared into white fog. I closed my right eye. Its light vanished, but the light where my left eye should have been remained. I closed my left eye and opened my right. Same thing, on the other side. I turned my head, and the lights moved as my head moved, not distorting at all when the angle of my face changed.

I called Terry in from his office a few rooms away.

"Look in the mirror. Can you *see* that?"

He leaned over so his face was reflected on the foggy, gray surface.

"Yes," he said quietly. I had no clue what he was making of this. I didn't have any idea what to think of it myself, for that matter.

I couldn't see his lights, and he couldn't see mine. But we could each see our own, shining brightly, unmistakeable, definitely disconcerting, but also *really cool*.

Terry went on his way, going back to whatever he was doing. I stayed in the bathroom, trying to make sense of what I was seeing. When the bottom half of the mirror cleared, I bent over, my face reflected, quite plainly and without any strangeness, in the clear glass. I straightened, and the rest of me disappeared while the lights immediately returned. Again, I moved to a clear section of the mirror. There was my normal face. I moved back into the fog, and there were those bright, haloed lights where my eyes should have been. In between these two extremes, where only a little fog clung to the surface of the glass, I could see my reflection *and* the lights, the lights appearing as a thin overlay, their rainbow colors paler, but still visible.

This continued for months. It had to be during the day, when natural light lit the room, and the light from the window had to be bright enough. For some reason, the cloudier the day, the dimmer the lights I saw. Either way, it's a very strange thing, to look into a completely foggy mirror and see freaking **headlights** staring back out at you. It is a bit stranger to only *slightly* be able to see through the condensation, able to make out a shadowy outline of your head and shoulders as your eyes shine like flashlights.

I wondered about this appearance – I'd seen myself in foggy mirrors all of my life, of course, and never before had this happened. What did it mean? I've never heard of it happening to anyone else either. And yet, there we were, both

Terry and I experiencing the same thing. I couldn't help remembering being afraid of monsters as a child, covering my eyes as children do, thinking that *if I can't see them, they can't see me.* Is there some truth to that? Is there some amount of light, emitted from the eyes, that can actually be seen and that children are hiding with an instinctive belief that we, as adults, laugh off and call immature?

As for why it began, I have no clue how to begin to figure it out. I'd found those amazing meditations the day before, but Terry hadn't done them and he could see the lights too. So that could not have been the correct explanation. The lights also began the day *before* Terry and I started our sungazing practice. If we had already been soaking our optic nerves in more light than usual from looking at the sun, and then emitting it later into the mirror, I'd understand that explanation, I guess. But the lights showed up the day *prior* to our first gazing day, so that couldn't have been the answer either.

Over the following weeks, I kept studying the phenomenon and learned a few things. The center of each light was white, with a rainbow-hued ring surrounding it beginning with red and fading into violet in that same order that any rainbows show. Next would come a ring of blue, around that would be a ring of white, and then the rainbow would begin with red again. The area of the light increased and decreased in a seemingly random fashion. Some days the lights would be bigger than sunglasses, some days they would barely take up the area of my eye socket in the mirror's reflection. I never figured out any explanation for the size changes either.

The lights didn't quite have their center aligned with my pupil. I had assumed, since the light was supposedly being emitted by my eyes, that it would have shone directly out from the center openings of each eye. For some reason, the center (so source, I suppose) of the lights were always slightly inside of and below this point. Was I seeing a light at all? Was this energy somehow emitted by my spirit body, which could have a different anatomy of sorts than my physical body, the way that one's heart chakra is lined up along the center core of the body while the organ of that chakra, the heart itself, is slightly to the left?

A week after the first day that I noticed the lights, I attended a lecture given by David Wolfe at a bookstore a few blocks away from our cottage in Santa Monica. Terry and I were both fans of Wolfe's writing. His *Sunfood Diet Success System* had been, more or less, our raw food handbook during our initial experimentation with that method of eating. We'd recommended it all over the place and even given copies as gifts to friends and members of our family. When I saw that Wolfe was giving a lecture near enough to our cottage that I could easily walk, I signed up immediately. Why not?

I arrived at the shop a few minutes before the talk was schedule to begin, and people had already begun to crowd into the small space. With only a few chairs available anyway, standing room was the only remaining option. I found a spot next to some interesting CDs and browsed through them until Wolfe appeared. By that time, people were shoulder to shoulder in the place. Some were sitting on the floor, which I would have gladly done, if my view from the floor wouldn't have been completely blocked by the people standing in front of me.

David Wolfe has an interesting charisma and an unlimited amount of energy. He talked for well over an hour, exploding with information and an excitement that was very contagious. There was an eclectic mix of people attending the talk. The audience consisted of some of those folks who just like to own signed books, and others who were obvious proponents of Wolfe's dietary recommendations. Once you start to notice it, you can often recognize raw foodists by their light body language and their bright, clear eyes. There is also a certain smoothness to the skin that is difficult to describe but easy to recognize that comes after when a person stops ingesting animal fats and eats only plant material. The effect is enhanced when that plant material is uncooked.

After the presentation was over, a line formed around the back of the store for people who would like to have their books signed. As he was signing my book soon afterward, I asked David Wolfe about the lights I'd been seeing in the mirror. I figured that if anyone would have come across such a thing before, surely he would have in all of his travels and interaction with people worldwide who live healthily alternative lifestyles. That said, I knew that I could also potentially sound like a nutcase, of course so even as I spoke, I was a slightly embarrassed.

David Wolfe listened intently while I spoke. Another common attribute among those of healthy bodies and spirits is their in-the-moment presence, which also makes them great listeners. After I'd finished describing my situation, he sat quietly for a moment, thinking.

"Hmm. No, I can't say I've heard of that before," he told me. "But you know, your eyes don't just absorb light, they also actually emit it. It sounds like that's what you might be seeing. What a cool thing though!"

I laughed and nodded. It *was* a cool thing. But I also knew now that this was definitely, authentically, *really **weird***. And no one could explain it to me. That said, I don't really mind being the first one to have strange things happen – I may as well be used to it by now! But the question of *why* it was happening still remained.

I couldn't say. I still can't say. I don't see the lights anymore. Perhaps the natural light coming at a particular angle into that room allowed a unique reflection. Perhaps the light I was emitting back then is now being transformed into another type of energy so it can be directed at other things, like the creation of this book. Perhaps I just don't shine the same way anymore – who knows?

I decided in early October that I wasn't getting out enough and that I needed to focus more of my attention on service to others, so I began to look for volunteering opportunities in areas that I was interested in. Almost immediately, I discovered a seminar that was going to be coming to town the next week given by Brian L. Weiss, the author of *Many Lives, Many Masters* – the same book that had served as my first real life validation after Susannah opened my mind, nearly a decade ago, to the idea of reincarnation.

I sent the organizers an email right away, volunteering to help with the day's events. After discussing it with them, I also volunteered my sister and Terry. Why not have company if you're doing something generally mundane all day? Conversation makes the time pass more quickly. Besides, they had both thought his book was interesting, so maybe they'd hear something informative.

A few days before the event, I got a phone call from my mother, telling me that my beloved Aunt Rose had been admitted to the hospital. Rose was the matriarch of our gigantic family; the glue that held us all together and kept us aware of what everyone else was up to, which isn't an easy task when you have a family as large and as spread out as ours is. Everyone loved her, and she was the only person in my extended family that I talked to regularly. We spoke about once a week, discussing education (she'd been a teacher for many decades,) the family, spirituality, and health. The week before she described a dream she had to me where she had been talking to my grandmother, her sister. Constance, my grandmother, had passed away about fifteen years before, and in the dream, Rose was bending down, trying to find something out about Constance's shoes. Rose told me that she didn't know what the dream meant, and a strange intuitive feeling made me wonder if what evidenced in the dream as my grandmother's shoes actually represented the way she'd crossed over from the physical world into the spirit one. Rose ended that conversation with me as she always did, with love and blessings and an assertion that she still enjoyed this life and wasn't ready to leave it yet. When I got the call about her, I wasn't completely surprised, although I also wasn't sure what the outcome was going to be.

Over the next few days, Rose alternatively rallied and faltered. She had a respirator tube inserted while in the hospital and could no longer speak, so she wrote notes to the droves of people at her bedside. I wrote a letter to Rose via my mother, giving her tips on how to minimize any pain she was feeling using her power of thought and attention. It was the same method I've described here already. My mother brought the note to her and Rose kept it next to her bed. My family does not, generally, handle death particularly well, so while I was hoping and praying for the best, I also knew that it would likely be beneficial, in case she was hanging on for everyone else's comfort, for someone to give her the verbal go ahead. I asked my mother to do this, since I was too far away to say these things myself. Although it would be difficult, Mom told me that she would. Not that this makes much of a difference if the person suffering isn't ready to go, but if they are, and if they are waiting for loved ones to be okay with it who won't think that way or accept the necessary change that all Humankind has faced since the beginning of our existence on this planet, then sometimes those simple words make a huge difference to the amount of peace a soul feels when leaving the body.

The night before the Brian Weiss workshop, I had a dream that I was teaching in a great big, brick school building in my hometown. I'd attended elementary school there, and years ago, the building had been a high school. In the dream I was wearing a dress that matched the styles in the mid-1900's as I walked the halls, intent on doing my job well. This was the school system that Rose not only taught in during her career, but that she helped build and shape, producing some of the brightest and most ambitious children for miles around and inspiring countless others.

My phone rang, pulling me out of the dream. It was my mother. She told me that Rose had crossed over. It was still dark outside, so I decided to wait until morning to tell Terry and my sister, who was asleep in the living room. She had spent the night in order to carpool to the workshop with us the following morning.

I got up to go to the bathroom after I hung up with my mother. For a moment, just after I closed the door separating the bedroom and bathroom, I smelled a strong, peculiar smell. It reminded me of perfume and books, and brought me back to my childhood in an instant. It was also completely foreign to my current life. The scent was only there for a moment, and as soon as I'd caught it well, I looked around for the cause, even as I knew that I wouldn't find anything to explain it. That had been Aunt Rose.

In the morning, the three of us drove to another part of Los Angeles where the workshop was being held in a beautiful old theater. We volunteered to be parking attendants, which really meant, to our delight, that we stood there chatting in our red t-shirts while people walked past us, having clearly seen the entrance to the theater themselves on their way to the parking lot across the street.

We stood shaded by an old olive tree on the side of the theater, remembering Aunt Rose and discussing whether we'd be able to make the trip home to her funeral. My sister and I did end up flying east the next weekend in order to attend.

As soon as everyone had parked and we'd spent some time chatting with the other volunteers, including a young woman named Krishanti who I developed an immediate liking for. She was sweet, friendly, and a professional intuitive. Our conversation flowed on that first day as though we'd known each other for years. Another volunteer came outside and surprised us by saying that that we were totally done! We could attend the workshop now like anyone else.

That was an unexpected perk. Ours mall group found a place in the upper balcony where we could see and hear Dr. Weiss quite well. He was the typical image of a psychiatrist – well dressed in that crisp academic fashion, and with impeccable posture. He also had a calm, smooth voice that could easily lull you into an inadvertent trance. He made jokes about that quality of his voice more than once over the course of the interesting day.

During the morning portion of the workshop, Dr. Weiss spoke about his experiences when he discovered, unexpectedly, that the client he wrote about in his famous book had lived before, many times. He described his skepticism, never having been one to be interested in the esoteric, and his change of heart when this client, while in the in-between state where she channeled the Masters, as he called them, told him things about himself and his life that she couldn't have possibly known. One of these was the diagnosis of his son, who had died in infancy from a rare and specific heart condition years before, which not many people knew about. His client, or rather, the Master who was speaking through her at the time, described the condition exactly and told Weiss details about the event which only he was aware of. This, he told us, was the moment where he *really* started to believe that what he'd been experiencing through this client's sessions was real. As always, it was refreshing to hear another person's account of the strange paradigm shifts that life sometimes brings. I had been so enamored by his book that listening to Weiss speak in person was quite a treat for me.

Dr. Weiss also led us through a group regression that morning, just before a lunch break. In it he took us back through our childhoods, encouraging us to remember a specific moment or two and find the meaning behind why it had been brought to the forefront of our awareness. I remembered a sunny afternoon when I'd been crushing up those little dangerously dark purple berries that grew abundantly in southern Virginia. The gray paint covering the concrete steps leading up to our front porch was chipping, so I was filling in the bare places with the rich purple dye made by my berry paste. I could remember being intent on my actions, moving the colored mash this way and that with a twig, completely covering any empty spots. I could feel the sunlight's warmth on the top of my head and gently pressing against my upper back. The message from this memory, I realized after Dr. Weiss's questions referring to it, was that nature was not a scary place for me. As a teenager and young adult, I'd gotten filled with ridiculous notions that the great outdoors is filled with unpleasant things, like bugs, creepy crawly animals, too much sun, and nameless other things that could, and probably would, hurt you. Coming through the memory, I heard that this assumption is a ridiculous fallacy and that I need to just get over it. Nature is my *home*. Go there. It will feel better than anything man made can.

Next, Dr. Weiss took us into our in vitro state, asking us how we felt in general, and what we though about coming into this life. He asked why we'd chosen to live this particular incarnation rather than any other. I was full of bliss and excitement, comfortable, warm, and very ready to be born. In response to Dr. Weiss's question about *why* I was incarnating here and now, the automatic response I received from my in vitro self was:

*The life was foretold, but **I** get to live it!*

That statement left me wondering about it for quite awhile. I still don't at all understand what it meant, not really. During the memory, I also got the feeling that I was ready to go before my mother was prepared to have me. I felt like I kept trying to begin the process of emergence for me – labor, for her – but that she halted me, wanting more time to pass before my birth.

A week later, when I was home for Rose's funeral, I wanted to confirm this with my mother. I asked her if I seemed ready to be born before my due date, and she cut me off with an exclamation before I'd even finished asking the question.

"Yes, you most *certainly **were**! I went into labor multiple times in the weeks before you were born. I had to keep using relaxation techniques that your father and I had learned in our Bradley classes to calm my body down. You tried to be born a *lot*."

As I've said before, it's always nice to have verification. I got such a thrill when my mother told me about this detail of her pregnancy. I hadn't known it before. She never mentioned that. I don't think she had even thought about it until that moment, when I asked her as we drove through Richmond during my visit..

Back to the reincarnation workshop. In the next portion of the regression, Dr. Weiss led us back into a past life, asking us to first notice ourselves. What did we look like? What we we wearing? What were we doing?

I was walking. There was dust on my feet. I was male. My skin was tanned from lots of time in the sun, and I was on a long road, stretching across several different landscapes. When I tried to see my clothing, I saw several different items, one on top of the other. This confused me until my understanding of what I was seeing crystallized enough for me to realize that I layered clothing a lot while on the road, depending on whatever the temperature was. I would do this throughout the day if I needed to, and it explained the visual I'd received at first of different pieces of clothing on top of each other. I always wore a certain type of clothing here, but put on and took off more layers that would keep me warm if the air grew cool.

What was I doing? First I thought I was simply traveling, but as my view of the surrounding time line of this particular life expanded, I saw that my traveling was actually something more than simply going from place to place. I was on a pilgrimage. I passed a family with a little girl, traveling on the road in the opposite direction. The girl's hair was tucked under a cloth, and she looked at me with calm, serene, knowing eyes. We understood each other. She'd seen it too.

Seen what? I wondered this even as I caught the answer. It was something about the spiritual place, or places, that I was visiting. Then I saw that I was some sort of spiritual person, and most of my life was spent going between different temples or holy places.

When Dr. Weiss directed us to see the most important event in that life, I got a flash of lying on my back, surrounded by chanting monks of some order I'm not now familiar with. Their appearance reminded me of pictures I've seen of Tibetan monks, although I don't think that these men were necessarily Tibetan at all. I was in the throes of a mind-bending spiritual experience, with the energy of the Cosmos flowing through me, filling my senses and my mind, carrying me away into spiritual ecstasy.

Oh, I see, I thought to myself. *I took part in the rituals. That was my mission in this life.* I had no idea what this meant, but these were the words that formed in my mind.

Dr. Weiss then directed us to go to our death and see how it happened. I had grown into an old man and was lying in bed, aware that my life was ending and feeling acceptance and joy. Around my bed stood people of varying ages, most of them children and grandchildren of mine, I knew. At one side of my bed stood a little boy who eyes barely reached past the top of the bedclothes. I looked into those eyes, and with a small shock, subtly felt because my present consciousness was mostly occupied with the man's thoughts in this incarnation, I recognized *Terry.* I'd heard before, more than once, that although much of our physical appearance changes from lifetime to lifetime, we can always be recognized by something in our eyes. I'd obviously had this happen before in regressions I'd done myself. In the lifetime I was currently remembering, Terry had been a descendant of mine. He was either my grandson or my great-grandson, I wasn't sure which. I tucked the information away as a fascinating piece to turn over in my mind another time. I was already aware that we tend to often incarnate with certain people, over and over, in different relationships throughout our lifetimes and I'd known from early on in our relationship that Terry and I had been together before, and probably with several different types of connections bonding us.

After we'd finished the memory portion of this regression, Dr. Weiss suggested that we spend some time *between* places, interacting with a guide that we would find there. I expected to see a human's form approach as I floated in darkness, relaxed and waiting for someone to come to me. When I saw who actually *did* approach, my heart leaped with a recognition that I had no idea how to interpret. Slowly floating towards me with exquisitely graceful movements was a being made of colored light. It did not look remotely human. The details of its appearance were difficult to see because it was always moving, but I was aware of two great, glowing eyes staring into me filled with more love and welcome than I can describe in words. There were streams of colored light in blues, greens, and purples coming off of this being, creating a formation that almost reminded me of giant butterfly wings, although they weren't like butterfly wings at all, not really. Tears broke through my closed eyelids, there in the theater, which felt quite far away and at the back of my mind. All I could say to this being was a joy-filled, soft, "Hi."

A great deal of information was transmitted between us, although barely any of it was verbal. I asked to see my Aunt Rose, knowing that she was also probably quite busy. Not even a day had passed since she'd left the physical plane, so I wasn't sure whether I would be granted my request. I'd forgotten that time worked differently in other dimensions.

Suddenly, there she was, with my grandmother and, in the background, a young man I recognized as their brother, Jerry, who crossed over many years before my birth and who I didn't even have a clear mental image of before this moment. When looking through the eyes of the spirit, you don't need an image of one of the random physical bodies another soul has lived in to recognize someone, I guess. Rose was not the elderly woman I remembered, but a young, vibrant, smiling lady at the prime of her life, wearing a dress and high heels. My grandmother was just as young, and dressed in a similar fashion. I asked Rose if she was all right, and she told me that yes, of course she was. I could feel her joy at being released from her painful, slow, awkward body, and I sent her, as well as my grandmother and my Uncle Jerry, waves of love from my heart as they retreated into the distance. I then thought to look at myself (again, when you're using the eyes of spirit I suppose you don't need a mirror,) and to my complete shock, I too looked like that beautiful being made of light, only I was of a slightly different overall color. My emotional state grew then to a level of excitement, surprise, and joy that defies words, and just at that moment, Dr. Weiss began to bring us out of the meditation.

During the lunch break, Terry and I volunteered to be carpool drivers and took a couple of our fellow volunteers to the closest grocery store so we could each pick up a quick and relatively healthy lunch. We chatted as we ate, sitting on the steps to one of the side entrances to the theater, shaded by more olive trees and enjoying a soothing breeze. Krishanti and I exchanged information after we realized that we had a great deal in common, saying that we should get together soon and share stories.

Before long, it was time to return to the darkened interior of the theater. In the afternoon, Dr. Weiss led the audience through a longer, more detailed regression. These regressions were where the major benefit of sitting in the deserted balcony came in. While the people downstairs were crowded together and so had to attempt to create comfortable seated positions in their chairs as they slipped into altered states, the few of us up above could lie prone in the aisles, spread out and with plenty of room to spare.

After the initial calming and centering beginning of the regression, Dr. Weiss took us through a few different visualizations, culminating in an immersion of one out of six lifetimes that were glimpsed through different "doors" created in our imagination. He gave us time periods for each of these imaginary doors except for the last one. This door was reserved for a time, he said, that may have come *before* any recorded history. This is the door I was drawn to with the greatest intensity out of the six.

I walked through the door and found myself in an underground chamber. It was extremely large, bigger than any ballroom I've ever been in, and it was filled with giant crystals. Some of these crystals were as large as a house. The ones I recall seeing, as I walked past them in the body that lived this long ago life, were egg shaped and quite beautiful. There was a soft glow in the chamber, a glow that wasn't electrical in nature like the artificial lighting that we have nowadays, but that reminded me of the bioluminescence emitted by creatures that live in the deepest parts of the sea. This particular glow also reminded me of the lit number "1" I see embedded on the bottom stone step of the journey I take to start a self-guided regression. The first time I saw it, this strange number's appearance was spontaneous and unplanned until I was already in the meditation. Was the luminous light in this chamber from my ancient memory reflecting some part of my subconscious that I'd already seen evidenced in my meditations? Was that luminous number in my meditation a reflection of ancient memories I held that only surfaced when I accessed the deepest part of my mind, since, after all, the "1" represents the most relaxed and deepest level that you can reach in a self-guided meditation? I didn't know. But as I looked at the hollowed walls of the chamber that seamlessly met the floor in an unbroken curve, as smoothly as if they had been naturally formed, but with a spacing and regular curvature that suggested otherwise, I noticed that the light was coming from delicate, intricate inlaid scroll work buried in the walls and floor that looked like softly glowing blue-silver wires. The same ones that made up that number "1." Interesting. I didn't let my mind wander farther than it had to in order to take note of the similarity, however. I was very curious about this lifetime.

I stretched my thought to be able to understand more of this life. I knew what I looked like – I was very thin, but not as if I lacked nourishment, rather as if my genetic makeup carried this thinness. This is where things began to feel even stranger, but in a different, hypnotic way that made me want to learn more. My skin was a shade of light, dusky, **blue**. I moved slowly and my internal emotional state was always serene and very present in the moment. The crystals all around me emitted such intense vibrations that it was almost as if they were continually humming – but not in a machine's irritating, one dimensional hum. This was a symphony, a living, pulsing, unimaginably beautiful vibratory feeling that translated to me as sound.

I was the keeper of this place. As I understood more about this life, the idea came to mind that this chamber was under the mountain that we now call Mount Shasta, which is located in the area of our land mass that we now call California. I also knew that there were great crystal chambers such as this all over the Earth. We didn't call her the Earth back then, and we didn't call her Gaia. She had a different name entirely and we knew that she was a living being. We were stewarding her growth and progress through the work we did here. I was in the member of my race who served in this chamber, as others of my race and other races did, in other chambers, all over the globe. We could communicate at any time, and I was always aware of what was happening across the planet. We also had the potential to work together by creating great shifts in the vibration of the Earth, interacting with her via these crystals. I loved what I did. It was not a job, it was my life. I relished this existence, with gratitude, love, and presence.

I didn't go outside very often. The surface above me was was covered by an ancient forest, and although I would go up for occasional late night walks when the air was dark and cool, the daylight was much too bright for my liking.

I became aware that I knew I was of mixed genetic heritage. I was partly of the Earth, and partly from elsewhere. I remembered standing on a ramp that extended down from a ship. This ramp looked like metal as I would recognize it now, but beneath my bare feet, it was warm, liquid (although it looked completely solid and I walked on it as such,) and *alive*.

Dr. Weiss suggested that we go to the most important event of that life. I made that intention and was immediately standing outside, at night, looking out over the view that my position on the mountain gave me. I saw many ships slowly lifting off of the ground and gently, gracefully floating upward. I was sorrowful because I knew that I would never see the ones on the ships – my family and friends – again in a physical sense, however, I had telepathic communication with them whenever I wished so my sadness didn't run incredibly deep. I was watching them leave for the last time.

Then, back in the theater, we were told to go witness our death. I was back in the chamber, and there seemed to be what felt like an earthquake. The floor was moving and things were falling, and I was trying to get out, but without the anxious fear or terror that you might expect in such a situation. Those emotions simply weren't part of my knowledge base or emotional vocabulary. Something fell from above and killed my body. I floated upward, free of my body, seeing the events of the moments unfold as I left the space, aware that this life was over and feeling perfectly at peace with that.

As I floated up and out of that lifetime, I wondered if I knew that the delicate balance of the Earth would shift and be destroyed, at least on the surface, in the time to come through the experience of duality that we currently face now, in this lifetime. I found that I did know this at the time, back in the chamber, and I also knew that this unbalanced time period was beginning, which had likely been partially, if not entirely, the reason for the earthquake, or vice-versa. The crystals which had kept Gaia's vibratory frequency so finely tuned were being disrupted and possibly broken. I also knew, however, that this coming difficult time was as transient as anything else and so I was not anxious at all about it. It simply *was*. In any event, this difficult period would only be temporary.

With a few more parting visuals, Dr. Weiss brought us out of the meditation. Then he led us through a exercise in psychometry, where we exchanged an item with a stranger, holding it in our hand and quieting our minds to see what images or sensations arose. I exchanged my engagement ring with a ring worn by one of the other volunteers that was sitting in our group. I saw plush furniture, a balcony looking out into a night filled with warm breezes, and two people dancing, around and around. It was a very romantic collection of images. I also saw a big red, cartoon-like heart in my mind's eye.

After the exercise when we shared our impressions, my partner told me what my visions meant. This ring had just been given to her by her sister who lives in Spain. My partner had traveled to visit her sister a few months ago. She said that her sister and her sister's husband were part of a dancing group, who gathered regularly to dance in different places, and that her sister had told her that this group was one of the great sources of love in her life.

I was floored. I hadn't tried much psychometry before, but the images I'd gotten were pretty dead-on. When our roles switched, my partner told me that she felt a lot of love and brightness, as well as a lightness that was almost airy. She said I was like a bird, or a butterfly, that could fly away at any moment.

I couldn't say what that meant with much clarity, but I certainly liked it. Later, after the seminar had ended and I'd stood in line for a good half hour to get my old, well-worn copy of *Many Lives, Many Masters* signed by Dr. Weiss, I gathered my courage and asked him whether people ever report experiences having to do with extra terrestrials after their past life regressions. He told me that while this was uncommon, it was not unheard of, and suggested that I email the experience to him so he and his daughter, who works with him, could review it. He'd told the entire audience to do the same during his presentation. Weiss had also said that he and his daughter were working on more writing projects, so reading other people's experiences would aid in their research.

I told him that I would send the email. And I did, a several weeks afterward.

Months later I remembered Susannah's reading about my past life as one of the Crystal People. I had all but forgotten about the story she'd told me years ago about my blue-skinned heritage. She hadn't mentioned that, during one of those lifetimes, I may have traveled to this planet. Given that last detail, this memory certainly seemed to match what she had told me.

Krishanti and I sat on my living room couch, facing each other, chatting. It was so nice to finally speak to someone else who was as "odd" as I was. She came from a conventional background as well, and her gifts essentially pestered her until she let that part of her natural skill set direct her life, leaving her normal, run-of-the mill career behind in order to focus on her career as an intuitive. She was a good one too.

We spoke about our poor husbands, having to deal with their wives' quirky personalities and behavior, which were decidedly stranger than other women who weren't concerned with the mystical side of life. We took out our Tarot cards and exchanged them, comparing decks and giving each other mini-readings. We also gave each other purely intuitive readings. Sometimes it's just fun to get to flex those "muscles" with a friend.

During one of these readings, Krishanti told me that she saw a guide next to me. This was a new discovery for me – I thought that I already knew all of my guides. She said that she saw him sitting surrounded by drums, and that he would teach me about rhythms, but not rhythms made by sound. He would teach me the rhythms of life and of energy, and he'd also teach me lessons about the stillness beneath the rhythms. I believe she called it the "order of the Cosmos."

He would use symbols, too, and she described a rune to me which I instantly recognized – yes, I told her, I'd done work with runes before after a friend brought me a little purple bag of wooden runes from a week-long trip he'd taken to New Orleans. I couldn't recall what that particular rune meant, however. I'd have to look it up later.

I tried to research the rune after she left. I couldn't find anything that matched. It could also have been a cuneiform symbol, considering the look of it, and perhaps that was what it was. I haven't found out yet, either way.

The next morning, during my meditation, I began to picture my rhythm teacher's rune. Right away, I felt his presence in my mind, strong, stoic, and focused. He told me, on that first day, through words spoken in a new thought voice in my head, that my rhythm, meaning my vibration – the frequency of my thought, my breathing, my words and my steps, would set the rhythm of everything around me. *Everything.* So I should always **choose** my rhythm.

I began recording what he said to me on that first day in my journal. I drew his rune, then wrote his words below the symbol, adding a box around what I had just written to separate it from the other contents of my journal. I then drew another box around the first one, and placed a line of dots between the two nested boxes, creating a pattern that I hadn't seen before, but that just felt right somehow. I've done that ever since. I can't say why other than that it seems the correct thing to do with this new serious guide's words of instruction. Nowadays, however, having discovered what I've discovered since our first meeting, I type his words as he speaks them to me each day, and I've been able to go from only being able to record a few lines of text to entire paragraphs. I suppose some would call this channeling, but I don't consider it that. I think of it as transcribing.

The next morning, my rhythm teacher told me that I didn't know how strong I was, and to claim my birthright. He also showed me the symbol of a spiraling triquetra, each of the spirals traveling in a clockwise direction, going inward. I've drawn spirals in the margins of my notebooks, traced them in the sand, and chosen spiraling designs for everything ranging from jewelry to furniture since I was a teenager. Now that I've become more aware of this symbol's significance for me, I know to *pay attention* whenever I see a spiral. I've been surprised at the odd places where it shows up.

The following day, my rhythm teacher instructed me to let my breath serve as my rhythm for that day. I didn't visit him for a few days, and when I called him again during my meditation by picturing his rune in my mind, he instructed me again to create my own rhythm using my breath. He grew more specific with his instruction as the days passed and I continued to visit him, expanding the idea to include a description of how I should determine my own rhythms, rather than letting the rhythms around me determine my inner state. He also told me that, at the time, I was more powerful than I could imagine.

This seems like it should have been flattering, but it wasn't. He was strict with me, and over the following weeks I discovered that when I didn't followed his lessons, he would give me the same directions over and over, becoming exasperated when I failed to exhibit the control that he was teaching me how to master over myself and over the world around me, through that initial self-mastery. Sometimes his words would be encouraging and make me think about myself in a new way, like on December 3, 2010, when I wrote the following in my journal, under his rune and inside the double layered, dotted box:

"BE AS YOU ARE. There is no need to temper yourself for other people. You are a gem among humans. Let yourself shine."

(*A gem among humans?* Interesting and confusing wording...but I went with it.)

A week later, on December 11, 2010, he grew frustrated with me, saying the following:

"I cannot teach you until you have mastered your lessons – use breath as your rhythm. Set <u>your</u> rhythms, not to be disturbed by others'. Claim your birthright."

(What he meant by all this *claim your birthright* and *remember who you are* stuff, both phrases he had said several times already, I had no idea. But I figured I'd understand eventually, and when I did understand, I was glad that I hadn't spent time trying to figure it out. The truth was so strange that I *never* would have been able to predict what was coming.)

Although he was tough, my guide did offer me encouragement too, when I needed it. Whenever I did listen and learn to grow via his teachings, which always corresponded with other ancient wisdom traditions I've studied before, although I obviously had not quite adopted them as part of my daily practice, he would progress with a new lesson. He gave me one of these new lessons after I'd finally learned how to stay aware of my breath over the course of each day.

This lesson was not as verbal as the others. It didn't fit into a couple of neat, easy-to-write sentences that I could jot down in my journal, surrounding them with their dotted box. Instead, he showed me what I suppose I'll call a vision, although it was much more than that. Sure, there were visual elements, but the majority of his lesson was in a language that almost defies description. Over time, this language has become more familiar to me through practice. Once you get the hang of it, you realize that this type of communication is the most familiar thing in the world.

The sense that this way of communicating and understanding uses is mostly an **emotional** sense. It is more refined that the pure emotions that you can draw with a pencil by making a couple dots and a squiggly line, but it is emotional nonetheless. Think about how love feels, or how frustration feels, or relief. These are actual visceral *feelings*, in your chest or your stomach. They are subtle, and we've been taught to ignore and deny them, so they can be hard to put a finger on, yet when you find yourself in a situation where this type of thinking is the point of the entire darned thing and it is more clear and solid than anything else, you'll see that it isn't *actually* more difficult to grasp. We're just out of practice.

In this lesson, I was shown how energy flows. This isn't a new idea. Feng Shui, for instance, has been used for centuries, and this was somewhat related to Feng Shui's description of the flow of energy moving through any given space. I saw and felt that I was standing just inside the doorway to a room. The room didn't matter – I understood that this could be any room, anywhere, with anything in it. Subsequently, I've come to understand that this is also true on a much larger scale and can be done anywhere, and in fact, *is* done whether you want to be doing it or not. By now, I've realized that it was kept at a non-threatening size so I would not be overwhelmed with the implications of what I was being taught. So I was in a room. Okay.

Around me, continuously moving, flowed what looked and felt like ribbons. I knew they weren't *actually* ribbons, they were streams of energy of all shapes and sizes and strengths, but for now, the ribbon idea worked well. There were lots of types, coming from everywhere and moving around everything that was in the space the way that filtered water moves in a fish tank. Actually, that is a perfect example. If an opening appeared in the tank, the water would spill out, interacting with whatever was on the side of the wall. But when the tank is closed, the water inside is always moving and flowing and interacting with everything inside the walls. That is how these energy ribbons worked.

Then I noticed that once I was in that room, I was affecting its energy. No matter what I was feeling, and whether or not I wanted to, I was changing everything around me because of the way I was influencing these constant streams of energy. I also understood that this was true for everyone. The simplified images I was seeing combined with feelings I was receiving showed me that I made a literal imprint in the field created by those ribbons. After they had passed me, the ribbons held the shape of my body like a plastic mold would as they continued around the room. Of course, my body, in this lesson, represented other things, like my mood, how happy or unhappy I was, how kind or unkind I was, and on and on. I saw that after leaving me, this energy affected everything else, bringing the energy from one person to another, and affecting all of the inanimate objects in the room as well.

Just about all of us has heard it said about someone, or made the comment ourselves that a person has a sort of "presence." This is often true for performers and strong personalities, but it can be true for everyone. And whether or not you want to, we **all** have some sort of presence, and it affects everyone and everything around us.

I saw that I could either ignore this fact and remain careless with what I brought to a place, flinging around whatever mood and mindset I happened to be in at the moment, or I could control it and consciously affect my surroundings. I saw that yes, this is done with emotion and mental clarity, but that it is also done by posture and by the pace and depth of one's breathing. Good posture and proper oxygenation literally open up the chakras, so the web of "ribbons" that we all have flowing around us at all times which are just as much a part of us as our ear or our pinky toe are, will be healthier, cleaner, bigger, and more vibrant. We'll also simply *feel* better – happier and more intelligent, not to mention physically healthier.

All that said, the thing that makes the most difference in how we impact those around us is our *intention*. Once we **know** that we can, and do, influence any space in that way, and once we choose to consciously interact with the energy around us, a larger and more significant effect is had on everyone in that space than by any freak-out or temper tantrum (or intended manipulation, for that matter) by a person unaware of this fact. The power and effect increases exponentially *again* when we decide to make our presence aid in the highest and best outcome of everyone affected by the energy we put off – not only of the Human kingdom, but from *all* kingdoms. This is especially true when we are spending time in nature, even if that nature is just outside our back door. We don't have to understand at all what that best outcome would be, we just have to want it to come, and define our intentions that simply. It will work.

Of course, this is a lot to remember. So if all you do is focus on your breath, posture, and presence (rather than being off somewhere in your memory or your mental to-do list or the like,) this makes a beneficial difference.

All that was given to me in about 30 seconds, including more detail than I have written here, and more multi-leveled information than I'm probably capable of writing at all. This mind-to-mind (or whatever it is) teaching is much more developed than any other type of information transfer I'd ever seen. The closest thing I can compare it to is plugging a storage device into your computer and literally downloading a file or program from it – you, like a computer would, understand **everything**. Not just the outline of a concept but the ins and outs of the entire thing. Quick, effortless, and comfortable. If only I'd been able to learn algebra that way!

In late October of 2010, I had a strange dream. This was the first of its kind, but it wouldn't be the last. For the past few years, I've kept a dream journal. The secret to doing this is in writing your dreams down the moment you wake up. It's even handy to keep an uncapped pen in the book, sitting on the next blank page. If you catch the dream just as you emerge from sleep, you can remember details that will dissolve if you wait even a few minutes to begin writing. You also retain comprehension of strange situations that will vanish as you wake up more fully and return to your waking life. That is what I've found to be true, especially in the type of dream I'm about to describe.

In my dream journal, I wrote that I was taken up into an "enormous alien ship." The dream began with me and at least five other people on a smaller craft during the journey to the actual ship. I didn't remember any faces or names of my fellow travelers, but I did know that most of us were disoriented and confused, and that some were pretty shaken up. I remember sitting down, talking to the others. We were forming the emotional bonds that usually come in the middle of strange and frightening situations. We didn't know where we were being taken exactly, or why, and we were imagining the worst, aware that we had no clue what would happen to us once we arrived at whatever destination we were nearing.

The next thing I remembered, I was alone in a room in the main ship, which was, as I wrote in my journal, "larger than any city." I'd been separated from my group and I knew that my fellow group members were off on some type of "mission," and I was stuck in the medical area. I was unhappy about this because I wanted to do the exciting things too, not just sit in a boring, empty doctor's office. I decided to sneak out and find my group.

I was wearing a metallic jumper that rustled awkwardly as I moved, making quite a lot of noise, or so it seemed to me, especially when I exited the medical room and saw that no one else was wearing this type of garment. I was standing in a large, curving hallway. There were people walking around who all looked pretty human, with no differences that stood out to me, aside from the fact that everyone looked extremely healthy. You don't often find that level of health in any group of people these days, it seems. I began to walk around and explore, realizing information about the ship as I did. After I woke up, I recognized that this wasn't normal. It was as if I was being instructed about the ship as I explored it, almost like a museum audio tour. The only difference was that this was not auditory at all, but purely mental. I just *knew* things. It was as though facts and information were being "downloaded" directly into my mind. Every time I saw something new, I would understand it and have a knowledge base connected to it almost instantly, as if I were remembering or becoming newly aware of volumes of information, moment by moment.

None of the people I saw seemed to be in a hurry, but everyone was very focused and intent on their various tasks, though not overly serious or at all stressed. Each person seemed pleasant and happy, and as I realized this, I also knew, in that "downloading" way, that the jobs that individual performed were perfectly aligned with what he or she naturally enjoyed doing. That explained the generally happy mood, I supposed.

I also realized that, although *I* felt as if I was on the run, no one else took even the slightest notice of me. At that moment I knew that here, in this place, everyone always did whatever they were "supposed" to do – it wasn't a law-abiding type of situation, but rather, a society in which the way that things were done was agreed upon and everyone was happy to do their part. There was no reason, therefore, for any of these people to begin to assume that I wasn't doing whatever *I* was supposed to be doing.

This was interesting. I'd never seen people act like this before. It was nice though. I started to become uncomfortable again as soon as I realized that I would be discovered as missing any minute. Just then, I saw small metallic machines flying around with no apparent method of propulsion. They were gliding at a height that was slightly above the general level of everyone's faces, at about seven or eight feet off of the floor. They would fly from person to person, stopping before each individual for a moment. The individual would, in turn, pause, and allow their face to be scanned. The actual scanning was invisible, but I knew that it was happening in the same way that I knew all of the other things I was discovering. I also knew that those scanners were searching for *me*. I certainly didn't want to be caught by them. I had no way to escape though. There was nowhere to hide and a scanner was coming towards me. What could I do?

Down the hallway from, a man caught my eye. He was staring at me in a way that told me he wanted to help. As we looked at each other, he silently pantomimed getting down, very close to the floor, and crawling on hands and feet, making his body as flat as possible. I understood that I could avoid the face scanners by doing this as well. My heart racing, I tried it, and, sure enough, the scanner that had been closing in on my position flew right over me, not even registering me as being there. This was another example, I realized, of people here didn't really *rebel*. I was sure it would have been easy to change the settings on the scanner, so that it would register any faces, not only faces that happened to be at the proper height. No one needed to do this, apparently, because the people here all allowed their faces to be scanned.

To the left of the door I had first entered the hallway from, an open area stood with doors lining nearly every surrounding wall. There were also ramps, stairwells, and elevators that traveled between the ship's many levels. Here, I "downloaded" information that told me that these structures were used by different people, depending on mood, task, and even physiology. There was also a smaller, daintier, more focally-based spiral staircase that could be used to go from level to level if you were only going a short distance. Behind large doors were big, industrial stairwells, the kind you see in large office buildings, universities, and hospitals. The elevators were for going *long* distances. I realized that the ship had several hundred levels and the elevators could take you from the bottom level to the top one in only a few seconds, and with no discomfort resulting from the speed at which you would be moving. There were at least two elevators. I did not see one in use, nor use one myself, but I had the awareness of how they worked just by looking at them, as it was with so many other things in this dream.

I walked up a flight of stairs. I didn't use the spiral staircase, nor the industrial one, but rather a generally normal, functional, and relatively small stairwell, walking up for a couple of levels. I still naively thought that by my own searching on this ridiculously enormous ship, I could find my group. The level where I emerged, I realized, consisted entirely of living quarters. I'd begun on a business and medical level, and now I was seeing where some of the inhabitants of the ship lived. I realized, while walking down hallways and looking into suites, which were all the size of a large hotel suite or small apartment, that each living level had a different type of "style," and that there were probably about as many styles available as you could imagine.

Very efficient, I thought to myself. This level reminded me of a spa. There were many white towels and rugs, and light golden brown mats that seemed to be woven of straw, or a similar material. Those were, I realized, basically the only colors I saw on this level – the soft white of the textiles and golden color of the mats. The walls and furniture were white as well. The doorways to almost all of the living quarters were open, and I didn't see doors there at all. Perhaps they slid into the wall, I figured. I realized too that crime was not an issue here, as everyone had whatever they needed with no struggle or competition in the equation at all. Most of the suites were empty. I realized then that just about everyone was at work during this time.

I walked up to another level. This one, a living level as well, had a distinctly different feel. The furniture was made in a style I've seen occasionally, where the piece is creating using natural curves in the pieces of wood used to make its design. This creates smooth, undulating, natural-looking and unique furniture. These pieces were everywhere, along with "furs" of every texture and earth-toned color imaginable. I knew that these weren't actual furs of animals, but rather a type of synthetic replacement that was as good, or better, than the real thing. This level reminded me of indigenous, ancient Native American dwellings somehow, although I have no memory of seeing any of those dwellings before.

On the spa-like living level, I had heard an alarm begin to sound. In retrospect, once I had awakened from the dream and was recording it, I realized that no one else I saw seemed to hear this alarm and that I was the likely only one aware of it. I knew that the alarm was sounding because **I** wasn't where I was supposed to be. It got progressively louder and more difficult to ignore as I visited the next living level, the one with with unique wooden furniture and furs.

Someone was following me. I knew that it was a man somehow, and I could hear his steps. He was far enough behind me that I couldn't see him yet. I forgot about my exploration and walked more quickly, twisting and turning this way and that down hallways, trying to lose him. Somehow, he constantly gained on me, walking with a brisk, determined step. I wondered how he always knew where I was going. Afterward I realized what a silly question that was. I kept increasing my speed in vain as he consistently gained ground.

He was nearly upon me, and I knew that in only a few more seconds, he'd be able to see me. In a last ditch effort I ducked behind a rack of clothing in someone's empty suite. I wasn't hidden very well, but hoped that the varying colors and textures of the clothing on the rack would hide me from his gaze. I also practiced a type of invisibility shielding trick that I had no clue I knew how to do at all until the moment that I put it into use. I made all of my thoughts center on what was immediately around me, filling my mind with the textures, colors and shapes of the clothing I was buried in. I knew that this would make me less visible (I re-examined this practice later and, sure enough, it makes sense if you're trying to make yourself psychically invisible. How the heck did I know that? A question for another time...)

My face was blocked, but I could hear him walk into the room and stop directly in front of me. Then he turned to his right and started to slowly circle the interior of the room, all the while saying something. I knew that the words he was saying were the same statement, over and over, repeated in many different languages. He spoke in a calm, self assured, commanding voice. I was hoping against hope that he didn't know I was there and would leave as soon as he finished his tour of the room.

The man completed his circle and came to stand in front of me again. He said in English that he knew I was there, and told me to come out. What could I do? He *knew* I was there. I couldn't run or hide. My time was up.

I emerged from the rack of clothing. More people (male, I believe,) dressed in dark colors and holding long objects that I took to be guns or weapons of some sort had filed in behind him and were standing by the door of the suite, all of them looking at me. I was terrified but resigned, sure that I was about to be imprisoned, or killed, or both.

We all began to silently walk back down the corridor in a group. The man, walking next to me, told me in that serious way that I'd done well. I was absolutely floored. Here I was, thinking that my life was over, and he thought I'd done *well*? What?!

Now he was saying that, after some training, I'd be ready for a mission of my own. I was shocked, relieved, and proud. I had a feeling that my knowledge and use of the mental invisibility practice had won me some points.

The dream ended in that moment. As I felt myself begin to awaken, I realized that Terry hadn't been with me on the ship. I told someone firmly, who I knew was listening and monitoring me as I settled back into my body, that I **wouldn't go unless he went too.**

In the following weeks, before my next encounter, my husband began to become very interested in this phenomena as well. Until he was, I didn't have any other similar experiences. However, after he did become interested, my experiences picked up again and happened with a frequency and intensity they hadn't had before.

In my dream diary, I thought back to various other thoughts I'd had lately about related subjects and wrote, in all capital letters, "WAS THIS FIRST CONTACT??" I didn't know. Now, I doubt that it was. First *conscious* contact perhaps, but I've learned that my first contact probably came long before this.

Over the Christmas holiday, Terry and I visited our families on the East Coast. My extended family lives in in southern Virginia, and his in northeastern Pennsylvania. As usual, the holidays were a welcome break from the worries and stresses of our ordinary lives. We reveled in the temporary escape.

One day, driving back to his home town after an afternoon in Jim Thorpe, an incredibly picturesque town with a rich history of its own, I mentioned to Terry that I wondered whether there was much UFO activity in this part of the country. I didn't dwell too long on the topic, figuring that if there was anything to discover, I'd discover it. If not, then I wouldn't. It didn't really matter. I'd come down to Earth for once. Anyway, I loved this snowy, wintry week in the mountains.

We stopped at the town's antique store, which contains a unique collection of clothing, books, jewelry, and old housewares that could keep me entertained for hours. A few days ago I had seen a beautiful green beaded necklace there that I wanted to buy, and when we'd been in town earlier in the summer, I'd noticed a full boxed set of the *Dune* trilogy by Frank Herbert. I'd listened to the audio version of his first book, *Dune*, and I was captivated by the story. I'd noticed the set during a visit earlier that year. It was a few decades old and the better for wear, the gentle lived-in feel of the books giving them a great character. I wanted to pick the set up if it was still there in the shop.

We went inside and looked around a bit, entertaining ourselves by looking at all of the interesting sights. The hats alone could have taken up an entire afternoon. We also chatted with the shop's owner, who obviously loved what she did for a living. This is always a refreshing thing to see in today's drone-filled world. Necessity drives so many people to work in jobs that put them into an unhappy, sleep-walking existence during most of their day, so it was refreshing to interact with someone whose job invigorated her.

Eventually I made my way to the small room in the back corner of the store that contained two large, overstuffed bookshelves. I remembered just where the box set had been sitting the last time I'd been in, and like many antique stores in towns where people don't exactly go bananas over antiques, these books didn't look like they'd been moved in awhile.

I scanned the shelf where I remembered *Dune* sitting. I didn't see it. I recalled the color of the binding and the size of the set, but nothing that fit that description caught my eye. I widened my search, looking above and below the space where I'd focused at first, and then moving to stacks lined up against the wall, finally reading the spine of every book just before finally relegating my search to a lost cause.

I walked slowly back up to the counter where my new necklace was waiting. I figured that this was my last chance to find out about the books I was looking for, so I asked the owner if she remembered the set,. Sure enough, she did. She remembered most of the things she sold, she said, and she didn't remember selling the books. She suggested that I try looking behind the books I could see on the shelf. Sometimes volumes fell and could only be found by moving the visible books out of the way.

It was worth a shot. I went back into the little room, deciding that I may as well try the shelf that I remembered the trilogy sitting on. I began with a horizontal stack of books on the right side of the shelf. As I pulled the top two or three books out of the way, the cover of the book underneath surprised me into complete stillness.

It was Whitley Streiber's book entitled *Communion*, which has a cover that is a portrait of the race of ETs known as the "Greys." The painting is a close-up, showing the head and shoulders only. The ET's large, dark eyes are staring directly off of the book cover. I took it down slowly, opening the front cover to read the synopsis and discovering that it was a true recording of the author's abduction and contact experiences. There was no doubt that I'd be buying this book and reading it immediately. I laughed to myself quietly, realizing that this was a pretty clear answer to the question I'd just asked in the car less than a half hour ago. As I straightened from returning the other books to their previous position, I went still again. At eye level, and just at the exact spot where I remembered it, sat the *Dune* trilogy box set. I hadn't missed it before – it was exactly as I'd remembered, of the same color and size, and even in the same position. **It hadn't been there before.**

Okay, I thought, *I get it. I had to find this one in order to get what I wanted. Good trick.*

I think it's pretty needless to say that Streiber's book was absolutely what I'd been looking for. Set all over the country, but largely in New York (only a couple of hours from where I was staying,) this book explained a **lot.** When he first realized that he was interacting on a regular basis with ETs, Streiber's initial reaction was one of denial and terror. Who could blame him? Every contactee experience is not as gentle as mine has been. And even though mine has been very gentle, I've been terrified enough times over the past year to be able to identify with his fear. Over the course of the book, however, Streiber was moved to curiosity, and finally acceptance and cooperation with his connections from above.

During one part of the book the anatomy of the ETs that Streiber interacted with was described, down to the smallest detail. After reading this,I couldn't get the idea out of my mind that I was, in a gentle, believable way, being *introduced* to these beings. I felt as if I were being given all of the possible information to calm me and help me understand their appearance and mannerisms, so that when I had my own meeting, I wouldn't be dealing with something completely new.

Then I told myself that I must have been imagining things. This was an interesting story, and I believed him, but nothing like that happened to *me.* I didn't have contact with ETs. They hadn't been picking *me* up since I was a little kid. But his experiences were interesting to know, anyway.

My quest for knowledge continued to grow in speed and intensity during the following months. As it turned out, there seems to be quite a bit of truth regarding the nature of various things that is not considered in modern society or science. Often, as new paradigms tend to be, this information is even laughed at and automatically discounted.

An example of this is the Hollow Earth Theory. It is laughable at first, I thought so myself, but once I read the theories of its proponents and noticed that many of them also created theories that are still in use today, I started to wonder whether the Hollow Earth Theory was really as ridiculous as I had assumed. After I read accounts written by individuals who had apparently reached the interior of our planet, almost always by accident, I noticed that, although centuries and cultures varied, the content was uncannily similar. I grew curious about this. I decided to research what we actually know about the interior of our planet, and how we know it. According to the Hollow Earth Theory, our planet's crust is about eight hundred miles thick. The deepest we've ever drilled has been twelve miles down (according to the official story. If we've drilled deeper than that, no one has publicized it.) I was beginning to change my mind. I found out that the only way we've formulated *our* theories (which we don't call theories, we call fact, by the way) about what is inside of our globe is by measuring seismic vibrations recorded in labs here and there on various points of the globe. We've then made educated guesses about what the recordings indicate. That's it.

I can't help but wonder the educated guesses. Most of the experimentation we've ever done with things like physics and gravity, although it has been extensive, sure, has only really been within our measly vertical mile or so of readily inhabitable land, here on the surface of our planet. According to Hollow Earth Theory, the eight hundred mile thick crust of our planet also holds the center of gravity within it. The theory states that the gravity that keeps us floating away doesn't actually originate in the core of our planet, but rather from a point about four hundred miles down, or halfway through the crust.

Long ago, I grew certain that our Earth is not a hunk of rock that, luckily, has somehow managed to keep air around it and maintain life, but that she is a living, breathing organism, much more evolved and intelligent than we give her credit for. Now that I had discovered it and found that my automatic discrediting of the Hollow Earth Theory may be wrong, the explanation it gives regarding Earth's anatomy couldn't be tossed out the window anymore in my mind.

As I was doing all of this research, I was drifting off to sleep one afternoon after a busy and difficult morning when I found myself somewhere *else*. My physical body was still lying in bed. My consciousness alone was traveling. In some back part of my mind, I knew that I was also still lying there with the covers pulled over my head to block out the light from my window. I was also in that other place, walking slowly, wearing a white robe with a hood that seemed to be faintly glowing. Walking beside me, to my right, was a very tall person who was definitely male. He was wearing a dark robe of either a black or gray color. There was something interesting about the way his robe was arranged. It reminded me, in a way, of bat wings wrapped around him, rather than a fabric cloak like my white one, Only after I'd come back from this little trip and a couple of days passed did I consciously remember the mythological tales told all over the world about people who dwell below ground with bat-like wings.

We were walking down a gently sloping landscape that was quite dark. Somehow my eyes had adjusted and I could see clearly the stalactites and stalagmites all around us. We were not on any path that I would have been able to follow on my own, but he was walking next to me, guiding me on a specific route downward. I asked him if I could see his face, but he declined, saying that he didn't want to startle me, and that if he did show me his face, I'd be distracted from our conversation. As we walked, I noticed a subtle glow ahead. Soon a path came into view that looked much like the cobblestone streets common a century or more ago. These stones were different than the cobblestones I've seen before in a very important way. They were glowing. This was not a light that came from electricity. Rather, it reminded me of the bioluminescence you see in certain insects and fish. He explained to me now that "they" (his people, I'd assume,) didn't pave or decorate the paths too close to the surface. This kept any of the people living on the planet's surface from accidentally finding a way into the lands underground, where, it was implied, the generally primitive and war-mongering surface people weren't generally welcomed.

I returned to my body then. At first I was bewildered and disbelieving of what had just happened, assuming that I had imagined the experience. Later, I discovered more accounts of people's inadvertent trips to the inner world, both by land – through deep caverns – or by sea, invariably after becoming lost and passing through certain interesting abnormal oceanic conditions such as fresh water that floated on top of salty water, and a compass needle that kept "sticking," pressing against the glass that covered the compass and rendering it unusable. In my opinion, this compass phenomenon probably happened while the boat that the compass was being utilized on was actually floating from the outer edge of our world into the inner surface, or one of them, and thereby passing the actual place where the Earth's magnetic field points compass all needles toward the north. I also found that there were other accounts of people who wore bat wing-like contraptions as cloaks when not in use to fly, and who had faces so intense that they were terrifying. This intensity was as a result of technology that has been discovered there that puts many of the things we fight about up here into the realm of non issue, and even into the realm of nonsense. This was a long and drawn out process of research and shocking discovery for me, and the description of it would take up at least one entire book, all on its own. Perhaps I'll eventually write about it. I haven't decided yet. For now, I'll give an example of an experiment I tried myself from a text entitled *Etidorhpa*, written by John Uri Lloyd and published in the late 1800s. Here is a journal entry dated March 12, 2011:

> *I've read a couple of accounts already of individuals' journeys to the Inner Earth, but Etidorhpa, the one I'm currently immersed in, is the most interesting so far. Not only limited to one person's traveling tale, which others have been, this book deals with all types of scientific phenomena, providing experiment after experiment. Most of them, though simple, require objects (certain types of vials, glass tubing, sand, etc.) that I don't have on hand, so I hadn't tried any of the experiments for myself yet. However, about a week ago, I read of an*

*intensely interesting, extremely simple experiment that I just **had** to try. It must be done in a very dark space, so there was about a three-day delay due to my nighttime forgetfulness, but eventually I tried this for myself.*

The experiment simply calls for heavy darkness and a candle. In the book, the process came as a result of a debate between the book's author, a young man at the time of the telling (though the book wasn't published until at least three decades later,) and an older man, who dictated much of the information in the book to the younger author of the finished work, and who had actually gone on the Inner Earth journey described therein. He was also something of an alchemist.

After an argument about the plausibility of some natural phenomena reported by the older gentleman as happening deep underground that would not have happened here on the surface, a comment was made about seeing one's own brain. The younger man demanded to be able to do this, and after some verbal struggle, the older man took the younger out into the country and showed him the trick.

Here's how you do it: sit in an extremely dark room. The closer to pitch black the room is, the better. The way it was done in the book was by sitting in a dark, empty farmhouse, in front of a window that showed the black night sky. As I only had a basement at my disposal, I used that room – and the experiment probably would have worked better with the sky view, since even the one candle flame did provide enough illumination to the room to be somewhat distracting.

Before the experiment was done in Etidorhpa, the elder man described how modern surface society does not embrace any authentically new idea. True creativity is discouraged, and true individuality when it comes to thoughts and connections is rejected outright. We simply build on what we have, never allowing for a real jump forward or progression.

As this has been one of my main criticisms of the fields of science and academia for years, my attention was caught by the beginnings of the argument. Yes, I agreed with that. So how in the world was this experiment going to happen? I was officially paying attention now.

The elder gentleman explained how one usually perceives the world around himself visually by light entering the pupil after bouncing off of outside objects. A reflection of those objects is picked up by the retina, and that image is transmitted to the brain. Yes, I believed that. Then the older gentleman went on to say that if light could enter the retina and somehow be made to bounce against what lies behind the eye rather than only what is in front of it, then one can perceive his own brain.

He did this by sitting in front of the dark window, holding his eyes open and upward at roughly a 45 degree angle (possibly higher,) then holding the candle at 6 inches in front of his nose. Keeping his eyes still, he moved the candle up and down, in a perpendicular line to his line of sight. He then gave the candle to his young, doubting companion, who tried the same thing, and wrote excitedly in the account I was reading of a ghostly shadow appearing before him, slowly solidifying into wrinkles and pulsing blood veins – it was his brain! Or so he thought. On a second attempt, a few moments later, the image sprang into sight more quickly.

So I tried it. I sat on the basement floor, with a large candle in a jar held before me. I gazed upward into a shadowy corner of the room and moved the candle back and forth. At first, nothing happened. Then, as described in the book, an image began to subtly solidify in my field of vision. Yes, it was gray, and yes, it was covered with a network of lines that certainly appeared to be blood vessels. I was absolutely floored.

I don't know if I believe that I was looking at my brain – perhaps I was simply seeing my own retina. There were wrinkles on the edges of the image I saw, or so it appeared, in addition to the blood veins crossing the surface of the gray mass, but this could have been an optical illusion. Either way, this was a fantastic discovery!

I ran up the stairs, calling to Terry that it had worked! It had definitely, actually worked! At first he had no clue what I was talking about, then remembered and tried the experiment for himself. Yes, he saw it too.

I have an idea that every experiment in the book would work. This, combined with my small alchemical knowledge and its consistent agreement with statements in the book have all but convinced me that this is an absolutely true account. There are many interesting details therein, and I haven't even gotten to the most exciting portions of the book, as far as I can tell...so I'll stop typing now and get to reading more.

Mark, my mentor, who directs me with short and sweet (but intensely thought provoking) questions and statements here and there after years of reading whatever dross I've felt like jotting down and sending his way, asked me if it were possible that I had simply been looking at a reflection of the veins in the back of my eye. My answer? Of course. Definitely possible. I'd even mentioned it in the entry. But the whole experiment was shocking, either way. If it were a trick, explained as something more outrageous than it actually was for the shock value it would and did create, then the method still worked – I was surprised, and my attention was captured. Given that other details in this particular text reminded me of experiences I'd had in the recesses of my own mind (or its unbounded frontiers, whichever way you choose to look at it,) I recognized truth in the manuscript.

This brings me to another issue – t he recognition of truth. As my presence and focus has grown, I (and others I've spoken to as well) have picked up an interesting knack for catching lies. It isn't that we know what the truth is; we aren't mind readers. However, you can literally *feel* a lie. It does something to a person's energy field, and even something to the facial features. Who knows? Perhaps it's a micro expression that your unconscious fully reads while your aware, conscious mind has no real hook to hang the feeling on. Maybe it's an energetic fluctuation alone. In any event, pay attention – it's easy to see, once you've got it.

My obsessive searching waned again and I found a happy medium in our Santa Monica cottage between work and play – my time wasn't taken up anymore by research, but any time I was doing a silent activity like cleaning, cooking, laundry, home spa self-care, and the like, I would watch interesting videos or listen to interviews with knowledgeable people in the field of UFO or esoteric research. One evening, alone at home for a couple of hours, I found an audio video on the internet that was given by a woman who called herself ArcturianStar (AS.) She gave herself a pseudonym because, as she explained, she knew how strange all this sounded, and she didn't want any backlash coming into her personal life or the life of her family. I could certainly agree with that. As she spoke, the first thing I noticed was her voice. As AS is from France, there was a bit of a French accent there, but that was not what I felt drawn to. I was so drawn, in fact, that I stopped what I was doing just to listen, standing still in the middle of my living room.

Her voice reminded me of *my voice*. I can't exactly say what it was – something in the way she said her consonants and in the slight huskiness or throatiness of her voice, although it was of quite a high timbre. *My* voice does that. I was riveted.

AS told of a "trip" she had where there were about ten people with her, called her "Mission Group." The group went up into a large spaceship. She went on to describe three women (actually ETs) who were explaining the process that the group was undergoing to AS and the others. The main woman who AS was most familiar with had long, wavy, auburn hair and big, purple eyes.

I dropped my broom.

She was talking about my Anam Cara.

I'd had about 10 people, give or take a few, in *my* group, and I was left out of their "mission" because of further training I needed in my dream – the one that didn't seem like a dream at all.

Trembling, I walked over and sat down on my couch next to my lap desk and little netbook computer, watching the screen as AS continued to speak, giving details about her interactions on a ship. She also spoke about people's fears and prejudices about this subject, including the prejudice that anyone who has these experiences must be, at least to some extent, insane, and explained, at the same time, how limited the current information given to us is about this, and related, subjects.

By the time the video ended, several mouse clicks and about thirty minutes later, because it was broken into a few different parts, I was completely convinced that I *had* to get in touch with this person. Finally, someone who felt like I felt and thought like I thought – and not only that, but who'd actually *had* these experiences too! Even if we turned out to have nothing else in common, I would be able to ask her questions about what she had experienced. Her story was close enough to my dream that surely she'd be able to shed some kind of light on what was happening to me.

Finally a chance to talk on an **equal** level with a person who I wasn't, at best, pushing the fringe of understanding for about reality and the world we live in, but someone who already stood where I stood on the edge of this frontier. Finally!

So, still shaking, I sent her an email. I wrote that I had no idea *why* I was contacting her, and that I **never** did this. In fact, I told her, if she watched my own videos on the same site that she was on, she would see that all I ever talked about was health stuff, giving out natural beauty, diet, and nutrition tips. I wrote that, although I would *never* say this out in the open, that what she was discussing in her video was probably the MOST important thing happening to me in my personal life, and had been for several months.

When Terry returned home, I told him about my little adventure and played a bit of her video for him. He agreed that yes, our voices certainly did sound similar in a way difficult to put your finger on. After I told him about the email I'd sent, he said that I'd just have to wait and see what happened.

Needless to say, I spent that evening and the next morning barely thinking about anything else. I expected either no reply at all, or some off handed one-liner telling me that she was flattered, but also getting the point across that she wanted to be left alone.

When I saw at midday that AS had replied to my note, I was nervous, but very excited to read what she'd written. She replied that she was glad to hear from me and she invited me to join a forum she'd just created called CosmicYou. She said that although she didn't know why I'd contacted her either, if I felt compelled to do so, then there must be a reason.

I sent her back a note, thanking her and saying that I'd go check CosmicYou out. I did, immediately, and I spent the next ten hours or so glued to my laptop. CosmicYou was a forum full of great articles, videos, and other sources of information. It was also full of seekers much like me, with one main difference.

I was surprised and thrilled to discover that all of my obsessive research over the past year had paid off! I was spending all of those hours on the forum answering questions left and right, giving encouragement, and explaining concepts, as well as experiences, that people didn't understand. Somehow I felt *maternal* here – and I was actually, truly, directly, helping people! I had no clue of how much information and knowledge I'd amassed through all of my countless hours searching and reading, not to mention my previous education and experiences of an esoteric nature, way before I had even become consciously aware of UFOs and ETs. I'd remained unaware of my own level of awareness up until now because I had had nothing to compare it to. Just about everyone I had contact with were complete novices in this subject, and deliberately so. No one I knew really wanted to learn more – heck, no one I knew even wanted to **know at all**.

And here I was, my fingers a blur as they moved across the keyboard, providing direction to people asking questions, giving references and offering information that those who I gave it to weren't already aware of. I was in heaven. Terry even had to remind me to eat that day, which is always a good sign that I'm on to something.

CosmicYou was, in function, an ordinary forum. There was a chat room, and interest groups, as well as a document library and video collection. Each member had a home page and a profile picture. For my picture, I decided, since I was in a hurry, to use the same photo that I happened to be using at the time in another social networking site profile I was on. It happened to be a black and white image of my right eye.

I figured this was safe because, although, yes, it was *my* eye, no one would be able to recognize me unless they either already knew of the picture from the other site I had it up on (which I doubted because my "normal life" contacts were not interested in these subjects, as I've already said,) or they would have to know me well enough to pick my random eye out. This was unlikely for the same reason.

I spent that evening updating Terry on my fabulous new experiences on the CosmicYou forum, telling him that after much searching, I'd finally seemed to find a place where I belonged. He was happy for me, of course, but he had things he was focusing on that were of greater importance to him than my current obsession, so he didn't think all that much of this new fascination of mine.

A couple of days later, I opened a private message from AS sent to my CosmicYou inbox. She told me that she'd read every single one of my comments and posts on the forum and that she hoped that her following request wouldn't seem too forward or hasty. She also told me that the forum had two administrators – herself, and Virajelix, a man who'd been a yogic monk for 18 years of his life. She told me that since she'd created the forum a few months ago, her private, "normal world" life had become much busier and that she'd been hoping to find someone else who could serve as an administrator for CosmicYou, along with herself and Viraj. There was simply too much going on for the two of them alone to handle.

AS wrote to me that the previous night, as she had been drifting off to sleep, she'd seen our three profile pictures arranged in a triangle in her mind's eye. My profile picture was on the right, hers was on the left, and Viraj's was between the two of ours and above them, his making the uppermost point of the triangular shape. She asked me if I'd noticed the similarity between my and her profile pictures. She said that she didn't believe in coincidences, and if I was open to it, she would like me to serve as the third administrator on CosmicYou.

I had noticed the similarity between our profile pictures before, but I decided to visit her page and check again, to make sure I knew what she was getting at. Sure enough, there in the top left corner of her personal page was her photo. It was a zoomed in, black and white picture of her *left* eye, with a miniature Earth sitting where her iris and pupil should have been. Her image was zoomed in a little closer to her eye than mine, and mine was only a plain picture, including my iris and pupil the way that they were when I snapped the photo **Still**.

Coincidence? When mine was a zoomed in right eye, in black and white? And when Viraj's was a picture zoomed in on the top half of a person's face with a third eye sitting vertically in the center of the forehead?

Hmm. I had become less and less a believer in "coincidences," and this pushed me over the edge. I scrolled down AS's page and there, on the bottom, was a picture of her, showing only her head and shoulders. My breath caught.

She was smiling slightly, her face turned a little bit to the left. She had dark, curly hair, almond eyes, and lightly bronzed skin. I called Terry to come look at this.

AS looked like me. Not exactly, but **certainly** enough to shock me, and Terry too. After showing him both of our profile pictures, I scrolled down to the image of her and swiveled my laptop around to face him directly. His face went still. He couldn't deny the similarity either.

How was this *possible*? What did it *mean*? I still don't know the answer to these questions, but I do know that AS and I (familiar on an actual first name basis now) talk to each other regularly now. During our first telephone conversation I learned that her initial spiritual awakening began a few years ago after a nighttime stroll on **Santa Monica beach**, where I was located as all of this was happening for me in its new depth. Since then, I've discovered much more information that makes all of this experience richer, more complex, and of course, more confusing – like the fact that there is apparently an entire *race* of beings who resemble my Anam Cara and the purple eyed woman she described in her video. It actually isn't likely at all that they were the remotely the same person. In that first moment, though, hearing someone described who looked *exactly* like who I'd seen, of course I would assume that they were the same. Who wouldn't? Being taken up to a large ship in groups of about ten is common as well. Things are always more complex and interesting than they may seem at first, and this subject is no exception to that rule.

AS's experiences have also been largely of a very different strain than mine. We've gone to different places and seen different things, both in our sleeping and our waking hours. Also, and most importantly – she has been having these things happen for much longer than I have, and her experiences are often absolutely three dimensional and physical. So far, mine have only been mental – in the same category of distinct, detailed experience as my shamanistic journeys used to be – this makes the experiences very different between the two of us as well. We don't have the same guides, and our lessons and contacts come in different forms compared to each other. However, since that first conversation, we've spoken for many hours, considering our number of long talks, and there are often similarities that are more than uncanny. Speaking to her serves as a great grounding experience for me – especially because when there are things happening in your mind that you can't explain to anyone else without sounding off your noodle, having another person who is as sane as you (or the opposite as the case may be, whichever way you believe, although neither of us evidence any off-balanced behavior – I've watched myself quite closely for this, can you blame me?) describing nearly identical experiences from time to time can be a priceless thing. I can say with full confidence that no, I don't believe our meeting, or my current Administrator status on CosmicYou, have been coincidental at all.

The bathroom in a Santa Monica cafe that Terry and I frequented about once a week didn't have a mirror. Where the mirror should have been was a blank, chipping square of paint colored a different shade than the rest of the wall. I figured that, at some point in history and since the last time the bathroom had been painted, a mirror had been attached there. This couldn't have been very recent history, however, because there had been time for people to scribble all sorts of things on the space where the mirror should be.

"Get a mirror!"

"You don't need a mirror. I think you look great."

"This is better, homeless people can't take FOREVER to shave in here."

I didn't particularly like that last one. The thought of someone shaving in the bathroom didn't bother me much, especially if the only mirror that this someone had access to was in a random cafe. Let them shave, I say.

In the top right corner of this space was a line of script that caught my eye every time I reread the assorted comments written there while washing my hands. It was small and written using only capital letters. This is what it said.

"TALK TO YOUR DNA. THEY CAN HEAR YOU. TELL THEM TO CONTAIN MORE OF YOUR **SOUL**."

This concept intrigued me. Since each of our cells is a living, independent entity, and even some of our intracellular bodies are, such as mitochondria which have actually evolved along *with* us, rather than as part of us, it wasn't very much of a stretch to believe that DNA could be living entities too.

So I started to talk to my DNA. I imagined communicating over sort of a mental loudspeaker that sounded throughout every part of my body, calling the attention of my DNA first. Then I would tell them to reconfigure themselves, changing and growing to hold more of my Soul. It was worth a shot. And if it was nothing, then I'd only wasted about forty five seconds. I had nothing to lose.

I'd also been keeping up a daily meditation practice for quite a while now. In addition to this, I was taking part in interesting guided meditations I'd stumbled across online that claimed to open and activate various chakras. Whether they actually did or didn't live up to the hype, I felt fantastic every time I completed one.

At some point around the turn of the year, I began to have periods where I would be able to keep that calm, serene, and completely present feeling for longer than the five or ten minutes after a meditation, after which I'd be back to my ordinary self. My ordinary self was always stressed to some degree and often worried about menial things. When I wasn't worried I was planning, or analyzing, or thinking up new issues to gripe over or protect myself from. No one would have guessed that I was thinking these things, as I remained cheerful and upbeat most of the time. I showed the world a happy, calm, confident face, and on the inside I was usually some degree of self-conscious, insecure, or worried. I think nearly everyone does this – it's part of the Human condition. This is also why, in my opinion, a daily meditation practice is actually a mandatory part of being a Human adult – we *need* that unplugged time in order to keep ourselves sane.

I think that I must have reached some sort of critical mass level where the meditative Self that I was when I slowed down and focused on the **real** world simply began to *stick*. And it did so in an amazing way – one that astounded me and that shocked Terry because we seemed to trigger each other, so when I would take on this calm way of being, so would he.

My posture would change. I would reclaim the upright, straight spine that I'd lost over the years since I's taught yoga and Pilates on a daily basis. My emotions would smooth and calm themselves, and I would be able to effortlessly focus on whatever was happening just then, in the moment. I was *never* bored. My insecurity completely vanished, replaced by a complete trust in the truth that it didn't matter what anyone thought about me – I was who I was, and I liked that person. Funnily enough, once I made that decision, everyone I met seemed drawn to talk to me. Terry and I would attend events together when both of us were in this state and it was as if every presenter or lecturer we saw was speaking directly to *us*. They spent their entire time at the podium or on the stage looking into our eyes, no matter where in the audience we sat. It was kind of freaky. And *awesome*.

I felt as if I had been set free.

It was if – and I quote, from my journal – I had "stepped into a Universal flow that was always there, yet I was mistakenly under the impression that I paddled against it." I began to surrender to that Universal flow, no longer feeling the need to direct events, which never works anyway, instead opting to enjoy each moment of each day, practicing full awareness and presence, seeing the world in a new light.

I didn't know how it had happened, but it was as if I'd reached some type of internal critical mass that allowed me to graduate from a life of struggle and worry to one of enjoyment and peace. Nothing drastic changed in my objective life nor my external circumstances, and yet I felt completely different on the inside.

It felt, at times, as if *more* of my soul could literally **fit** into my body. Maybe this was what that DNA comment had been all about. When this subtle change came over me, as it came and went sometimes multiple times per day, I felt as if I'd become another person. I thought differently. I spoke differently, talking deeper in my vocal register and with a more relaxed and slower cadence. My emotions worked differently. I even carried myself differently. I was attracted to different clothing, feeling an affinity for scarves (so much so that jokes were made about often I wore them) and always wanting to wear long, flowing dresses, as strange as that sounds. People began to treat me differently as well.

On Monday, January 17, 2011, I sat in the living room of our little cottage and prepared to meditate. I added a new crystal today to my meditation today – my big, rough citrine. I used this one to clear my energy field and ground myself. According to my journal, "I emptied myself of the mental gunk and felt my true spirit return to my body. Ah. That was it. I remembered who I am and what my mission is. I remembered that all my obstacles are just perceived ones that actually have no power over me. They just direct the shape of my path to walk. This doesn't have to be unpleasant."

Once I felt as if I'd fully returned, I called my rhythm teacher by picturing his rune strongly in my mind. The first thing I heard was a great big, deep, belly laugh. I'd never heard him laugh before. I was surprised, and thrilled. This was a welcome change.

*Finally **you've** come to see me,* he said in my mind.

I could see now that his previous sternness had been a result of my own laziness. He was preparing me to be able to visit with him so we could actually begin the next phase of our work together. Today he gave me a different kind of rhythm lesson. He showed me, through that way he had of transferring information along with a complete understanding of that information directly into my mind, how to move slowly and with great focus. This, he shared, would direct that same energy constantly flowing around me that he'd shown me in the ribbon lesson weeks before.

I saw again that there is always movement, in every space you ever step into, and that by entering that space, you have now made a change in the energy flow inside it. I was reminded that depending on your own rhythms and vibrations, which are caused by things like your physical and emotional health, your literal movements – breathing, moving, walking, and the like, the words you speak through the tone of your voice and the meaning and energy that the words carry, and even your posture and how well your own energetic field is running, you can, and do, whether you like it or not, impact the room in meaningful and significant ways.

He also showed me how important and useful **true stillness** is. I learned that I usually fidget in some way or another, whether it is noticeable or not. I'm definitely guilty of covert fidgeting. When one fidgets, they are literally throwing off and dispersing energy that could be put to more useful and purposeful means. When true stillness is allowed to settle around you as you are listening, concentrating, or focusing on any activity, there is a quiet power that gathers in and around you that is impossible to deny or ignore.

It is also extremely rare, in our society, to ever allow stillness within ourselves from the time we awaken until our bedtime. We are taught to be in constant movement and to, therefore, constantly waste our energy, rather than to conserve it until there is a useful cause to direct it toward, and then to focus unwaveringly on our task until that task is not only completed, but mastered.

Interesting. I definitely had my work cut out for me until I mastered this new "level." Somewhere along the way I've begun to, only halfway jokingly, see life as similar to a video game. We have the certain tests repeat themselves until we master them and the skills that are needed to deal with them. Sometimes we never do master these things, and so the same problems that we never learned to grow beyond can follow us over the course of an entire lifetime.

Whenever we do master a level, the next level is more difficult. It definitely holds greater benefits once it is won, but if it is lost, the defeat is worse than it would have been before, on simpler and easier levels. This knowledge of directing energy by my mere presence and self awareness, as well as my conscious choices of how I would impact the people and things around me, was a new level for me. It was a different angle on the last teaching, and it provided me with more detailed tools to master whatever I was supposed to me mastering.

After my lesson was over, and for the first time since I'd owned this crystal (why this never occurred to me at any point in the past seven years, I have no clue,) I decided to ask my small, round, rutilated smoky citrine that Susannah had introduced me to, which I held in my left hand at the time, if it wanted to share any information with me or teach me anything.

I warmed and awoke the crystal, asked the open ended question mentally, and then I cleared my mind to see what would happen.

First there was blackness. Silence. Expectancy.

And then there were great pillars, supporting a grand, enormous structure reminiscent of the ancient Greek architecture that we're all familiar with, but not identical to it, and even more beautiful and intricate. I was walking up a long flight of wide steps that led through the pillars, and then I went through the big, heavy door. I wore a long, flowing gown, that left my shoulders bare and that had matching sleeves that only began at the upper portion of my arms and hung down to my wrists. I wore my hair in an elaborate style, and I wore jewelry everywhere. This was the fashion that I'd found myself suddenly drawn to recently. I didn't have time to ponder this connection, though, because I wasn't remotely in charge of this sudden vision. I was simply a spectator, watching from inside myself.

I was striding quickly, not running – I *never* ran, and never even hurried much (the thought of it was ridiculous, in whatever incarnation or in-between stage this memory or vision occurred in,) but I had very little time and this task that I was about to do was of the utmost importance.

I walked down a hallway, then turned into a large room on my left. A great book sat on a stand near the center of the room. I flipped through the book, skimming various pages, retaining certain information with single-minded focus and great purpose, shoving information into little packets with my willpower and tucking them away. I'd studied these subjects for a long time in this place – the Truth of things, of existence, such as the way that matter interacts with Spirit and the anatomy of planets, as well as physics, energy, and the way that this system and dimension, as well as nearby others work in general.

As I recalled each subject during this final cram session (because that's what it felt like,) it was as if I placed each folded, tightly compressed bit of information into my future mind, ready to be unpacked whenever it was needed. I realized, as I witnessed this event, that this is what is currently happening to me. It explains some of my downloads regarding the spiritual anatomy of things, as well as other Truths. These moments of unpacking seemingly happen through coincidence or serendipity, but I realized that I'm being *activated*, somehow, according to some type of schedule or the accomplishment of tasks (or levels, perhaps?) This memory or vision was allowing me to see was how I prepared for what is happening to me now, and what has been happening during the past decade. In this memory, I knew that it was imperative that I remember these things when the proper time came for me to remember them.

I wanted to know more, but I received a firm, non-verbal reply from my crystal that this was all I was allowed to see at this time. I wondered, however, how this little crystal held such information. At the same time, I became aware that there is much more stored in this crystal for me to discover in the future.

I was then instructed, in the next moment, as to how to use this small, round, beautiful crystal. I was to sit in the sun, then handle and warm the crystal with my body heat in the same way that you awaken many of them, by using the warmth of your hands to warm the crystal. Then, I was to hold it between a finger and thumb even with my eye level, where the sunlight could fall uninterrupted onto the crystal. I was to slowly pivot the crystal each way between my fingers so that the light glistened off of the golden filaments inside. This transfer of sunlight to the filaments, and then to my brain, would carry the information stored in the crystal. I wasn't told, however, how to put information *in* to the crystal, but I got the idea that I would learn this eventually.

I then left that thought stream and found myself in some type of amphitheater. I was wearing something that felt like a type of head or hair jewelry where a crystal hangs down onto the center of the forehead, and I was calling in my guides and guardians from the non-physical plane.

I gave them instructions for the day, requesting help on certain matters and asking advice on others. This was the first day that I added this detail to my meditation, and I've done it ever since, with a few interesting changes over the months.

I suppose that now is as good a time as any to describe how to use crystals. Of course, as Humans, we're all different, with different energetic blueprints and natural affinities, so I don't believe at all that my method will work the same way for every person that may try it. That said, it can serve as a jumping off point, and after that, you can do whatever feels right for you. The way you work with your own crystals will just sort of *make sense*. You'll know what I mean once you start experimenting.

When picking a crystal, go to a store where they are sold. Try not to order your first crystal from the internet. It will be tempting, but picking one out at the store is bound to give you better results as a beginner. Just look around, noticing which ones stand out for you.

It may be because of their color, or their shape, or they may call to you for a reason you can't quite put your finger on

– that intuitive sense is the one you want to go with for this particular shopping trip. Pay attention to your feelings; don't go off of preconceived notions telling you which crystal **should** be the most powerful. You can never tell what you will resonate with, it may not be what you expect. My rutilated citrine, the one that has seemingly effortlessly cleared people's chakras and caused intense cleansing physical effects within twenty four hours of holding it for less than five minutes looked simple and uninteresting in the store. Its beauty has grown since I've been using it, and in the sunlight it is nothing short of breathtaking. You can't tell just by looking which one will be best for you.

When you find a crystal that gets your attention, hover your left hand over it. If this is a box full of crystals, do the same thing, noticing which one causes a subtle sensation in your hand. As I've mentioned before, the left side is the receptive side of your body, so it's often easier to pick up on energy and vibrations with that hand versus your right one. The feeling may be cool, or warm, or like a soft pressure or pulling. You may just want to hold one, without knowing why (this happened to me a lot at first.) Then try picking a couple different ones up, one at a time, feeling them and discovering what type of subtle sensations they cause. Hold each one, in the center of your left palm for a moment. That is where your palm chakra opens and where you're likely to get the clearest indication possible of whether or not you *like* holding this crystal. You'll eventually find one that you just want to hang on to. That's your crystal.

Once you get it home, it's beneficial to rinse most crystals in cool water (check the internet or ask at the shop before you do this though ,because a few types of crystal can dissolve in water. Many shops also have reference books on the premises that you can look through to find the attributes, best uses, and particularities about your new crystal.)

As the cool water runs over the crystal, intend firmly that any old energy remaining in the crystal be washed away. This will clear it for you. Many crystals are excellent recorders of information, and you don't want to accidentally pick up anything you'd rather not have around. Of course, you could be more specific and say that anything negative be washed away, and that the positive information and energy can stay. It's up to you.

Then leave the crystal out on a counter or in a windowsill the next day. Sunlight "charges" a crystal, the light particles coming from the sun awakening the energies of the crystal. Don't worry, real crystals shouldn't ever fade in the sun (I've been asked about that,) but when in doubt, check first. Also, on the next full moon, set the crystal somewhere that the moon will shine on it. Light reflected from the moon's surface helps to strengthen the subtle energies present in a crystal as well. If you're skeptical about this full moon stuff, ask anyone who works in a hospital emergency room or a psychiatric ward. They'll tell you that there is definitely something odd about full moons. The energy isn't intrinsically *bad*, it just stirs things up. In this case, it can be put to very good use.

Once your crystal has been charged (and even before this, if the full moon is a while off,) start to interact with it. You'll want to warm it first, by alternately squeezing it in your palms and and running your fingers along its surface. This will also connect your energy field to its energy field, so you'll be, more or less, "plugged in" to it, in a good way. Once it is warm, hold the crystal so that some light is shining onto or through it, and look deeply into the interior of the crystal. Clear your mind as best as you can, breathe deeply, and simply listen with your thoughts. See what happens. Perhaps nothing will. Perhaps something will. A lot of this has to do with the type and shape of your crystal. That research you did at first will be very helpful here – once you know the properties and strengths of your crystal, you can work more easily with it.

Here's the thing. Crystals can't *make* things happen. What they do is focus or amplify *your* energy. They are, quite literally, tools. And different ones will do different things. For instance, Rae gave me the large orange clearing and cleansing citrine crystal that I've already mentioned as a birthday gift several years ago. This type of citrine clears out negativity and enhances clarity. I hold it when I'm struggling with something – a problem, a stressful situation, or even an illness. Illnesses, after all, are simply physical manifestations of negativity or blockages in our energetic circulatory system. After I've been holding the citrine for awhile, no matter how grumpy I am, I find myself feeling better.

Could this be my imagination? Logically, sure. But I've also seen crystals do amazing things, and I've felt energy from them running through my body, giving me chills. There's something to it. When in doubt, go buy a five dollar crystal that appeals to you and try it out for yourself.

A loud, shrill noise woke both Terry and me out of a sound sleep. It was the smoke alarm in our bedroom. The high pitched beep repeated itself again, lasting for a second or two before it stopped abruptly.

"The battery must be dying," we whispered to each other, and winced for the next sound. I cracked an eyelid and looked up at the small red light shining from the ceiling, checking for that familiar blinking pattern that means the battery needs to be changed.

There wasn't any blinking. And the sound didn't come again. Strange. As we settled in to go back to sleep and Terry grabbed a pillow that had fallen off of the bed during the night, folding it in half and stuffing it under his head, I saw a large, dark blotch on the pillow.

"Oh no, honey, there's ink on the pillow case," I said as I reached out and touched the black spot. It was damp. I looked at my fingers in the near darkness and saw a thin layer of ink on them.

Terry sleepily apologized. He'd accidentally left a pen open by the side of the bed about a week before, leaving a similar spot on one of our sheets.

"That's okay. We'll get it in the morning," I replied. We both went back to sleep.

While we were making the bed in the morning, Terry looked for the ink-filled culprit. There was no pen on his side of the bed, where the pillow had fallen. No pen on the bedside table either. There was a pen on the floor, way under the edge of the bed, near the middle of our mattress, but it was firmly capped. The ink blot was still on the pillow case, and my fingers still showed the dark remnants that had transferred as I'd touched the spot.

"That's *really* weird," I said to him. "Do you think..."

"I don't know, but look at this," he said, laying his often-worn gray Notre Dame sweatshirt on the bed. There was a large inkblot on the front pocket, and another on the back of the sweatshirt.

"I don't know how those got there either," he told me.

"Whoa. *Weird.*"

"Yeah, I know."

And that was all. What more was there to say?

Not long after that, I sat down for my daily meditation. I visited my amphitheater as usual, making requests and giving instructions, and at the end of my little spiel, the child-like guide (who I'd always known wasn't *actually* a child, although his or her size and movement reminded me of one,) walked up to the stage where I was standing. This guide had done this before, and he (I'll say "he" from now on because I *think* this guide is male, but I'm not completely sure) always gave me little pieces of advice, or tips about the upcoming day. He was also always right, although this private conversation had been rare until recently.

On this morning, it was as if my vision of him, all of the sudden, *cleared* somehow. I'd never been able to picture him completely clearly before. It had been as if I were looking through textured glass whenever he came up and spoke to me. Before this morning, I'd been able to see his size and how he moved, and I could "hear" him with my mind, but that was it. That's how it usually goes in the amphitheater. I can't see detail. I just get the general feel of things.

He was, as it turned out, a Grey – one of the smaller ones, roughly three feet tall. After my initial surprise, my mind started whirling with ideas and realizations.

So many things made sense now! I'd heard before that they seemed childlike, but I hadn't really understood what that meant until this moment. Although his height of about three feet and his movements reminded me of a Human child, his personality didn't *feel* childlike at all. When I expressed incredulity at his transformation, he pointed out to me that this was always what he'd looked like, and my mind had been screening him out because I would not have accepted what I was seeing before.

I asked him why things seemed to be moving so slowly. Why was I made to want to see things so badly before anything happened?

In response, he halfway told, halfway showed, and directly downloaded a lot of the following information right into my conscious mind. Apparently, it isn't a difficult thing at all for them to show themselves to people in the three dimensional "flesh." However, when a person isn't prepared for this drastic paradigm shift (and also because we've been partially designed to literally be afraid of them, to our core, which also explained a lot to me about my different responses in three dimensional reality and in my meditations,) appearing to Humans all at once like that isn't "maximally efficient." That choice of words was his. Very logical. He then told me that it takes roughly three years for most people to recover from the shock, much less become comfortable with the idea of interacting, and that there wasn't that much time available now. That was why people often have to *beg* (at least that's how it feels to us who are doing the begging) to see the ETs who are interacting with them in other, non-physical ways, before they'll show themselves openly. That way, the shock is diminished to a manageable level.

The small Grey also told me that the fire alarm we'd heard earlier that morning hadn't been a fire alarm at all. (It never did go off again after that, by the way.) The sound had been a test to see how we'd react to unusual things that were uncomfortably surprising. And the ink blots *were* their doing as well – this was a way they'd chosen to, in our case, slowly begin to become present in our three dimensional reality in ways that were impossible to argue, but also very non-threatening.

Okay, I understood that pretty well. It made a lot of sense, actually. I asked about my sister's memory troubles. I had a hunch that it may have to do with those guys.

He explained what happened with her to me then. He said that she'd been created, and that she was the initial experiment of the three of us. She worked so well, he said, that the other two of us were then brought in. He gave me some more details, which have to do with another large issue that would require much more space to explain than I have here. Then we completed our conversation. I grabbed both of his hands in a gesture of affection, which made him a little uncomfortable, although I could also tell that he liked it. They don't use emotion in the same way that we do, I realized.

Okay, well...that was odd. Through my previous searching, I had come across a hint of the idea that occasionally, maybe more often than we'd expect, genetic alterations are made to infants when still in vitro. This sounded simply ridiculous to me at first – aliens screwing around with our DNA while we're forming into babies? Whatever.

And yet...after giving this idea time to rattle around in my head and finding more information about the theories mentioning it, I had to admit that this could be very much linked to stories my siblings and I have always heard about our conceptions.

My parents wanted to wait to have children. In fact, they always used two forms of birth control.

No condom ever broke. My mother never forgot to take a pill. There were other contraceptives that also seemed to work perfectly well. And yet, here we all are.

I asked my mother soon after my conversation with the little Grey whether she remembered anything odd about her pregnancies with us.

"No, not really," she said. "I just remember that my dreams were very vividly colored."

"Okay, do you remember what the dreams were *about*?"

"No, I don't remember that at all. I just remember the colors."

Dreams like this have been reported by other women who had contact with ETs during their pregnancies. Of course, I didn't mention this to my mother right away. I don't think my parents can be blamed for it, but I have a hunch that they may think I've gone off the deep end from time to time. I didn't want to push it.

However, this new knowledge rattled around in my mind for quite a while before I began to really accept it.

Could this be **true**?

I did more research and found out that there are certain characteristics that "starseeds," or people with a genetic makeup that includes human genes as well as *something else*, have in common much of the time.

They often have brightly colored eyes. All of our lives, my sister and I have had our eyes commented on by strangers and friends alike.

They often have the O blood type. So do I.

They tend to have a lower body temperature than what is considered normal. My basal body temperature is usually below ninety seven degrees.

They often feel a connection to the Orion constellation. Ever since high school, I have pointed out the middle star in Orion's belt, claiming it as "**my** star." I never had any idea why I felt that way, I'd just say it without much thought. I still don't really know why I feel such a connection to that star. But it sure is an interesting coincidence.

Another story from my childhood returned to me as I learned that if someone is a contactee as an adult, it is nearly certain that they've actually been contacted throughout their entire lives. Contactees have often simply had their memories of their interactions with ETs blocked.

This sounds like a strange, unrealistic thing at first, but when you think about the type of technology that must be available to the ones doing the contacting, it becomes pretty much impossible to assume what they are and aren't capable of.

When I started going over my history of strange experiences after my initial denial that this had ever happened before to me at all, I remembered a repeated interaction during my childhood that I confirmed within a couple weeks with both of my parents.

I know that this happened before I was five years old, which is easy to be sure of because my family moved across the country, from Southern California to Virginia, when I was five. These events happened when we were still on the west coast.

My father told me, when I brought the subject up with him and asked for anything that he could remember, that I was a child who loved art. I was constantly drawing or painting or otherwise creating something, a habit that continued until my early teenage years, when hormones shifted the objects of my attention (predictably, I might add. You know how it works. Who wants to paint a picture when you can giggle about boys?)

In our conversation, Dad reminded me of the way in which most children progress in their artistic ability when they are very young. Initially, they can barely control the crayon. Then they move to drawing circles, dots, and scribbles that represent things to their own eyes but no one else's. Next come stick people and cartoonish objects, like the familiar house made of a square and triangle and that same tree we've all seen that actually looks more like a lollypop than anything else. Finally, more realistic interpretations are produced.

"You completely skipped the stick people stage," he told me, a memory of his obvious perplexity moving across his brow. "All of the sudden, as if overnight, you started drawing very realistic renditions of everything, except that there was a major difference in the way that you drew *people*."

This I remembered. I recall sitting at our kitchen table with my art supplies spread out before me and my mother moving around throughout the room, doing the mysterious things that mothers do when we are young children and still assume that the world revolves around our simple affairs.

I'd just finished another picture, adjusting things here and there, making the eyes bigger and the waist smaller once or twice. I can remember rubbing the eraser across my paper, unhappy with the messy way the pencil line smudged instead of completely disappearing. Oh well. It would just have to do. I called my mother over to see my new accomplishment.

She stood next to my chair, sliding the picture across the table with her fingertips to look at it more closely. Her face looked very serious as she looked from the picture to me, to the other already completed images scattered across the table, all drawing of basically the same thing.

"Charis," she said softly, "your people look very interesting. Have you *seen* anyone who looked like this?"

She was speaking slowly, and I could feel the waves of worry and trepidation come from her that sometimes appeared after I'd been drawing. I didn't like this feeling, and I certainly knew which answer would make the feeling grow, and which one would make it shrink back into safety and comfort.

So, no. Of course not. I hadn't seen anyone like that.

I've tried to probe my memory to get more specific answers than this about what I felt and where I'd gotten the ideas for my drawings, but I can't seem to dig out any more details. All I know is that I thought people who looked like this were the epitome of beauty, so of course, they were what I wanted my people to look like.

You may be wondering what they looked like. You probably already have an idea. The faces of these people were wide at the top and ended in small, pointed chins. They had tiny mouths and tinier noses. Their eyes took up most of their faces, and were almond shaped and slightly tilted upward at the outer corners. The bodies of these "people" were tall and very, very thin, with spindly arms and long hands. The legs were usually covered up by their clothes, which tended to be princess dresses and fairy outfits – after all, I was a normal three or four year old. I was drawing what I was thinking about.

As a child, we weren't allowed to watch anything out of the very generic mainstream. No movies about aliens, or ghosts, or even angels. So I hadn't been exposed to any character or illustration who would have looked like this. Where did this strange pervasive idea of what a person *should* look like come from? I never thought much about it until this past year.

After meeting AS and seeing our similarities, as well as witnessing my sister's amazing and unique progress as she incorporates a spiritual practice into her life, I'll admit that this idea of being a starseed doesn't seem so far fetched anymore.

I'm not the only one; apparently there are tons of us walking around and there always have been. The fun thing is recognizing others that have no clue about their starseed identity yet. There's often something about the eyes...however, sometimes a starseed's eyes aren't brightly colored at all. It's not about the color, really – it's about the clarity of those eyes and the presence behind them. We also tend to have certain personality traits and affinities. I'll let it go there, because I'm still not well versed enough in *all* the starseed research to go into much more detail with much confidence.

Since my unexpected anvil cloud experience last year, I have become somehow more adept at being able to tell the difference between clouds that are made up of simple water vapor and "clouds" that aren't really made up of *only* water vapor at all.

This knowledge began in earnest on the Santa Monica, California beaches. After watching online videos where the presence of ships were only thinly veiled by what look like clouds (and what could certainly have been water vapor, even still, but that was cloaking something definitely solid inside,) I would occasionally recognize something that I thought *could* have been more than just a lump of gaseous H_2O.

One morning after a meditation and during a moment when I *knew* that I was being monitored, I asked to be shown something **real**. Something that was obvious and that I could perceive with my normal senses. All this "belief" and "faith" stuff was fine, but I was in need of an extra bit of proof to both make sure that I wasn't losing it and to keep me interested. One gets tired of having to work at making connections and defend one's sanity, both to myself and to others, because of a lack of physical proof *all* the time.

Later that afternoon, Terry and I decided to walk down to Santa Monica beach. The beach was about a fifteen minute stroll from our house. The walk provided us with a nice, stimulating bit of exercise because of the hilly route we usually chose to take, as well as an opportunity for us both to unplug from our current solitary interests and reconnect with each other.

I didn't tell Terry about my earlier request to see something a little more solid, but the request came in and out of my awareness throughout the day. When we found a place to spread our sheet out on the sand (sheets work much better on the beach than blankets or towels by the way – they pack into smaller spaces and are easier to clean,) we spent the next couple of hours lying in the sun and talking. I also worked with my crystal a bit, holding it between two fingers the way I'd been shown in my meditation that day and tilting it back and forth, slowly, letting the sparks of colored sunlight glinting off of the internal filaments softly hypnotize me. I didn't know logically what information was being transmitted, but I did know that every now and then, when I'd turn the crystal so a certain blast of light would enter my eye, a wave of pleasurable sensation would run through my brain that I can't describe, even now. The intensity would make me shudder. There wasn't much rhyme or reason that I could figure out as to why certain filaments would affect my mind in this way. It wasn't necessarily the brightest or longest glints of light that had the greatest effect on me, and it wouldn't last beyond three or four repetitions. Something was definitely happening there, but I didn't question it, or try to logically figure it out, opting instead to simply do what I'd been told and see what happened – there was no real reason not to.

After several minutes, I eventually tired of this exercise, and Terry and I began to talk again, about some philosophical thing or the other. We tend to discuss philosophical things. As we conversed, my eyes traveled past Terry to rest on the mountains that run along the coast just north of Santa Monica. The shore curves there, so all of the mountains are visible in a beautiful display, including the one that the Pacific Palisades portion of Los Angeles is built on. If you pay attention, you can also see how the top of that mountain is much more flat than the others around it. We discussed whether or not this flatness was a natural formation, possibly even the thing that made that particular mountain fit for building on, or whether it was made by people carving out the rock, bit by bit, to create level areas.

Although it was an interesting line of thought, there isn't very far that you can go with this subject if you don't have any hard evidence behind you, which we didn't, so our minds began to wander relatively quickly. I glanced up at the sky above the mountains. What looked like a storm was coming in, and my vision traced the edges of that cloud as it appeared over the horizon, in a somewhat circular overall shape. Something struck me as odd about that cloud, although I couldn't determine what exactly that "something" was. I kept looking.

The dark layer of clouds coming over the mountain was sitting at an altitude that was fairly low and close to the mountains that they were crossing. Nearer to us was another area of cloud. These clouds were of a lighter, wispier color and consistency, but they still weren't the fluffy white color you see in most thin, wispy clouds. I pointed this out to Terry, and showed him how, in another area of the sky, there were more "normal" looking clouds – white, wispy, and without form. The thin ones I had initially noticed, however, became more and more defined as I continued to watch them. As I've said, they were nearer to us, and after a few minutes, they separated into horizontal stripes of a uniform length and with an even amount of spacing between the five or six of them that I could see. I tried to make out exactly what I was looking at, because it was becoming more and more clear to me as I watched, however, it took me a few more minutes to really wrap my head around what was up there.

These stripes of light gray, wispy cloud were not, themselves, forming any shape. What they *were* doing, however, was **outlining** something *else*. There was a mass of air, probably of a different temperature and density, moving through the sky. Yes, this is normal, and it's also what causes thunderstorms, right? But when have you ever seen a mass of air that has a solid, ribbed front edge? I'd seen clouds swirling and moving along with a mass of air coming in, but I had never, in my entire life, seen a huge, horizon-wide area of sky that had ripples going across its entire length. These particular thin pieces of cloud stopped and started, stretching along the whole length of the northeastern horizon, spreading out so that the "air" that they were on the edge of had a circular shape, with the corrugated edge that was becoming more clear with every passing minute. I was looking at *something*. Well, actually, I wasn't looking at anything – rather, I was looking at the outline of *something*. And it was definitely bigger, by many, many times, than the mountain range that it was slowly crossing over.

I couldn't believe my eyes. As the minutes passed, I kept watching the large invisible object traverse the sky, slowly, smoothly, and completely silently. To the south an airplane flew across the sky, going into the city. I saw that it was so infinitesimally small compared to this monstrosity, whatever it was, that you could easily compare it to the tiniest ant standing next to a six-foot-tall human being. There was no chance that *we'd* built this thing. Not if it was so invisible that there was nothing to be seen if you weren't watching it. Not if it was this completely silent.

I looked to my left and my right – no one else on the beach had noticed a thing. Of course they hadn't. Isn't this how such things happen?

The nearest I could tell, the dark clouds at the horizon were covering the central portion of this huge thing that was moving across the sky. The wispy clouds I saw being pushed, farther each moment, by a gigantic rippled front, were covering (or perhaps even forming against, like condensation,) the leading edge of the huge – what? Ship? Mothership? Either way, I couldn't even see half of it, much less the whole thing, and by now it was taking up nearly a third of the entire Southern California sky that I could see from my position there on the beach.

Nearly speechless, I tried to show Terry what I was seeing. I pointed it out, showing him how the leading edge was pushing the perfectly spaced ripples of cloud, or condensation, across the sky, and how they stopped and started, showing that the thing that they were outlining took up more area than the mountain range that it was passing over. He didn't see anything. He said that the clouds may have just been pushed by a new bit of air coming through.

"Terry," I said, "I've been a sky watcher all my life. So much so that my friends in high school made fun of me for it. When have you ever seen clouds as perfectly spaced as that, moving like that?"

He couldn't answer. But he also still didn't buy it. I understood. Seeing something invisible is weird, and different, and if you aren't the one who discovers it, then I get how it may take some convincing.

On the same token, he also couldn't convince me that I **wasn't** seeing what I was seeing. There was something *there*.

Even though I couldn't share the experience, I was incredibly grateful to have finally seem something, with my actual, physical *eyes*, that reflected all that was going on in my internal world.

I only remembered later where I'd seen that same rippled edge – on the anvil cloud that we had driven beneath on our road trip, the year before.

AS and I were on the phone again having another one of our long conversations. It is always a refreshing eye opener to be able to talk to her. I'm reminded that I'm not the lone crazy person who fixes my hair and wears mascara by day and travels to spaceships at night, having knowings and random conversations in my head throughout both times and pretending that nothing strange is going on for everyone who would scream and run the other way.

We were talking about guides and interactions, and I told her about my newly discovered (or re-discovered, to be more specific) rhythm teacher guide. I described how Krishanti had "introduced" us and how I now visited him daily, always unable to make out his form very clearly, but very open to our thought interactions.

"You know," she said, "usually what we think are our guides are actually our ET contacts, disguising themselves."

"Yes, I know, I'd definitely heard that-" and then I stopped, realizing that I was did so often, brush off something that I was supposed to hear, assuming it was meant for other people.

Was my guide actually someone else? Could he be what she was saying he was?

YES. It wasn't a word, it was a *feeling* and *knowledge* that resonated throughout my entire mind and body once I asked the question. It felt almost as if he had been wanting me to ask this question all along. The answer came with a great wave of relief and a feeling of "Finally!"

I was reminded, in that moment, of the mythology touched on here and there that discusses how the "angels" are unable to help us if we don't ask. Before and since this moment, I've had the impression of all of the non-physical (or of a different dimension than our three dimensional one, to be more specific,) entities that are on our side sitting on the edge of their seats, just *itching* to help us, unable to do so until we simply *ask them to.*

That knowledge certainly changed everything. Yes, the fact about the asking makes a huge difference, it's true. But wrapping my mind around the fact that this whole time, the rhythm teacher who's been so stoic and hard on me, accepting nothing but the best and the highest self-control on my part, telling me in no uncertain terms that yes, my rhythms *do* affect everyone and everything around me, that it is my responsibility to make sure I was controlling myself and choosing who I wanted to be, rather than letting myself be buffeted by the winds of emotional immaturity, fear, and reaction (not to mention learned helplessness, which is a **huge** problem with the lot of us, apparently,) has been a freaking *alien?* Now that was just plain **weird**.

But I went with it. What else could I do? And I had learned by now to not be afraid, especially because, when I thought about it, everything he told me to do was perfectly in line with what the world's sacred wisdom and religious teachings have been teaching us for thousands of years. In fact, what he was offering me was even a much more user-friendly version of this information.

I've heard that some of the entities interacting with people on our planet aren't out for our health and happiness, and that some are, in fact, quite intent on the opposite. I believe this to be true. Just like there are people whose intentions run the gamut from giving life to taking it, this is also true on all levels and in many other dimensions.

In my opinion, the way to know the difference between those who would encourage growth and those who would cause harm is to pay attention to **what is being asked of you**. Are the suggestions made and directions given ones that would stem the flow of your personal power, your creativity, or your life choices? Are you bothered when you want to be left alone? Are you encouraged to manipulate or control others? If so, then there may be a problem. But I can also say that if, in your interactions with other beings, you are made aware of your *own* power that you've always had, if you're encouraged and taught how to keep control of yourself and therefore have a say in how you're already affecting others *anyway*, and if you're given information that is corroborated by other sources that you didn't know existed before you heard it during that contact you experienced, then you're more likely safe and dealing with a helpful entity.

But always, always, always remember to use your own judgment. Everyone can't be trusted. That goes for *all* levels and dimensions. Pay attention to your heart, and you'll know the difference.

I had that conversation with AS on January 28, 2011. On January 29, 2011, I recorded the following experience in a journal I started that day in order to keep track of these experiences, once I realized that this ship may be a place that I'd be visiting on a semi regular basis.

*Shockingly, this happened while I was completely wide awake. I was in the middle of my morning meditation, when completely unexpectedly, I found myself on the deck of the ship again, in the curving hallway, just where I'd emerged from the medical area last time I was here. My first response was to question whether I was imagining this, but a moment later I came to the conclusion that I hadn't ever done so before, so I decided to just go with the experience and see what happened. True to form, the following events unfolded in real time, with me not expecting what was to come. **I didn't make this up.** When I direct my meditations, I decide what will happen, and then it does. This experience was* *nothing like that. Things just happened, without me thinking anything at all beforehand that would have shaped them.*

There was a hard railing against the wall of the hallway, and I leaned against it, arms crossed over my chest, in amused amazement that I was here again. Then I remembered myself and stood up straight. I realized now that I was wearing a flowing dress.

*The man who followed and instructed me (I now realized) on my last visit walked up to me. We shook hands warmly, using both hands to clasp during the handshake (with our right hands shaking as is normally done on Earth, and our left hands clasping the outside of the other's right hand.) I realized at this moment that **this** is what our handshakes evolved from – when you greet someone in that way, opening up your palm chakras and exchanging information, it is a true greeting, especially when this is done with affection.*

He turned and led me (or walked with me, which is perhaps a better description) up the white spiral staircase to the next level. We turned right and walked down the curving hallway, which I realized was open to the lower level in the middle, where I'd begun, in the same way that I've seen many indoor shopping malls designed today. Soon, on our left, against the wall, was a door that looked like rich, dark wood, but was of a much lighter weight. I realized it was some sort of synthetic material. We went through it and inside was a room with a long, thin table which seemed to almost materialize as my eyes ran down its length. I think that I was only allowed to see what I paid attention to, or something like that. The table was a dark color, possibly that same "wood" substance as the door but I wasn't sure. I sat down in either the first or second chair from the end, on the long side nearest to the door where I'd entered. I realized as I sat down that I was wearing some sort of diadem with a stone resting against my third eye center on my forehead. I also realized that others were seated around the table as well.

I was told that the near future would hold a test to see if I was "ready to come be a part of the Council." I was told to do my best, because they did want me there! This last statement was made with calm, but significant, passion, and even urgency. There was a distinct "hurry up" feeling implied in it as well. I smiled and placed my hands together before me in a Namaste gesture, familiar to yoga practitioners and people who meditate in groups here, thanking them, promising that I'd do my best, and then I got up, turned around, walked through the door, shut it behind me, and was instantly back in my living room. That was it.

A question that I often ask myself after these types of experiences is whether my experiences were real, or just my imagination. I'd just had a talk with AS where she described a long table in a room. Was I projecting? Was this all my subconscious feeding delusions? Then, I usually recall that these occurrences startle me, and that I'm always shown details that I didn't know existed, and that are later confirmed. In our next conversation, AS would tell me about another long shiny table where **she** sat and spoke to some type of Council. Was this my imagination? I don't think so. *Could* it have been? Absolutely. How can one be sure, when traveling in other dimensions? Those dimensions could be purely imaginary, or they may not be. In graduate school I wrote a paper on shamanism and used, as a reference, some book I'd found from the middle twentieth century about European and American researchers' experiences while studying shamans in the Australian outback. One researcher wrote that he'd seen, with his *own eyes*, a shaman throw an invisible "rope" to the top of a tree and walk upward, through thin air, to reach that treetop. He was with a group of others and they all saw it.

What did he use to explain this? Mass hypnosis. Sure. Somehow a shaman hypnotized over twenty fully grown, wide awake men, without the aid of anything other than his presence.

I considered that explanation a perfect example of the way that the science worshipers in our culture attempt to stick to paradigms that don't explain the unexplainable by forcing a ridiculous, nonsensical argument onto a space where it doesn't actually fit, rather than just expand the paradigm. This rigidity has existed for all of recorded scientific history, and it remains now.

Eventually we'll all get the point and realize that truly understanding the way that things work doesn't necessarily threaten us, even if we have to admit that what we previously thought was true may not be the whole truth, in light of new evidence (or, for that matter, in light of old, even ancient, evidence that we've ignored.)

Something is happening to Humanity on this planet, and has been for quite a while. From time to time, when I open up a book about contact, abductions, or angelic encounters and I see an author discrediting perfectly reasonable and sane people's experiences, or talking to or about these people in a condescending manner, I'll openly admit that I feel irritated.

Guy, I can't help but think, *when you say these things and you seem so sure and so smug, but you have no idea what you're talking about, you just look like a jackass. Do your research with an open mind and you'll discover the truth. Don't just say the same things others have said and keep your blinders up – or else, what's the point of researching anything?*

Yes, it's scary to jump out of a new paradigm. Look what they did to Galileo. Look what they did to *Jesus*. And yet, here we are, finally **just** starting to understand what Christ meant, although it's been hijacked for thousands of years by powerful people who would rather keep all of the ones who would follow Christ's true teaching in a slave mentality, unaware of our own power and natural divinity. This is the same power and divinity that Jesus spoke of, reminding us over and over that we could do the same things he did and more. This is not heresy, it's truth. *He said it*. The question is, how do we learn how to do these things? How do we become empowered to the same degree that the greatest sages of recorded Human history were? We *pay attention*. And we simply have to **want to learn**. The great all-pervasive power that we've named "God" will feel this desire and jump for joy, sending that information along directly. That knowledge is where we're headed. We're better off if we just go with it. Things will be easier all around.

Terry and I decided on the spur of the moment to attend a lecture on UFOs given at one of Los Angeles's more well known esoteric bookstores in the heart of the city. We wanted to see what we could learn there, since it wasn't often that we got to interact with other people who were having similar thoughts or experiences. We were both looking forward to it.

After fighting traffic and finding a parking spot (which was quite a crusade on its own,) we walked into the bookstore's meeting room. We were some of the first people to arrive, and we picked seats toward the front of the room. I wanted to sit close because I was always interested in seeing whatever visual images were presented having to do with this subject. Photography and photo editing are hobbies of mine, and I can usually pick out the fakes, although, to be honest, I haven't seen many manufactured pictures when used as part of the few presentations I've attended. Online, however, most of them are created. Just so you know.

When the presentation began, it seemed to be going well. The beginning portion of a new documentary on UFOs and disclosure was shown, which didn't give Terry and I any *new* information, but rather regurgitated things we already knew in a new format, and a good one for people who hadn't already done lots of their own research, I supposed.

Next, the speeches began. My hopes were high, but as the people at the podium became less logical and increasingly forceful with the religious dogma they were shoving at their small audience, telling us that all of the UFO sightings world wide in recent years have only heralded the return of one religious figurehead whom I'd never heard of before, Terry and I glanced at each other out of the corners of our eyes. Okay. This was one of *those* events.

After a woman at the podium sharply told an audience member who'd had an abduction experience that it was completely impossible and that the ETs would *never* do anything like that, I was done. This guy was not crazy. He was not lying. He was, in fact, reporting very similar events to others I'd read and heard about over the course of the research I've done. And here was this woman, completely out of her element but blindly believing some dogma she'd been handed, acting like an expert and discounting his somewhat traumatic experience. Ridiculous. Things only went downhill from there.

Terry and I walked back down the sidewalk afterward, discussing our surprise when we each independently realized that we not only knew a little more, but that our knowledge base was a *lot* larger and more complex concerning this subject than the speakers' had been. And not only that – but the force they were speaking with and the nearly fanatical way that they were acting gave us both the heebie jeebies.

On the drive home that night, we stopped at the grocery store to pick up a light dinner. It was late and all of the nearby restaurants had already closed. Besides, a light meal was certain to make sleeping more pleasant than it would have been if we had stuffed ourselves before going to bed. We went into the store and came out about ten minutes later, emerging into a parking lot filled with fog.

That was odd. Santa Monica is not an especially foggy place, and when fog does roll in, it never moves that quickly. We drove slowly down the empty streets, wondering at what was going on. I couldn't keep the thought out of my mind that fog is often reported during physical encounters with ETs – were we about to have one? The timing would make sense. But as we parked our car in front of our cottage, the fog here swirling thicker than it had been anywhere else, I fought down a deep, cold fear. As badly as I wanted to, if I were to actually see an ET walking towards me through the mist, I was going to *freak out*.

I didn't understand this fear response. Why would I be afraid? I never had an ounce of fear in any of my interactions with ETs during meditations or dreams, no matter how odd the entity I was in front of seemed to me. Why would the thought of this encounter scare me so much? I thought about what the small Grey in my meditation had told me about maximum efficiency and the shock to the system that seeing ETs in the flesh may cause. Somewhat familiar with such things from my formal education, I recognized my nonsensical fear response as being trauma-based. That's what happens when, for no apparent reason and against your logical judgment, your emotions are powerful enough to change your behavior and kick your mind right into panic mode. I also thought about a question my younger brother had asked me a few months before.

"Do you remember," he started with, "the night that all three of us had the same nightmare about that man, and then someone came to the house in the middle of the night to talk to us and we all forgot everything?"

What!? At first I didn't remember anything. But as he spoke, sure enough, something **did** stir, deeply buried in my memory. I couldn't recall exactly what it was, but his words rang true.

Since then, I've gone back into my memory and searched for this event. I think I may know what happened, and it not only explains the current traumatic response on my part in these situations, but it would also explain other strange things I've noticed about me and my family members, as well as strange lapses in memory that we all have...but I'm not sure about it. I also think that it will change as I discover more, so I'm not going to include that particular theory here.

If there is anything I've learned along this journey, it's that things are not very often at *all* exactly what they seem. As I've undergone the task of writing this book, my own understanding of some of the experiences I'm reporting in these pages is deepening and becoming increasingly complex. This is why I'm laying low on my interpretations of things. I don't know *why* many of them happen, or even *how* they happen. But I do know that things **are** happening, and that reporting them, for some reason, has become one of the most important things in the world to me, only months after I never would have agreed to even mention a *piece* of what I've experienced to anyone other than a close, trusted friend (or to a completely anonymous stranger, as long as I was anonymous too.)

My earlier training in energy work and shamanism has shown me that these strong intuitive feelings are not to be ignored, but to be followed. When left ignored, they always end up coming out anyway – and usually in a much less comfortable manner than would have happened if they'd been obeyed at first. So I'm going with it, making sure that I tell you over and over that these have been *my* experiences, and mine alone. Maybe no one else in the world is experiencing the same things. But I know that enough people are reporting uncannily similar and also unexplainable events to make ET contact a phenomenon that spans the globe. As I've said before, there is most definitely *something* happening. What this is exactly or how to explain it, I'm still unsure of. But to ignore its occurrence is to choose denial over truth – and that hardly ever ends well for anyone.

It had been a long night. My sister, Terry and I had taken a road trip up the California coast to visit my father for the weekend and I wasn't feeling well. I was having trouble falling asleep. Being in a different house and an unfamiliar bed didn't help either. Terry was beside me, fast asleep, and I could feel that still, quiet energy that told me that the other occupants of the cottage – my sister and my father, were sleeping as well. I turned over, began to breathe deeply, and willed myself into sleep again.

Finally I drifted off...

What the hell was *that*?

I was sitting up in bed, breathing quickly, blinking my eyes hard, and trying to *remember*. There had been someone **there**, in my dream.

I have active dreams, obviously, and some of them I recognize as being something other than simple situations and objects presented to me by my subconscious, unraveling and then winding itself back into order, assimilating events in my waking life through strange nighttime encounters and adventures.

But *this*...

This was unlike anything I'd ever seen before.

I had been sitting, or maybe I was standing – I didn't know. I didn't know the place. I didn't know anything but who was standing before me. Or perhaps he's been sitting down. Either way, he was very close – perhaps two or three feet away from me. I could only see his head and his shoulders, which were wide and muscular in a way that indicated natural living, probably outdoors in harmony with the elements. His skin was a deep, almost navy blue color, and his hair was long, wavy, and dark, with things tied into it that could have been flowers, beads, or bits of cord, in either a symbolic or a decorative fashion. Perhaps it was both. His skin was not *painted* blue, it *was* blue. And he didn't look exactly Human, although what I could see of his general form seemed to be largely the same. The main difference was in the bottom half of his face – it was as if he almost had some sort of a muzzle, rather than the flattish nose and mouth like we Humans have.

Even with all of that, his strange appearance wasn't what shocked me clean out of a much needed sleep. What shocked me was his pure, raw **intensity**. We were as close to each other as if we'd been talking already, but I don't know whether we had or not. I do know, however, that he was staring deeply, intently, and with an incredibly sharp focus into my eyes, as if he was looking through me, or as if he could see *inside of me*. But that wasn't only it – his consciousness was pushing at mine, trying to get something across. A concept? An idea? Another sort of communication? I had no clue. And I wasn't frightened, I was just totally shocked.

Considering some of the strange dreams I've had, I can't say that I understand why this one had such an effect on it. And of course the questions I was asked the following morning as to whether I'd seen the move *Avatar* recently were understandable – he did, after all, roughly resemble the type of creatures in the movie. The truth was, however, that he didn't really look like them at *all*. He was real, and wild, and **intense**. I didn't know what to make of it.

About two weeks later, AS and I had another telephone conversation. She told me that she'd just been surprised out of a deep sleep and into complete wakefulness by the appearance of a not-quite-Human seeming man, with deep blue skin, a nose and mouth that seemed more animal-like than Human-like, and an incredibly intense gaze. I asked her if he had long, messy, wild hair with things tied into it. She said she wasn't sure, but she thought that he might have.

The truth is that we didn't ever figure this experience out. Sometimes you don't. But I also know that the story isn't over yet. More will come, sooner or later.

I reclined on the sheet that Terry and I had just spread out on the sand, relaxing into the rhythmic sound of the waves crashing onto the shore below us and enjoying the warm pressure of sunlight on my skin.

Terry sat down on the other edge of the sheet, quietly looking out towards the ocean.

"I just wish I could see something *real*," he said. "If they're as prevalent as they supposedly are, why can't one walk up and shake my hand or something?"

I knew who he was talking about, and I could identify with how he felt. Hadn't I made that same request a few weeks ago? I also knew that when you ask for something like that and really want it to happen, it usually does. So I relayed that information to Terry and rolled over to get some sun on my shoulders.

An hour or so later we were lying on our backs, side by side with our heads nearly touching, discussing the static we could see in the sky. I haven't spoken of this to many people, so I don't know if it is a common thing or not, but whenever we've spent a decent amount of time outside and especially when we've been looking up into the blue sky – this doesn't happen as much when there are clouds – we see static. It's almost like the "snow" that you can see on a television screen that has no signal to broadcast. This static is more subtle though, and you can easily see through it. You have to focus to even notice it, unless you are looking up for at least a few undisturbed minutes. The effect is also reminiscent of the "stars" that you sometimes see when low blood pressure gives you that woozy feeling after standing up too quickly. The static in the sky, however, doesn't swim and dart like the "stars" do, it just blinks and crackles exactly like television static.

The effect is certainly disconcerting, so whenever one of us would see it, we'd mention it to the other to check and make sure we weren't imagining things. So far, we've probably spotted the static twenty times or less, and never has the other person not seen it as well.

This particular day was the only instance in which the static cleared after we saw it. Usually, once it's there, it's there, but on this day, we saw it and mentioned it, wondering aloud again what it actually *was* that we were looking at, and then we changed the subject. Awhile later, one of us (I forget whom) noticed that the static was gone. Yes, we discovered that it was gone for both of us. Hmm. Interesting.

"Charis, what's that? Do you see that?" Terry pointed his finger directly upward, indicating a spot in the cloudless, light blue Santa Monica sky.

"No, I don't see anything," I replied, trying to see whatever he was pointing at.

"It's right there! It's small, but look, something is moving. There are two of them now. Are those birds?" Terry kept pointing and moved closer to me, showing me exactly where to look.

And then I saw them. First I saw one, but then another one blinked into vision. High in the sky above us, tiny dots were moving. They were each about the size of a grain of pepper because they were so far away, and they were even too far to make out a proper shape. Maybe they were round, but maybe they weren't.

We thought they must be birds, because airplanes didn't fly like that, and they certainly didn't blink in and out like that. These things were moving effortlessly, completely free of the hanging awkwardness of helicopters or the slow forcefulness of airplanes. The way they came and went to our vision was as if they were moving in front of and behind clouds, but there wasn't a cloud in the sky. Why did they appear and disappear like that, seemingly at random?

Throughout the entire twenty minutes or so that we watched them, sometimes both of us would see them and sometimes only one of us would see them, taking a minute or two to point out the exact location to the other person. These things were so high up, and as a result, so tiny, that the fact that no one else on the beach remotely noticed anything didn't surprise me a bit. Also, this difficulty is what made the next thing I saw so controversial where our subsequent conversations have been concerned – Terry didn't see it, but this was the very evidence, in my mind, that proved that what we were looking at were definitely UFOs of some type or another.

I saw one of these dots blink in, moving across the sky in a slow, straight line. Then it split into *four* dots, each of them moving outward from the center, creating a diamond formation which they held for a few seconds as they continued to go across the sky, toward the ocean. Then the bottom and right dot completely disappeared, and the other two kept moving at the same speed and in the same direction until the right one, which had been the top dot of the diamond formation, moved to the right instantly – making a ninety degree turn without any curvature at all. After going in this new direction (towards my right) for about a second or less, it moved to the left, instantly. No turn, no hesitation. This was done for about a second again, until it was about the same distance to the left of its original turning place as it had been to the right of that turning place when it went made its first complete reversal in direction. Then both movements repeated, the dot I was watching bouncing left, then right, then left again – in essence, it was moving one hundred and eighty degrees every few seconds, *instantly* shifting its direction, with no slowing at all. And though it just seemed to go a few inches to me, I knew that, given the distance, this craft, whatever it was, was traveling hundreds of feet with each "bounce."

Birds don't fly like that. Neither does any airplane I've ever seen. Sure, this could have been a test flight made by some sort of new aircraft that no one knows about yet, because there was an Air Force base reasonably close by. But if these *were* crafts that hadn't been released to the public yet, then why would they be flown over Los Angeles, one of the most densely populated cities on the west coast? That explanation didn't add up.

After that display, the two dots I was watching disappeared, and that was the end of it. On our walk home, Terry and I discussed what we'd seen in the sky. He still wasn't sure what they had been – what we saw could have been birds, in his opinion – but I haven't seen birds blink in and out like that. And I saw what *I saw*, which allowed no argument in my mind. Instant ninety degree and one hundred eighty degree turns, with no curve and no pausing? I've only heard of *one* thing that can fly like that.

On March 14, 2011, I had another experience on the ship I found myself visiting from time to time. Here's what I wrote as soon as I returned fully to my body enough to record the experience:

For the third clear time (there may have been more that I don't know about,) I was taken up into the ship with the curved hallway. This was prior to sleep, and I'd had a feeling all afternoon that something like this might happen tonight – I didn't know exactly who I would talk to, or where I would go, but I felt a sort to excitement come over me a few hours ago that indicated something was going to happen. This isn't the first time this has happened – sometimes I get it before interesting things happen during other waking times as well.

As bedtime neared, I became more and more sure that I'd go somewhere or see something when I laid down to sleep. Sure enough, relatively soon after stilling myself for sleep, I felt my consciousness (NOT my physical body, just my consciousness, which makes these things harder to confirm within myself as true, and not just my imagination) drifting up and up and up, into the curved hallway of the same ship I'd visited before.

For the first few moments, I oscillated between acceptance of this experience and the opposite. **Seriously though**, I wondered to myself, **am I imagining this?** But, as I've done before – the last time I "visited" this same place, actually, I decided to just go along, as best I could, and not interpret anything until after the experience ended, so as to pick up all the detail possible.

I'm standing in the big curved hallway, facing toward the "center" area with the stairwells, my left side close to the wall. This is where I always begin these visits – it is also outside the door to the "medical area" where I emerged from on my first conscious memory of being here on the ship.

I'm wearing the same "uniform" I've worn over the past months during any of my "travels" - a long, flowing, ornate dress. My hair is up, as it usually is, and I'm wearing lots of jewelry – big earrings, bracelets and arm cuffs, and something across my forehead.

I'm more aware than ever that this is NOT the time to get caught up in surprise or selfish examination of my surroundings – I feel strongly that this is a time to work, not play.

My old friend from the ship, the tall man with the light hair, walks up to me, and I give him the double handed handshake that he taught me during my last visit. After greeting him, I look to his left, and see, standing there, my rhythm guide! This is the first time I've seen him in company of anyone *else, and in any other environment than ones unique to him during our lessons. He is certainly tall, probably closer to six or seven feet, and his skin is a color between tan and gray – not either, but more in the middle. We exchange a double hand shake as well, warmly, and the others turn around and begin to walk, obviously expecting me to follow. I do.*

This is when I become aware that I'm not imagining this. The way I know it is similar to how I did the last time I was here – things keep happening that I don't expect. It's also as if my awareness is like a spotlight – I can only see things that I focus my attention on specifically, the rest of the environment and goings-on therein are somewhat blurry.

I realize that I'm not imagining this specifically when we walk down the curved hallway, to the other side of the stairwell, where this hallway becomes smaller and less open, and then continues deep into the great big ship. I had never even remotely concerned myself before with what was down this hallway. My attention has always been quite taken up while I've been here with whatever was going on at the time. Now, as we walked, I realized that we were going someplace I hadn't been before. At some point on the short walk we ascended two steps, and shortly down the hallways past the central area with stairs and the "elevator," we enter a room on the right side of the hallway.

In it, as in the last room I visited, is a long table. Today, I calmly sit at the head of the table. At *this point, the smaller, less sure-of-myself piece of my consciousness that has been observing all of this is quite surprised – **Me?** At the head of the table? What the heck? And yet, the part of myself that is quite calmly and confidently acting and speaking in this environment, not only takes the spot like it is completely normal to sit here, but stands up just afterward and begins to give a presentation, it seems.*

*I stand and tell those seated at the long table (I receive an impression of many types of creatures, some humanoid, some less so) that of the population I've had access to, people are quite ready to accept what is happening, and will probably be happy to do so. However, in order for that to happen, they need solid, irrefutable **proof**. Stories of others' experiences will be inadequate for this. Something physical and undeniably real will do the job. Not necessarily an experience for themselves, but something that they can clearly **see**. I say this in much fewer (and more eloquent) words than I have typed here, by the way. For some reason I believe it is necessary to involve this detail.*

Others stand and begin to discuss what I've said with me. Much of this is blurry, but I do know that there must have been some prior, perhaps ongoing, discussion as to whether I was ready to be doing this (to sit on the council? I suppose?) - everyone there was not necessarily ready to listen to my take at all. A tall being stands up. He is a light green color, and has some type of three-

pointed head and very smooth skin, almost exoskeleton-like. He also (it was a "he," I'm pretty sure) has three-fingered hands, with, rather than "fingers," long, hard, curving claws. He uses them to gesture to me as he criticizes my current mental state, affirming that I am still doubting that this is even happening (which I am, actually,) and implying that because of this, I am not ready to be offering up opinions yet that should be heard and considered.

There are others arguing for my place here – more seem for me than against me – and one that stays in my mind is a woman with large, intensely blue eyes (possibly with no pupils.) I don't believe she says much, if anything, but rather simply gazes at me encouragingly and deeply in such a way that when I look at her, her eyes seem to take up my entire field of vision. I believe this is the same woman that came to me in guided meditations before I was even aware of these experiences at all. She has long, slightly curled, deep red hair and pale skin.

At this point, the sights and sounds around me almost begin to vibrate. I know that the vibration is in my mind, and that I am losing my ability to be consciously aware of what is happening. Some more things happen that are less clear – I looked out of a great big window, for instance, seeing one of Earth's oceans below, but I don't know which ocean it is. I try to hold on as best I can, but the visual and auditory experiences begin to fade, with those woman's blue eyes being one of the last things I see.

*I feel it necessary to put in here that **I was never asleep**. This entire experience likely took less than fifteen minutes, and I was never close to being asleep. This is the second time that I've visited this particular ship when what appears to be a "council meeting" is being held. An interesting progression though, between the last time and this time...*

I'll also note here that earlier this evening, as I was beginning to wind down for bed, I saw a picture of a Grey (actually on the cover of a book I have,) and "felt" the presence of one of my watchers (I'm not sure if there's more than one, but I think that yes, there is.) I asked when I'd be taken up again. There was a distinct reply in my mind asking if I wanted to go up this evening. Yes! I replied. The response that came down was something akin to, "Sure, we can pick you up today."

I sat there numb for a second after I heard those words – I'd never had them say so clearly to me anything of the sort. I also didn't really believe it, and assumed that I was imagining things.

Since I've spoken so much about meditation in these pages, I think it is only fair that I describe my method of meditation. It has evolved over the years both from a combination of meditative techniques I've been consciously exposed to as well as from simply feeling my way through the process, adjusting my routine as certain things feel right or make sense. I've said it before and I'll say it again – I think that we are, at our cores, deeply spiritual beings and that meditation is a necessary daily part of being a Human adult – without it, we go a little insane. This insanity can manifest in an infinite number of ways, but insanity it is.

Anyway, if you've never meditated before, then feel free to use my process as a beginning point for your own practice. If you already have a practice that works for you, stick with it. I prefer meditating in the morning, before I've enmeshed myself firmly in my day and after I've done other necessary morning routines such as exercising, showering and dressing – this is just the most logical time for me to clear my mind and set my intentions for the day.

My meditation practice is also continually changing and evolving. It is likely that, by the time you read this, I'll do something at least slightly different than what I'm about to describe. In any event, here it is, as it stands.

I sit on the floor or on a piece of furniture, my legs curled into the lotus position, as the yogis say, or Indian-style, as many Americans say. I nearly always meditate with my small rutilated smoky citrine crystal, spending a few minutes prior to my meditation holding it my palms, warming it and activating its energetic field. Then I "plug it in" to my left hand, aligning the place where its rutilated lines of gold emerge to the surface of the crystal in what looks like a tiny tree trunk with the center of my palm chakra. This is done by feel more than by knowledge, and it came to me one day in a meditation, so I've continued the routine ever since then, because I've enjoyed the effects. Nowadays, since a project I am working on requires me to have both hands free to type as I meditate, I tuck the crystal into my shirt, where it can sit against my sternum and therefore my heart chakra. This works reasonably well too. You don't have to use a crystal at all during meditation. Only do so if you feel the desire to have any extra assistance from the energetic field put out by a certain crystal (they all have unique vibrations, depending both on the type and shape of crystal and on the actual unique crystal itself. Handle enough of them, and you'll find one that feels natural to work with.)

I then make sure my spine is erect, each vertebra stacked on the one below so that I use balance, rather than muscular control, to hold myself upright, and I slow and deepen my breathing pattern, taking care to maintain full and complete inhalations and exhalations.

Once my breath has reached a steady rhythm that doesn't require my direction anymore, I focus all of my attention on the top of my head – the area just under the very top portion of my skull. This is where the crown chakra, or the seventh chakra, interacts with the physical body. The seventh chakra is usually portrayed as having a brilliant, glowing white light with a hint of violet in it. I focus my attention here until I can feel a pulse. It is not my heart beat, which is obvious because my heart rate moves much more quickly than this pulse does. I'd say that there is one energetic pulse for every three or four heart beats. The pulse often starts out subtle and uneven, but as I continue to focus on the place where I can feel it and pay attention, the rhythm always smooths and strengthens.

Once my crown chakra has regulated into an even, steady pulse, I focus all of my attention on my third eye chakra, or my sixth chakra. This chakra is colored a deep indigo color, and it sits just about even with the bridge of your nose or the place between your eyebrows, and about two and half inches inside your head, if you start at the front of your head. This is where your pituitary and pineal glands sit, and I focus there until I can feel that same pulse, with the same rhythm, moving in that central part of my head.

Then I focus on the back of my head, just inside the back portion of my skull, about where the brain's occipital lobes are, I suppose. Some have referred to this area as the "ascension chakra," and although I never thought much about it, I have included it in my routine for the past several months. When this one starts to pulse for me, it moves from the left side of my head to the right side, and it often corresponds with cracks and pops in my ears, in the back of my head, and in my neck. Sometimes my head even jerks a little bit as the bones adjust. I can't explain why this happens, but it doesn't hurt at all – actually, it's quite pleasant – so I just go with it.

Next I move my attention to my throat chakra. This is just below where a man's Adam's Apple is located, at the front of the throat. It is the fifth chakra, and its color is blue. I focus there until I feel the same pulse at the same rhythm, and then I move my attention down to my heart chakra.

A common question I've been asked about the heart chakra is whether it is in the center of the chest, or to the left of the body's center, where the actual physical heart organ is located. The chakra is in the center, basically sitting just behind the sternum. It is colored green, and it is the body's fourth chakra. Often this one feels as if it is becoming warm and fluid as I focus there, and sometimes I feel as if it is opening like a flower. After its pulsing has become regular, I move my attention to my third chakra.

The third chakra is sometimes called the solar plexus chakra. It is located just a couple of inches below where the ribcage meets at the sternum, and deep within the center of the body. This is where you sometimes get "gut feelings," and also, I've found, where hiccups originate much of the time. The solar plexus chakra is colored a bright yellow. In my body, it often pulses in the shape of an upside-down mushroom, spreading out into my middle abdomen.

After my solar plexus chakra is pulsing steadily, I focus on my second chakra, sometimes colored the sacral, or sexual chakra and colored a deep orange. This chakra is located in the center of the body, a few inches below the belly button and just between the two hip bones. In women, it corresponds with the uterus's location. In men, it's in the same place (only with no uterus, of course.)

After this chakra is pulsing along with the rest of them, I focus on my root chakra. This is the body's first chakra. It is colored a deep red, and is actually located a few inches below the junction of the legs. It is actually outside of the physical body, as the crown chakra is, but it can be felt in the perineum area, or just between the sit bones (which seems strange, if you're new to this, but is true.)

Once my root chakra is pulsing at the same rhythm as the rest of my chakras have been moving, I know that my energetic body is aligned. Some days this process either takes longer than usual, or I finish it with time to spare. I've had a throat infection spontaneously heal within about ten seconds as I directed energy to my throat chakra during this morning routine, and I've also regulated menstrual cramps using it. One's mood and energy level will be more regulated and healthy by doing this every day. Everyone knows that the body generates electricity, but not many people who aren't already interested in meditation realize that this electricity is not simply sparking about the body in random bursts or floating in a homogenous field – it has channels and organs just as the rest of our physiological systems do. There are even organs that correspond in location and purpose to the chakras. For instance, the heart chakra deals with love and compassion, and individuals who often have rage responses are much more likely to suffer from heart disease then those who take the same things more lightly that the ragers go nuts over. The hard part with this is that often we aren't all that aware where we carry our stress or where our energy pathways are blocked. Reading books like Louise Hay's *You Can Heal Your Life* are great ways to figure out our own energetic patterns and blockages.

After all of my chakras have been balanced by this exercise and while my attention is still on my root chakra, I send my energy down into the Earth to unite with Gaia's core. This sounds odd if you've never used this type of visualization before, but that's just what it is – a visualization. Imagine that you're doing it and soon, after a few (or many, depending on your level of focus) attempts at it, you'll feel something when the connection is made. I usually feel a deep vibration resonate through me that is reminiscent of a large wind instrument. Then I feel a resultant wave of energy move back up that "root" I sent down into the earth, and rise through the center of my entire body. Once it reaches my head and my crown chakra, I send that same energy, combined with my own, upward in another long line, intending that it unite with the center of our galaxy, or the Galactic Center. Often I imagine that it is uniting with the center of our entire Universe (or Multiverse, as the case may be.) You don't, of course, have to know the specific locations of these places – thought and visualization practices don't work in this way. All you need to do is intend that you go there, and you will.

After I've connected to both places and am now sitting along an energetic line running from Gaia's core to the Galactic Center, I usually feel a very high and fast vibration, like a high-pitched, clean, clear, spinning note, resonating through me. It feels very expansive and open. Everyone's experiences are different, however, and you may feel or hear, or even see, something totally unrelated to what I report if you try the same practice.

After I've formed this column or pillar of energy, I start to direct some of it. I form it into a bubble around me, cleansing and strengthening my aura (which you'll be surprised at the results of – just a few weeks ago at a crowded concert I was tired of being jostled and nearly knocked over, and I also felt like experimenting, so I envisioned that same clean, pure, strong light around me, and instantly people totally stopped bumping into me. They simply avoided me, completely, leaving a space between us of three or four inches, which was all I needed to be comfortable. It was fantastic.) Then I start to imagine things I'd like to manifest in as much detail as possible – both things for myself and for others, as well as for the Earth as a whole, as well as her population. When doing this exercise, you think of an experience of the creation you want to manifest. For instance, if I want to build my dream home, I will imagine walking into that home – what does it look like, smell like, and *feel* like? What is the yard like? Who is with me as I walk through the door? As the image, in all of its detail, becomes clearer and clearer, you fill it with the emotions you'd like to feel in that moment – love, peace, joy, or whatever else comes to mind. It's also important to add gratitude in there too, loads and loads of it, because that is how the overall consciousness of the Universal presence around you fuels itself. The more gratitude you feel, the more you'll get that matches up with your feelings, in order to justify that gratitude. Also, this doesn't work as well if it is fear-based. You may manifest what you want, but since fear is a broken emotion (literally,) things won't turn out quite right. They'll be *twisted* in a sense, and they won't make you happy anyway. You also can't manipulate or harm anyone by doing this, not without a major backlash that will make you sorry you ever had the idea in the first place. So manifest good things all around, and fill them with love and gratitude and any other positive emotions you'd like. Then, once you have that image or situation clearly in your mind, direct some of the light from that column you've created into the image. There is an infinite amount of light there, and its purpose is to be used to create with, so if you fill this image you have made with the light, working until it is shining and glowing from within, that light will help it become true, faster and more completely. Once the image is full of light and your positive emotions are as strong as you can make them, release everything (not the pillar, but the image and its associated light and emotion) in a great rushing wave that travels out and away from you in every direction. That will bring your creations back.

After I do my manifestation work, I give thanks again (remember that gratitude tip?) and go visiting. I first visit an amphitheater filled with my guides. This was not in a book anywhere, it just occurred to me to do that day in my living room and I've been making it a part of my meditations ever since (and it has provided me with a great deal of information, as you read before in the ink blot encounter.) I interact with the beings in the amphitheater in certain ways that are unique to me, sharing information and ideas, sometimes talking for awhile, and sometimes only exchanging a few words.

After that, and after I send out gratitude and love toward my guides in the amphitheater, I leave that room (just using my thoughts to guide me) and float in nothingness for a few moments, picturing the rune of my rhythm teacher, whom I've also already mentioned in detail. He appears in one way or another — sometimes I only feel his presence and hear him, sometimes I fully see him and his surroundings, and sometimes I am sitting next to him, sipping a cup of tea, or walking down a hallway, passing others in conversation like we are. We converse as long as that particular day calls for, and after we part company, I imagine myself floating upward from my body and viewing Gaia from the outside. I do work, at this point, to clean and heal her, as well as all of the creatures who live on her surface and in her interior. The work I do is different every day, but it always has to do with using light, color and visualization. Sometimes she gives me direction, makes requests, or offers advice. Sometimes she is silent. On occasion I see her in other shapes, which make it easier for us to communicate from time to time.

After I've finished with this work, I return to my body. That ends the daily meditation. The entire process usually takes less than twenty minutes. My meditations have never been very long, and I find them to be a lot like dreams — what seems like a long time can pass in a very short period, if you measure it using a clock.

I was cleaning the bathroom, listening to music on my computer and letting my mind drift. The sun was shining outside and I looked at my forearm, glowing as a shaft of light slanting in the bedroom window a couple of feet from the bathroom door shone across my skin. I thought about the sun, and how so many things on our world need sunlight, specifically, in order to thrive. There is something in the sun's light that our science can't yet explain, isolate, or duplicate, and that gives life to people, animals, and plants alike. I've even heard that leaving water in glass containers will purify it after eight hours of direct sunlight, and also fill it with something that makes it effective as an energy drink. I haven't tried that experiment out myself yet, so I can't be sure, but it's an interesting idea.

I angled my head to see the sun standing in the blue sky, and all of a sudden, I *understood*.

Yes, **the sun is a conscious being**. I received, in the next five or ten seconds, a quantity of knowledge that flashed through my mind like a fully narrated moving visual presentation that, if spoken out loud, would have been a few hours, at the very least, to repeat.

I'd already known that the Earth, or Gaia, is a living entity herself, and that other planets probably are as well. I figured, when I realized this, that the sun would likely be alive too, albeit in a different way than what we Humans living on the surface of this planet currently qualify as "life."

I saw now that yes, the sun is absolutely alive, and that its body does not end where we *think* it does – that is, where the actual fires stop and where "space" begins. Rather, each particle of light emitted by the sun is still connected to it in a very literal way. In fact, each piece of light that comes from the sun is connected to it the way that our fingertips are connected to us – those particles are extensions that touch, and feel, and *interact* with other things.

That explains the pressure you feel on your skin when the sun is shining on it. No matter how bright a fluorescent light is, you never feel that same *pressure*. Sure, we explain it by assigning names to parts of it like UVA and UVB and whatever else, but we really still haven't much of a clue about how this light, as a whole, actually works. The entity that we call the sun actually *feels* whatever it touches by shining light onto that thing, be it a building, a plant, an animal, or even the inside of a human brain, via sungazing. That one blew my mind, and it explained a lot. When Terry and I sungazed, waiting until an hour within sunset or sunrise so that the rays were safely filtered through as much atmosphere as possible, we were never bored. This was something I'd worried about prior to beginning the practice. I knew we would eventually work up to minutes and minutes of gazing – would I be able to stand the monotony of it? And yet, no matter how long we stood there, I was always completely captivated. I can't give a logical explanation as to why this happened, or even as to what was going on in my brain. I just knew *something* was. Kind of like (excuse this explanation, but it's the best thing I can think of) after you've eaten something that your digestion doesn't really agree with and you feel movement in your abdomen. You don't know exactly *what* is moving, and you know even know exactly where the movement is, you just know that some adjustments are taking place. That's what sungazing is like, except that it is absolutely painless (and actually feels quite good,) and the movement is in your **brain**. Weird, but true.

I also realized, as I received this burst of information, that this is why stargazing is so important. I'd had a theory about our relationship with stars developing for a few months. I'd even written a children's story romanticizing this theory, because it was so easy to translate into such a container. It seemed to me that the point where things like greed and murder began often happened (not always, but often) after Humans stopped living out in nature and started living in cities.

What if, I wondered to myself, *the "illness" we got was something so simple as not being able to see the stars each night?*

I sat on that for awhile, writing the little story and not thinking much more about it until this moment as I was receiving this new download. I now understood that every time we let ourselves get lost in the stars overhead, they are actually *touching* us – and not only touching us, but traveling through our eyes and deep into our brains. Who knows what adjustments those sentient light particles make once they have settled into our neural pathways? We evolved and developed into our current species with this information always being fed to us – the same information that makes a plant grow and that allows our body to do things like break down our food properly (via Vitamin D.) We *need* this, I realized, in order to be fully Human.

Sitting in the backseat, enjoying vista after vista of beautiful slopes and new spring green – there are definitely benefits to living in the mountains, even if only for a short while – I had one of my rare conversations with Gaia herself. After the few terrifying ones I've had before (and this was terrifying in its own right, as you'll see,) I can easily recognize her unique voice. It usually sounds to me like many women, all speaking together at the same time in a smooth, soft, whispery sort of way that is filled with immense power and strength. There is no accent, which doesn't surprise me when I think about it. I suppose that she would talk in the accent-free native language of anyone she happened to have a conversation with.

Left to my own devices as the two people in the front seats were having their own deep conversation, and with a, coincidentally, very open mind that day (sometimes I do these things on purpose, and sometimes I don't,) I relaxed and leaned my head against the head rest behind me, watching the blur made by dark brown tree trunks and light, new, soft green spring growth pass my window. Winter lasted a long time this year and everyone was ready for the warmer breezes to come for months before they actually showed up. This was all part of our current place in the cosmos, I knew, but that doesn't make it easier to take when another cold, rainy day sends you back indoors in a sweater and thick socks when you'd rather be wearing a sundress and feeling air on your skin.

As the car rose and fell over rolling hills and steep mountains, I became aware of another presence with me and *in* me, in the way that only happens when I'm about to have some sort of intense experience. I knew who it was, because as my awareness of this other consciousness deepened, I understood things about the landscape that I was gazing at. I saw that the trees are a part of a web of intelligence that absorbs information from the skies and the stars and then feeds this information down into the Earth, as well as routing it across the surface and keeping all of the life there informed. I saw that, on the other side of this surface, deep underground, there are other structures that serve corresponding functions. These may not look anything like trees, and if they do, there are definite marked differences because the versions we are familiar with here are specially adapted to surface life. I zoomed out in a little, and saw the beautiful and random-seeming (though not actually random at all) growth patterns of the trees passing by.

I was also aware of a few other, less pleasant things. Every little town I peered down at in valleys we passed looked unnatural and *wrong*- I could *feel* how it isn't the Human presence that is the problem, but that it is our incessant drawing up and polluting of parts of a natural system. We are acting, on the whole, as parasites at this time. Of course, this would all change if enough people even gave a thought to it, for all of the technology we would need to live in harmony with the planet already exists, but in our current state of hypnotic sleepwalking, most of us don't give the ecological impact of our everyday routines a second thought beyond what the other sleepwalking Humans will think of us. Our sensitive egos are the cause of so much trouble, wherever trouble is to be found.

I cringed every time we passed through what used to be a hill. Innocent undulations of the Earth had been painfully blasted and chipped away, and I wanted to cry as I looked that the naked, bare rock walls on either side of the cut where the road now sat. They looked like open sores to me, since the forest green is actually what Gaia's skin should have been in this part of the world.

I started to "download" more information then – knowledge about the origins of Humanity and the development of the Earth. Granted, I'd heard some of this before, but it was now being synthesized in a new way, along with added information that was coming into my mind faster than the speed of my thoughts could quite keep up with it.

For years I've been saying, even before I knew anything much (consciously, that is) about the Extra Terrestrial presence, that we as Humans do *not*, as a rule, treat Gaia like she is our home. We pollute and have extremely short-sighted thinking where our choices are concerned. That fact always made me wonder, but I didn't reach any conclusion until I understood some other pieces of the puzzle. Now I saw it, in beautiful complexity, as if a hologram slide show was playing in my mind, each thought image coming complete with an in-depth understanding about what I was looking at and experiencing. She hadn't spoken to me in her "voice" yet, but was communicating in pictures now. Here is the long and short of what I soaked up in those several moments, sitting stunned and silent in the backseat of the moving car.

Bi-pedal creatures who resemble Humans, more or less, and who have our particular brand of intelligence do not usually originate on planets. Yes, this did happen long, long, long ago, but that event is buried so deeply in ancient history that it is beyond my scope – and probably will be for awhile. In any event, it doesn't matter. Human-like species travel from planet to planet, sort of like a virus. However, this is a virus that a planet willingly accepts as a part of its own development – an evolutionary stage that can only be completed with our particular sort of parasite. In fact, our Gaia may have been the first to ever participate in this particular type of "arrangement." I'm getting ahead of myself though. Let's back up.

Gaia was evolving her own type of creatures – these creatures were mostly plants or plant like - I can't quite say whether or not movable animals were already here. I think they were, but I can't be sure so I won't give an opinion one way or the other. In any event, Gaia's creatures, already present, were extremely highly evolved and intelligent in an appropriate way for *her*. That intelligence, however, is very different than what we currently define intelligence as, although there are some similarities – such as an embodiment of love, mutual respect, and a knowledge that we are all part of the same great cosmic force that inhabits and animates all matter.

Gaia agreed to be an incubator to a new species of creature – as well as to give a part of herself in order to create that creature. This was done in much the same way as a woman both incubates and gives part of herself to create a child – hence our nickname for Gaia, "Mother Earth."

She was joined by several other races, who had also come from other places which helped to make these creatures as well. Let's just say, for clarity, that parts of these species' "DNA" were, in turn, made from their respective planets or environments (for they were not *always* from planets, as we consider planets to be.) By the way, I wish I could give more specific details here, and I have a hunch that I will be able to do so in the future, but I'm sharing my current farthest level of understanding as it exists at the moment. Back to our story.

I've heard that thirty-three species, all Human-like (generally) contributed their DNA to our creation. I've heard that there were thirty-seven species. I've heard that there were less than ten species and that there were over a hundred. I don't know what the true number is. However, I do know, as a result of what I've been shown, that we were created as a hybrid of different Human-like species and building blocks from Gaia herself.

Just to provide an example, form a mental image of your average, run-of-the-mill, Grey alien. You can even use Marvin the Martian if you like, because he's basically of the same form. You'll probably want to remove the helmet.

What do these beings look like? They walk upright on two legs. They have shoulders that extend out from each side of their body and arms that hang down toward the ground, but that are not used for walking. They have upright heads and necks, and their faces are flat, with barely a nose and no muzzle at all. They have large eyes that point forward rather than to the sides and they have large foreheads. They have opposable thumbs. Their feet are flat and their legs come straight downward from their hip joints. They are basically hairless, and are certainly without any thick fur. They have extremely small ears.

Now, in your mind's eye, picture an average Earthling mammal. Not a human, but, let's say, a dog, or a cow, or even a rabbit. These animals walk on all four legs. Their shoulders do not extend to the sides, but rather they round down so that their forelegs can carry part of the body's weight on a continual basis. They have separated back feet, and do not put weight on the "heel" portion of their foot. They have muzzles and, after infancy, do not have large foreheads. Their eyes often face to the sides. They have large ears, coming up and out from the skull. Their heads and necks curve upwards compared to the rest of their spine so that they can look forward while walking. They do not have opposable thumbs. They are covered, usually, in thick fur.

Now, picture Humans. We walk upright. Our eyes look forward. Our shoulders come to the side, our arms hang down, and we have opposable thumbs. However, we have defined noses and a very slight muzzle, compared to the image of that Grey alien. We have ears that slightly rise up and away from our skulls and that have intricate folds and curves like the Earthling mammalian creatures' ears do. We have patches of fur on our bodies at the tops of our heads, at our underarms, and at the junction of our legs.

When you look at the situation like that, is it really so hard to believe that we could be a hybrid species? When you compare the age-old accounts of "Gods" coming down from the sky in great, fiery ships, which exuded loud noises, created strong winds, and even put off noxious fumes, does it really, logically, seem out of the question that this could be a very important piece of our collective Human "birth story?"

Speaking of, let's get back to it. So Gaia agreed to host this species, knowing (for she is *extremely* highly evolved – she must be, for not only is she the host of all of the creatures that reside on her, but her intelligence and intellect is also partially made up of all the collective intelligences and intellects of those creatures, as well as more that we are not currently aware of,) that it would be a difficult process. She knew that she would have to make sacrifices as part of her journey through the time during which this new species was maturing and growing into its adult form. As we have seen and constantly attest to in environmental circles today, Humankind has used many of Gaia's resources without replacing them, but rather repaying her abundant nurturing of us as a species by injecting poisons deep into her oceans and into the land as well. Humankind not only makes the animal, plant, mineral, and environmental (meaning air and water) kingdoms suffer, but it turns on itself as a matter of course, killing members of its own species over ridiculous, imagined divisions. Because of this, Gaia suffers much – she feels the pain of all of her creatures and kingdoms, including the Humans, who are so intelligent and so emotionally developed.

The payoff in this equation, which seems like a gamble but isn't at all, because the outcome is assured, is that once

Humankind realizes its true nature and purpose, the damage can not only be completely healed much more quickly than it was created, but Gaia will be more beautiful, healthy, and abundant than she ever has been before. This new Humankind species, made of pieces from Gaia as well as from many far-reaching points in our Multiverse, has a new ability to create more effectively than has been seen in a very long time.

Not long ago, while driving and flipping through radio stations, I came upon a show by some Christian evangelist talking about how Humans are "God's children." *Yes!* I thought to myself, but then my heart sank as he went on to speak of us as perpetual, helpless, petulant, immature beings.

That's the main mistake, I realized all in an instant. *Yes, we were created in God's image. Yes, we are the children of God. However, we were always, always meant to* **grow up***!*

This "growing up" would, logically, be a maturation into Gods ourselves – no, not Gods who fight and rule over whatever groups they can, which isn't what the *actual* "God" is anyway – but Gods who are unlimited, loving creators.

That was the agreement that Gaia made. The Human children, once grown, would leave Gaia and be able to seed the Universe, possibly even the Multiverse, with life, transforming barren planets into beautiful jewels throughout the cosmos, jewels which would be able to hold all types of incredibly complex and unique life. Holding life on the surface is a developmental stage for planets in their own evolutionary ladder. For those planets who desire to take that step and are ready to do so, the new race, themselves children of Gaia and of the other star peoples who have contributed their "DNA" and efforts toward stewarding and assisting with Humanity's development in whatever ways they could (although those ways were limited because of the "free will" we hear of so often,) will be able to facilitate that holding and bearing of life more quickly and beautifully than has been done before in our current system of reality.

As I've said, I had understood pieces of this before, but on this day, gazing unfocused at the blur of forested lands we passed while driving down the highway, I realized much more of it. I also realized the nature of duality, or the knowledge that "Adam and Eve" gained in the Garden of Eden as they learned of "good *and* evil."

I'll come back to that in a moment. For now, let me tell you more about this particular conversation between me and Gaia.

After this knowledge descended upon me in detail, showing me that at first, the Human-like race or races who initially contacted and joined Gaia lived within her outer shell, in a much safer (at the time) environment. Then, over time, and through the great stories that make up all creation legends and that explain the ancient tales and histories of people like the Annunaki (or Anakim in the Bible,) who apparently created Humankind as we now are in order to assist the visiting species with their harvesting of Gaia's materials. These bits of legend and history are true in of themselves, more or less (many of them, at least, are true – probably more than we would assume at first glance or first hearing,) however they were also all ways in which the greater story could come to be.

Now my mind wandered. I started to hear Gaia's voice, or voices, in my mind first, bringing me back to the conversation. She told me of the changes on her surface and shared with me, in picturesque detail, that yes, America is the newest continent, compared to the others that we know of right now, and that this is why American thought has been so important in our current planetary story. She told me how people are differently molded depending on where they are born, as a result of the electromagnetic fields, as well as more methods of shaping and sharing information, at the area of the Earth where they are located during gestation and development. This I already knew, as it has been proven slightly through studies that measure body proportions, but I understood it in more detail after Gaia's description.

During this conversation, I was also acutely aware of the pain that Gaia is suffering, even more now than ever before in our recorded history. Although this pain isn't only because of Humanity's damage, that was what I was most focused on in this part of our conversation.

We were driving through mining country, and I could feel those scars in the land made from the mining done here as if they were old, festering wounds, perpetually torn open again and again to get out more of the resources that we don't *actually* need. We could stop this damage by using the new technologies that have been created at a great speed but that are being suppressed just as quickly by the powerful players who gain from using the old, dirty, harmful ways of operating our society. Gaia's pain, at this time, also comes from the great birthing she's doing, during our traveling into a new area of the cosmos. This coincides with events such as the Mayan prediction of the end of the fourth age and the beginning of the fifth age that they said would happen in late 2012 – this is what they were seeing, our solar system's, and therefore Gaia's, arrival in a new sector of the Milky Way, a sector where the vibrations on our planet will no longer be able to continue the way that they have been moving for eons because the vibratory environment will be different.

This also, in some way I don't quite understand, explains the natural cataclysms that are also happening to Gaia right now – it isn't the literal end of the world, not by any means – rather, it is a rebirthing. Gaia is giving birth to her own new form through all of the shifting that is happening now in her positioning, the strange weather, and in more ways. Also coinciding with this is Humanity's awakening and maturation into what we *actually* are.

As she shared this information with me in exquisite detail, I felt waves of her pain. At one point, I stared at tree trunks rushing by as she let out a sigh of pain, building into a crescendo that was louder and more intense than my mind could handle without injury, or so I thought. In my mind it sounded like all of those voices were sighing a great, painful *aaaaAAAAAAAHHHHH* – it filled my mind and bored into the deepest part of me so painfully and frighteningly that I tucked my head quickly and begged her to stop.

No more – please, no more, I can't take it, it's too much! Too much. Please, you're going to break me.

In that moment, maybe for the first time in my life, I was afraid of going insane *immediately*. The pain and intensity was so great that I thought it may create a break in my psyche, leaving me damaged beyond repair. I was terrified. But you can't cover your ears when the noise that is hurting you is inside you mind. I screwed my eyes shut and repeated my pleading mantra for the next few seconds.

And then came her reassurance:

*Don't be afraid. Don't be afraid. I won't hurt you. Don't be afraid. I **know** where your limits are.*

Gaia repeated that mantra in all of those calm, deep, whispery voices of hers until I calmed and slowly opened myself again to the knowledge streaming into me, this time with more confidence than before. Of **course** she knew where my limits were. She had created me, after all – at least in part.

And I'm a part of her. She probably knows my limits much better than I do.

Is my activation over? Not even *close*. I've begun to record my meditations, realizing the value of all those hours of tedious typing class in elementary school now that I'm able to transcribe what I'm experiencing and "hearing," word for word, with my eyes closed, saving what I've written on my computer to review later. You can never reach the end of Truth – it just keeps getting deeper and deeper and going farther and farther. Maybe it goes on forever, and maybe just until you don't need to know any more. I, obviously, haven't reached either of those places.

At the start of my awakening and learning process, I wondered more than once if I'd made the right decision. Did I want to take this leap? Was it safe? My life would probably change. And it certainly did. Nowadays I wonder, *what in the heck did I **think** about back then?* Mascara? Novels? The previous weekend's party? I don't know. But I do know that I would neither trade nor delete an ounce of what I've experienced – it's just too darned exciting.

Then there was another leap that had to be taken more recently. I knew that I had to "come out of the closet" about my experiences, and the thought of it was absolutely terrifying at first. In the same way that my paradigm shifts always do, this idea floated around me for awhile, finally landing in my head and rattling around uncomfortably until I began to talk about it. I talked about it to *everyone*. It was embarrassing, actually. I'd be chatting about something random, and all of the sudden, I'd let the cat out of the bag about my struggles with opening the door and allowing others to know the strange things that were going on with me. And invariably, completely unexpectedly, I was encouraged. Hmm.

Standing in the coffee shop line at a Los Angeles expo, I met Giorgio A. Tsoukalos, one of the brilliant minds behind the television show currently sweeping our nation entitled *Ancient Aliens* on The History Channel. The odd thing there was that Terry and I had been watching this show nonstop over the previous week or two. We were captivated, as just about everyone seems to be, by not only the spot-on logic and references given on the show, but also by Giorgio's charismatic personality and expansive intelligence. This was someone talking about things that everyone thought about – or at least, that *we'd* thought about. He was on television, discussing the very same ideas that had seemed so fringe when Terry and I brought them up beforehand in our own private, personal conversations, anticipating a huge backlash should we mention them to anyone else. Not only were we not alone, it turned out, but our peers, out there, speaking publicly, weren't afraid at all! And Giorgio was setting everyone who saw him on fire, opening minds in a decidedly non-aggressive manner that can make even the staunchest fundamentalist wonder, rather than immediately crying demonism or heresy and changing the channel.

Giorgio was delightful – he had coffee with us and we spoke about the state of this nation's education and what can be done to enhance the possibilities open to the young minds all around us. We spoke of UFOs, his magazine, *Legendary Times,* and of course *Ancient Aliens.* He was, refreshingly (especially in that environment,) **normal**.

"No," he told us, "I've never seen a UFO. I've never talked to an alien. I'm just telling the facts as I see them. It's clear. You just have to intelligently look at it, and the answers are right there. People always ask me when disclosure will happen. I always respond with the same thing – it *is* happening! **This is it, right here.**"

Amen to that.

Somewhere in our conversation, I, of course, let slip that I was feeling the pull to talk publicly about my very odd experiences, which I didn't specify because I remained afraid that I'd seem like a lunatic. I shared my fears about going public. Giorgio encouraged me to just come out with it, telling me that this field needed more young, intelligent, **sane** people, and *especially* women.

I thought about that for awhile.

Weeks later, AS put me in touch with Joe Montaldo, the head of the International Community for Alien Research (ICAR.) She said that he would likely be interested in what I'd seen and experienced, and to send him an email to ask if he wanted me to send anything I'd recorded to him. I did email him, he did want me to send my records over, and we've been corresponding here and there ever since. He was one of the main sources of information I had after my "visits," and he has helped to keep me secure in the knowledge that no, I'm not imagining things. He, of course, knows much more than I do and he gives me bits of information here and there about other contactees' experiences and recommends resources that can help me understand what's going on. He's been accumulating this information over the decades of in-depth research he's done for ICAR. If I were imagining my experiences, then how would I be able to refer to the same structures and technologies that other people have seen on similar ships? I haven't been exposed to that information. And ICAR doesn't release all of their data – as Joe has explained both to me directly and mentioned more than once on his radio show, *UFO Undercover*, if ICAR did release everything, it would be more difficult to spot those people that actually **are** making things up. Joe is refreshingly honest. On his radio show he interviews researchers and contactees that are also intelligent, balanced, **normal** people having seemingly abnormal experiences. Once you begin to pay attention, however, these experiences are less abnormal that you would originally assume. Joe's mixture of down-to-earth humor and a no-nonsense attitude paired with the incredibly out-of-the-box subjects he discusses are exactly what people who are curious about this subject need to hear – a balanced and extremely well researched perspective.

If you are curious about such things, I'd suggest that you take a look at the reference list I've included – those works have helped me on my journey and may help you too. When in doubt however, go to your library and walk the aisles, seeing what stands out for you, following your intuition, however it may arise for you. As for me, I'll be continuing my journey. It isn't as if I could stop it now anyway. Besides, I've been told in just the past several days that I have a growth spurt ahead of me that puts everything else in the dark. I can't even imagine what's coming; it's quite literally beyond my comprehension, by definition. That's how paradigms are stretched. But I'll be keeping you posted as to what happens next.

There is much talk about "disclosure." And it seems like a lot of people's automatic assumption of what this disclosure would appear as is a big press conference, led by government officials, telling us that yes, were are now, officially, no longer alone in the Universe. People expect it to be a big announcement:

"Ok, they're here. They've been here for awhile. Our bad for lying to you."

Honestly, I don't know whether this will ever happen in the exact way that people are wanting it to. I'm not saying that it *won't* happen, because I don't know. But I'm also definitely not holding my breath on that one.

In this case, I believe it necessary to think about what exactly disclosure might more realistically appear as. Does it *have* to be government and military officials making a mass announcement or gigantic ships unveiling in our skies so thickly that they block out the sun? Or could it be more subtle? Perhaps in the form of small news segments here and there, or educational television shows, or hints in entertainment media? But wait, those things have already been showing up for years. Just about a week ago I watched a clip from an extremely widely watched morning television show discussing the Indigo Children phenomenon. The guests on this segment were members of a family with three children - all of them having extremely bright blue eyes with multiple rings of color, the darker outside edges of their irises fading into centers so light that they were nearly white, ringing relatively ordinary black pupils. These eyes were so bright that they seemed to actually *glow*.

About a month ago I stumbled across an evening news segment a couple of years old discussing The Disclosure Project, which is a nonprofit research project containing over four hundred testimonies from individuals who either currently are involved with or have previously worked as government, military, or intelligence personnel. Videos of The Disclosure Project's events that you can pull up within a minute or two on the internet would very closely fit the image mentioned above of that press conference held by military and government officials. Also, if you but *slightly* pay attention, you'll notice right away that a few of the most popular musicians worldwide at this time often feature ETs as a subject for either open discussion in their music, or not-so-subtle inspiration for their costume and set designs.

The political powers who are the same ones we expect to appear at that disclosure press conference also control these lines of information. If they were adamant about keeping things quiet, we wouldn't be seeing such interesting images and soundbites coming across the airwaves.

In addition, things just might be easier for most of us to accept if they are put in a fictional, non-threatening package first. Especially when the paradigm shifts are as significant as the ones that would be needed in this case.

Afterwords

Here are some questions that I'm fully expecting to be asked about this book.

- *Question:* Do I realize that I could be imagining everything I've described in these pages?
- *Answer:* Yes, I do.
- *Question:* Do I know that there is no way (yet) to *prove* hardly any of this at all?
- *Answer:* Sure.
- *Question:* Am I aware that sharing what I've shared here may mark me as a complete lunatic?
- **Answer:** Uh-huh. I mean, yes.

So, *why* did I write it? Simply put – I had to. The darned thing wouldn't leave me alone until I did. I had strangers and friends alike popping out of the woodwork, telling me that I had to write what I'd experienced. Eventually I couldn't ignore what I was hearing anymore. And since I've begun the project, I've only found reason after reason to continue and to shed that ever pervading, inspiration-killing fear of the dreaded "what people will **think** of me" concept.

Here's what I figure. I've been afraid my whole life of "coming out of the [esoteric] closet," so to speak. I've held my tongue and watched my words, aware that if I revealed who I *actually* was, I'd lose friends and loved ones. I thought that I would be ridiculed. I thought that I'd be called crazy, or maybe even worse.

Now it occurs to me that, first of all, in real life, people aren't often as freaked out as you'd expect. Just about everyone has had the type of experience where you think of someone you haven't talked to in years and they call you the next day, or you know intuitively that something is wrong with someone you love. It's a normal thing, and a sense that Humans have always had. We've just forgotten how to use it as a part of normal, everyday life. Who knows? Maybe if enough of us *do* come out of the closet, than we can wake up as a species and actually progress to the next stage of our evolution, that is going to eventually come whether or not its arrival feels comfortable to us at the time. That said, I doubt that any significant shifts in evolution are ever completely comfortable. But the truth remains that after a certain point, keeping yourself from growing is more painful than the fears that may or may not be realized as a consequence of that growth.

In closing, I'll leave you with this. **These have been *my* experiences.** Yours are bound to be different. And yet, we are all of the same source – Spirit. We are all connected, and even if this book has you completely freaked out and convinced that I'm a lunatic, maybe when something like this happens to someone you love, or even to you, you won't be afraid. You'll realize that it's actually more normal than you thought, and you'll grow into the edges that are trying to expand in your mind, your spirit, and maybe even your body as well – I've heard of spontaneous vegetarianism and similar physical shifts happening as a result of a spiritual awakening. Who knows?

What I am completely sure of is the fact that many of the things that we used to label as something to be afraid of aren't at all fear-worthy. When in doubt, use your own best judgment. Don't listen to dogma – for that matter, take everything I've said here with a grain of salt, if you want. I'm always learning. My edges are being pushed, even now, tonight, as the clock reads 2:50am and I am wrapping up this book that has grown a life of its own. The next one I write will likely make this one look like kindergarten material. So don't worry. Things are always stranger than you think. And that's nothing to be uncomfortable with.

References

Andrews, Lynn V. (1991.) *The woman of wyrrd.* New York: HarperCollins Publishers.

Browne, Sylvia. (2001.) *Past lives, future healing: A psychic reveals the secrets to good health and great relationships.* Minneapolis, MN: HighBridge Company.

Burns, Kevin. [Producer.] (2010.) *Ancient Aliens.* [Television Series.] New York: A&E Television Networks.

Cameron, James. (Director.) Cameron, James. (Producer.) (2009.) Avatar. [Film.] Santa Monica, CA: Lightstorm Entertainment.

Conway, D. J. (1995.) *By oak, ash, & thorn: Modern celtic shamanism.* Woodbury, MN: Llewellyn Publications.

Hay, Louise. (1999.) *You can heal your life.* New York: Hay House.

Herbert, Frank. (1965.) *Dune.* New York: Chilton Books.

Lloyd, John U. (1895). *Etidorhpa.* Retrieved from http://etidorhpacontent.blogspot.com/.

McKinney, Donald. 2006.) *Anam Cara wisdom: Spiritual guidance from your personal Celtic angel.* Berkeley, CA:

Ulysses Press.

Montaldo, Joe. (2011.) *UFO Undercover Radio.* Retrieved from http://ufoundercover.homestead.com/.

Streiber, Whitley. (1988.) *Communion: A true story.* New York: Avon.

Summer Rain, Mary. (1989.) *Phantoms afoot: Journeys into the night.* Walsworth Publishing Company.

Tsoukalos, Giorgio A. (2010.) *Legendary Times Magazine.* Retrieved from http://www.legendarytimes.com.

The Disclosure Project. (2010.) *The Disclosure Project.* Retrieved from http://www.disclosureproject.org/.

Von Daniken, Erich. (1969.) *Chariots of the gods.* New York: Penguin Putnam.

Weiss, Brian. (1988.) *Many lives, many masters: The true s tory of a prominent psychiatrist, his young patient, and the past-life therapy that changed both their lives.* New York: Simon & Schuster Inc.

Zimmer Bradley, Marion. (1980.) *The mists of Avalon.* New York: Del Rey.

Made in the USA
Lexington, KY
04 January 2015